Praise for
CONFLICT ANALYSIS

"In this extraordinary volume, Matthew Levinger serves as a wise guide through a vast landscape of conflict, war, and peace. His chapters on the causes of war and violence are remarkably clear and thoughtful, followed by a seamless presentation of the most important tools for analyzing complex, chaotic conflict situations. He includes lively, concise case studies that bring his explanations to life, and he presents complex ideas in a way that both professionals and those new to the field can immediately grasp and appreciate. His chapter on "cognitive minefields" is a particularly helpful reminder that we are all hardwired to be susceptible to groupthink and miscalculation, yet some basic self-awareness can help avoid these traps. The central message of this book is one of empowerment: You do not need to be a peacebuilding professional to be able to analyze conflict, and we can all be more effective working in conflict areas if we are fluent with these tools. I recommend this book for anyone working in a conflict zone and for everyone who desires a deeper understanding of the forces for war and peace in our world."

—**Melanie Greenberg,** president and CEO, Alliance for Peacebuilding

"More than yet another conflict assessment framework, this comprehensive primer describes a wide array of analytical tools and processes that development, diplomacy, and humanitarian professionals can use to grasp complex conflict situations and avoid cognitive traps in order to engage effectively. Drawing from research in multiple disciplines, the author reviews global trends in conflict and major theories. Using diverse and interesting examples, he then ably explains the distinct functions as well as complementarities of conflict watch lists, early warning, analyses of drivers of conflict and of peace, narratives, conflict and systems mapping, scenarios, participatory rural appraisal, SWOT analysis, and collaborative planning. The appendices provide useful matrices and annotated links to leading conflict databases. Overall, a compelling case for understanding conflicts before responding."

—**Michael S. Lund,** senior specialist, conflict and peacebuilding, Management Systems International, Inc.

"This book is a must-read for all analysts and practitioners seeking to cope with conflict. It presents a wealth of techniques for assessing the nature of a conflict and the points of possible intervention. It also discusses the steps and pitfalls in developing a plan of action. Much attention is given to understanding the strengths and weaknesses of one's own organization and resources as well as the conflict environment. The book is broadly rooted in the literature on analysis and planning and provides good concrete examples at every point. It is a deep and thoroughly practical handbook."

—**Dean G. Pruitt,** Distinguished Scholar in Residence, The School for Conflict Analysis and Resolution, George Mason University

"A comprehensive description of the costs of deadly conflict and an important contribution on conflict analysis. Levinger describes how to take an analytical approach to identifying the diverse dimensions fueling conflict."

—**Lisa Schirch,** director, 3P Human Security: Partners for Peacebuilding Policy, and research professor, Center for Justice and Peacebuilding, Eastern Mennonite University

CONFLICT ANALYSIS

UNITED STATES
INSTITUTE OF PEACE
ACADEMY
GUIDES

CONFLICT ANALYSIS

UNDERSTANDING CAUSES, UNLOCKING SOLUTIONS

MATTHEW LEVINGER

The views expressed in this book are those of the author alone. They do not necessarily reflect the views of the United States Institute of Peace.

UNITED STATES INSTITUTE OF PEACE
2301 Constitution Avenue, NW
Washington, DC 20037
www.usip.org

First published 2013

Printed in the United States of America

The paper used in this publication meets the minimum requirements of American National Standards for Information Science—Permanence of Paper for Printed Library Materials, ANSI Z39.48-1984.

Library of Congress Cataloging-in-Publication Data

Levinger, Matthew Bernard, 1960-
Conflict analysis : understanding causes, unlocking solutions / Matthew Levinger.
p. cm. — (United States Institute of Peace Academy guides)
ISBN 978-1-60127-143-3 (alk. paper)
eISBN 978-1-60127-166-2
1. Conflict management. 2. Peace-building. I. Title.
JZ6368.L48 2012
303.6'9—dc23

2012018917

CONTENTS

FOREWORD

For practitioners in the field of conflict prevention and conflict management, effective action depends on insightful analysis. *Conflict Analysis: Understanding Causes, Unlocking Solutions* introduces practitioners to a wide range of analytical tools that will help them identify emerging threats of conflict and opportunities for managing or resolving a conflict. The tools include early warning watchlists and conflict metrics instruments, conflict assessment frameworks, narrative analysis, conflict mapping and systems mapping, and scenario analysis. The objective of the book is to give nonspecialists an understanding of the potential trajectories of a conflict situation so they can develop effective peacebuilding strategies.

The book is the second in the new Academy Guides series, following *Peace Economics: A Macroeconomic Primer for Violence-Afflicted States,* which was published in the fall of 2012. The purpose of the series is to introduce the reader to topics of conflict management and provide explanations of key concepts along with advice on how policymakers and implementers can make use of these concepts as they plan for and initiate operations in conflict zones. Other books in the series will focus on such topics as engaging with identity-based differences, and governance and democratic practices in war-to-peace transitions.

In our rapidly evolving and often unstable global environment, many institutions—including the U.S. government, the United Nations, regional organizations, and dozens of nongovernmental organizations (NGOs)—are devoting resources to preventing conflict and to postconflict operations. These organizations vary widely, however, in the training they provide, and many practitioners express a desire for more preparation for these complex operations.

Accordingly, the United States Institute of Peace (USIP) established the Academy for International Conflict Management and Peacebuilding in 2009 to prepare practitioners to work effectively in conflict zones abroad and to help decisionmakers develop effective strategies to prevent and resolve conflicts.

The USIP Academy is a professional education and training center offering practitioner courses on conflict prevention, management, and resolution. Drawing on USIP's twenty-five years of leadership in the field, these courses emphasize strategic thinking and practical skills. They include a mix of theory and practice. Participants come from a wide variety of backgrounds: U.S. government agencies, embassies, and foreign ministries of international partners, international organizations, the nonprofit sector, the military, international development agencies, educational institutions, and others. Typically, participants have several years of relevant experience in their fields.

As with the courses, the books should prove especially useful to people from government, the military, NGOs, and civil society who are engaged in conflict management and peacebuilding. They might also find a place in college courses and in bookstores.

We look forward to receiving our readers' feedback on this exciting new endeavor. You can reach us at academy@usip.org, and you can find the latest information on the Institute and the Academy at www.usip.org.

PAMELA AALL, PROVOST
Academy for International Conflict Management and Peacebuilding
United States Institute of Peace

ACKNOWLEDGMENTS

This guide is the product of my four years of work at USIP's Academy for International Conflict Management and Peacebuilding, where I developed and taught programs on conflict analysis and prevention for mid-career practitioners from around the world. Dozens of students in my courses have read and critiqued various drafts of the manuscript, and the final product has benefited immeasurably from their suggestions.

At USIP, Dan Snodderly has been a patient and attentive critic and coach who has provided invaluable guidance and encouragement throughout the writing process. Pamela Aall, provost of the USIP Academy, is an inspiring mentor and friend. Her incisive comments on the manuscript have been instrumental in refining its content and enhancing its utility for conflict management practitioners. Jeff Helsing, the Academy's dean of curriculum, has also played an important role in catching errors and sharpening the focus of the book.

Much of the content of the guide grew out of conversations with colleagues in the Academy and other programs at USIP. Perhaps my greatest intellectual debt is to Lauren Van Metre, who has educated me on a number of topics discussed in the guide, including scenario analysis, systems mapping, situation analysis, and adaptive leadership. Lawrence Woocher has helped refine the material on risk assessment, early warning, and conflict prevention. Peter Weinberger has enriched my understanding of the role of culture in conflict and other topics. Nadia Gerspacher has offered valuable insights into the role of conflict analysis in project planning and implementation. Conversations with Anthony Wanis–St. John have informed my discussion of how conflict analysis can support negotiation and mediation processes. Dominic Kiraly has helped me focus my ideas and communicate them more effectively. Debra Liang-Fenton has given wise and insightful advice on various chapters. Linda Bishai, Andy Blum, Veronica Eragu Bichetero, Mary Hope Schwoebel, and Jacki Wilson have all provided vivid anecdotes and useful reality checks on the nature and value of conflict analysis in difficult field-based conditions. Others at USIP who have provided useful input into the manuscript include Jonas Claes, Michael Dziedzic, Charles Martin-Shields, Vanessa Francis, Raymond Gilpin, Sheldon Himelfarb, Qamar-ul Huda, Maria Jessop, Kathleen Kuehnast, Michael Lund, Nina Sughrue, and Abiodun Williams.

I have received invaluable help from various experts outside USIP: above all, Dean Pruitt (who provided a detailed critique of the penultimate draft), Fen Osler Hampson, Randy Pherson, Koenraad Van Brabant, and an anonymous reader for USIP Press. Jim Levinger provided useful suggestions, including the book's subtitle. Thanks also to Valerie Norville, Michelle Slavin, Kay Hechler, and Marie Marr Jackson at USIP Press, as well as to Micha Archer and Manuel Leon for their illustrations. Any errors, of course, are my own responsibility.

I dedicate this book to my father, George Levinger—my first and most attentive editor, as well as the inspiration for much of my professional work. As a professor of social psychology, George did pioneering research into the connections between interpersonal and social conflict. In retirement, he remains active in the pursuit of a more just and peaceful world. I hope that this book may assist, at least in some small way, efforts to achieve this goal.

INTRODUCTION

Conflict is a central and enduring feature of human existence. It occurs whenever two or more individuals or groups perceive their interests as mutually incompatible and act on the basis of this perception. Conflicts can be waged violently, as in a war, or nonviolently, as in an election or an adversarial legal process. When channeled constructively, conflict can be beneficial. Peaceful competition can inspire the pursuit of excellence and lead to great economic, cultural, and political achievements.

This guide focuses on a darker phenomenon that we call *deadly conflict*: large-scale organized violence carried out by governments or nonstate actors. By some estimates, more than two hundred million people around the world died during the twentieth century as the result of military action or coercive political measures such as forced starvation or mass deportation. The opening years of the twenty-first century have witnessed the continuation of this grim legacy.

Since 2001, the U.S. government has spent more than a trillion dollars on military efforts to stabilize Afghanistan and Iraq after having defeated the Taliban and Baathist regimes in those countries. The United States and its international partners, including the United Nations (UN), have also an intuitive process that should complement rather than distract from other pressing tasks. To illustrate key points, it draws on a wide range of historical and contemporary cases, including the Cuban Missile Crisis, the Israeli-Palestinian conflict, the Yugoslav wars of secession, the Rwandan genocide, the 9/11 attacks, and the wars in Iraq and Afghanistan. It has three distinctive features that make its approach to this subject unique:

- *First, it integrates theoretical and practical knowledge.* The book presents research findings from a wide range of academic disciplines—including international relations, political science, history, economics, peace and conflict studies, psychology, and cultural anthropology—in easily accessible terms relevant to the work of conflict management practitioners. Our approach throughout is to simplify complex concepts without oversimplifying them. We illustrate key concepts with case studies and provide guidance on how to apply conflict analysis methods in practice. In each chapter, we also offer questions for practitioners. These questions are intended as a starting point for conversations about how an organization can use the analytical methods discussed here to increase its operational effectiveness.
- *Second, it emphasizes the importance of analyzing the causes of peace as well as of conflict.* Peace is not a static condition defined simply by the absence of war, but rather a dynamic process for managing conflicts without resort to violence. To develop effective peacebuilding strategies, it is essential to identify and understand both the connectors that bring people in a community together and the dividers that drive them apart.
- *Third, it stresses that conflict analysis is a social as well as an intellectual process.* A conflict analysis, whatever its quality, provides no value to an organization unless its audiences absorb its findings and act accordingly. Analysts can help frame the strategic narrative that informs decisions by an organization's leaders and staff. Moreover, by fostering conversation both within and across organizational boundaries, analysts can help forge a shared vocabulary and a shared story about the conflict that can support collaboration with partner organizations.

Part I of the book, "Understanding Deadly Conflict," examines contemporary global conflict trends and a range of intellectual perspectives on the causes of conflict and peace. It discusses quantitative models for conflict early warning and risk assessment, including early warning watchlists and conflict metrics instruments.

Part II, "Tools for the Trade," provides practitioners with a range of analytical tools that will enable them to systematically assess the causes and potential trajectories of deadly conflicts. The topics include how to conduct a qualitative conflict assessment, how to conduct a narrative analysis to identify key points of contention and potential paths to resolution, how to use conflict mapping and systems mapping tools, and how to use scenario analysis to manage uncertainty and anticipate change.

These chapters offer a flexible approach to conflict analysis, providing a menu of approaches to this subject to match the particular needs and objectives of diverse organizations and individuals. The success of a conflict analysis exercise depends not so much on the specific features of a framework as on how one uses it. Conflict analysis should ideally be a collaborative rather than a solitary process, so as to facilitate the formation of a common vocabulary and story regarding the conflict. It should encourage alternative points of view, against which the prevailing interpretation can be tested. Above all, the participants in a conflict analysis exercise should recognize that any assessment provides not the final word on a given conflict but rather a snapshot, which requires constant updating as the conflict dynamics evolve.

Part III, "From Analysis to Action," focuses on the role of conflict analysis in decision making and program implementation and explores the social dimensions of the conflict analysis process. It examines cognitive and institutional challenges that may prevent an organization from absorbing and acting upon important new information. It also presents strategies for maximizing the utility and effectiveness of analytical work within the organization. It discusses how analysts can contribute to creating a strategic narrative of the conflict for both their organization and other organizations operating in the conflict zone. It also explores the analyst's role in helping identify ways in which diverse organizations operating in zones of conflict can complement each other's work and capitalize on their distinctive comparative advantages.

How to Use the Book

The art of conflict analysis can be boiled down to one essential commandment: "Look and listen!" All of the analytical techniques discussed here are intended to help practitioners observe conflict environments more keenly in order to facilitate effective action.

For practitioners working in conflict zones, time is a precious commodity. This book is intended to lighten the burdens on busy professionals by helping them better anticipate emerging risks and develop more timely and effective responses. It is a reference guide rather than a compendium of mandatory analytical procedures.

One analytical method presented here, conflict assessment (chapter 4), is recommended for all conflict management practitioners as an essential exercise for a team working on or deploying to a conflict zone. Whenever possible, the team should devote at least a few hours to an initial conflict assessment and regularly revisit and refine this baseline assessment. Even in emergency situations, such as a natural disaster in a conflict-afflicted region, the team should take a few minutes to go through the steps of a conflict assessment before taking any action—just as an airplane pilot uses a checklist before takeoff. The assessment serves several critical functions:

- informing newcomers to the region or issue about key actors and key drivers of conflict and peace;
- enabling the team's experts to explicitly articulate and reexamine their assumptions about the conflict;
- helping develop a shared lexicon for discussions of the conflict, enabling greater transparency and mutual understanding within the team; and
- helping identify key points of consensus and disagreement about the nature of the conflict and about the team's strategic objectives, thus clarifying and sharpening issues that need further discussion.

The choice of analytical methods to use in a given situation will of course depend on needs and objectives. The goals that follow are characteristic:

- *Operating safely in a conflict zone. A conflict risk assessment* (chapter 3) is a good starting point. Macrolevel or microlevel *conflict metrics* (chapter 3) are also useful as indicators of rising or declining risk levels, and to inform decision making about whether and how to maintain operations in a given region.

- *Preparing for a negotiation or mediation.* A negotiation or mediation team may complement its conflict assessment with a *narrative analysis* exercise (chapter 5) to enrich its understanding of the rival parties' competing perspectives on the conflict, as well as a *conflict mapping* exercise (chapter 6) to chart the relationships among key actors in the conflict zone.

- *Planning conflict-sensitive humanitarian or development assistance programs.* The process should begin with a collaborative conflict assessment involving all program stakeholders, including local partners. A second valuable step is *scenario analysis* (chapter 7), which seeks to identify and explore the implications of a range of potential future trajectories of the conflict. It can thus be a powerful tool for enhancing strategic foresight. *Situation analysis* (chapter 9) is an important third step that helps identify the strengths and weaknesses of an organization with respect to the conflict dynamics and enables an organization to maximize its strengths and develop strategies to compensate for weaknesses.
- *Improving interagency and whole of community cooperation.* The term *whole of community* refers to the full range of stakeholder groups—governments, international and regional organizations, international NGOs, local civil society organizations, and private-sector firms—operating in a given region without a unified command structure or coordinating authority. *Systems mapping* (chapter 6) can be useful in enhancing cooperation across organizational lines.

All the analytical techniques discussed in this book can be used in either formal or informal settings and can involve greater or lesser investments of time and resources. The analytical methods discussed in chapter 7, for example, are sometimes used in multiple-day exercises involving dozens of experts from a diverse range of organizations. At the other extreme, the same methods can be used to organize brief brainstorming sessions during staff meetings. A team leader might ask, "Over the last week, has the situation on the ground moved closer to scenario A or scenario B? How do these developments affect our organization?"

Because violent conflicts are intrinsically volatile, and because human knowledge is always incomplete, a quick and dirty conflict analysis scrawled on a paper napkin may sometimes be more useful than a polished final report based on an elaborate and time-consuming series of workshops or field surveys. No matter how insightful and well-informed, any conflict analysis represents only a partial view of a constantly evolving environment. Curiosity, humility, and openness to new perspectives are essential traits for conflict analysis practitioners.

PART I

UNDERSTANDING DEADLY CONFLICT

try, or governments of other nations may sponsor competing factions. Such hybrid events are sometimes described as *internationalized intrastate war.* Deadly conflict can also involve campaigns of *one-sided violence* such as *genocide* or *mass atrocities.* In other cases, such as in Somalia or Iraq, conflicts may defy easy categorization: multiple factions may struggle for control over a territory that lacks an effective central government, or an interstate war may evolve into a complex conflict including elements of civil war, insurgency, terrorism, and one-sided violence by state authorities. In this book, the term *conflict* covers all these forms of organized violence.

Trends

Statistical surveys reveal several encouraging signs regarding global conflict trends since the end of the Cold War. In 1991, when the Soviet Union was transformed into the Commonwealth of Independent States, more than fifty armed conflicts in which at least one of the combatants was a sovereign state raged around the globe. By 2006, that number had declined to about thirty. This count excludes conflicts in which all of the combatants were nonstate actors, such as sectarian violence between Muslims and Christians in Nigeria's Plateau State. Estimated global battlefield deaths also declined by at least 50 percent between 1991 and 2006. The great majority of these events have been intrastate conflicts, and many of the rest have been categorized as internationalized intrastate conflicts. Interstate wars have constituted only a small fraction of the conflict events around the world since the end of World War II—although they have accounted for a substantial proportion of battlefield deaths (see figure 1.1).

But it is important to offer several qualifications to this optimistic picture. First, the data on battle-related deaths in figure 1.1 reflect only direct casualties from military conflicts between a state and another armed group, not one-sided campaigns of atrocities against unarmed civilians. These data also exclude civilian deaths from malnutrition and diseases that are caused indirectly by conflict. Second, the collection of mortality statistics from conflict zones is notoriously unreliable, both because of the difficulty of gaining access to conflict-torn regions and because the states typically lack the capacity to collect and process such statistical data (see appendix 1). Finally, past patterns do not necessarily predict future developments. The world is currently experiencing historically unprecedented social, political,

FIGURE 1.1 State-Based Armed Conflicts, 1946–2006

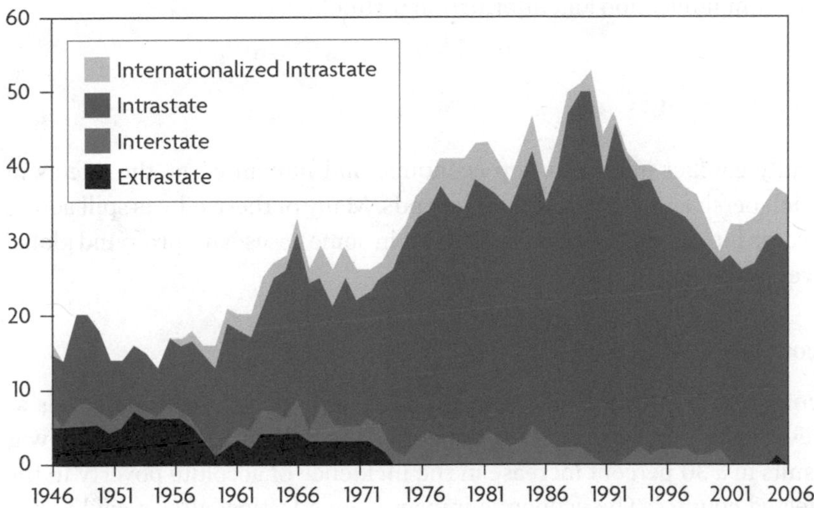

Source: Human Security Report Project, *Human Security Report 2012: Sexual Violence, Education, and War—Beyond the Mainstream Narrative* (Vancouver: Human Security Press, 2012). Reproduced with permission. Data source: Uppsala Conflict Data Program (UCDP), Uppsala University, Uppsala, Sweden/Centre for the Study of Civil War, International Peace Research Institute, Oslo (PRIO), Armed Conflict Dataset v4–2010, www.pcr.uu.se/research/ucdp/datasets/ucdp_prio_armed_conflict_dataset (accessed October 9, 2012).

economic, and technological transformations that may aggravate international tensions. Potentially disruptive forces include the following:

- environmental degradation—global climate change, pollution, shortages of water and arable land;
- resource competition—shortages of fossil fuels and other natural resources;
- economic disruptions—from globalization, financial crises, and market volatility;
- political forces—radical ideological and sectarian movements, erosion of international cooperation, and instability caused by authoritarian regimes and democratic transitions;
- military developments—nuclear proliferation, genetically engineered biological weapons, proliferation of small arms, and advanced precision weaponry; and

- technological transformations—continuing advances in and dispersion of communication and information technologies.

Costs of Conflict

Deadly conflict imposes steep economic and human costs, the effects of which persist long after the conflict ends. Many of these effects spill across borders into neighboring countries and in some cases have profound global reverberations.

Economic Costs

Economists sometimes describe civil war and other violent upheavals as "development in reverse," observing that the typical seven-year civil war results in a 30 percent increase in the incidence of absolute poverty in the affected country. The economic impact is long lasting: after a civil war, a country requires an average of fourteen years of peace to recover to its original growth path. According to a 2011 World Bank report,

> One-and-a-half billion people live in areas affected by fragility, conflict, or large-scale, organized criminal violence, and no low-income fragile or conflict-affected country has yet to achieve a single United Nations Millennium Development Goal. . . . While much of the world has made rapid progress in reducing poverty in the past 60 years, areas characterized by repeated cycles of political and criminal violence are being left far behind, their economic growth compromised and their human indicators stagnant.[1]

A comparison of two sub-Saharan countries, Burundi and Burkina Faso, illustrates the economic impact of civil war. From 1960 through 1990, economic growth rates in these two countries tracked each other fairly closely. But after the outbreak of civil war in Burundi in the early 1990s, real incomes plunged to 1970 levels. Burkina Faso, which had no major conflicts, experienced continued economic growth. By 2008, Burkina Faso had a per capita income level of $1,400, nearly two and a half times that of Burundi ($600).[2] These setbacks stem from a variety of factors:

- *Increased military spending.* During peacetime, the average developing country spent about 2.8 percent of gross domestic product (GDP) on the military in 1995, whereas this figure increased to 5 percent during civil war. During the first postconflict decade, countries continued to spend an average of 4.5 percent of GDP on the military—60 percent more than the prewar level.

- *Capital flight and destruction of infrastructure.* Civil wars often result in severe damage to railroads, bridges, ports, and electrical generation facilities and transmission lines, as well as the looting and destruction of housing, schools, and health facilities. International investors shy away from capital investments in conflict zones, resulting in further economic losses.
- *Loss of social capital.* Civilians in conflict zones lose homes, household possessions, livestock, and other assets. Violence also severs family and communal relationships and leads people to retreat from commerce and manufacturing into less risky subsistence activities.

A civil war can also have significant spillover effects on neighboring countries, which may lose access to vital transportation routes for trade. The civil war in Mozambique, for example, doubled Malawi's international transport costs and led to an economic downturn. Neighbor states may also face the economic and social stresses of accommodating large numbers of refugees. Pakistan, for example, hosted two million refugees from Afghanistan during the 1990s. About 70 percent of the world's refugees are hosted by neighboring countries. Furthermore, neighboring states may perceive the need to increase their own military spending to defend against cross-border threats, which in turn may adversely affect economic growth.[3]

Human Costs

The greatest human costs of conflict are often borne by civilians, whose daily lives are disrupted by violence. Infant mortality increases by an average of 13 percent during a five-year war, and adult mortality rates among refugees and internally displaced persons (IDPs) rise even more. Strikingly, heightened rates of mortality often persist long after the conflict ends.[4]

Beyond the direct toll of deaths, injuries, and other traumas, conflict results in high indirect costs. Taking into account both refugees across national borders and IDPs, the Office of the UN High Commissioner for Refugees (UNHCR) estimates that forty-three million civilians around the world were displaced by conflict in 2010—triple the number of thirty years ago.[5]

This displacement of civilians can have significant regional and global effects. For example, a 2005 World Bank study observed that the rising number of war refugees during the 1970s and 1980s was accompanied by a ten-fold increase in the global incidence of malaria, excluding cases in China and India. Strikingly, refugees from civil wars contracted malaria at a higher rate than refugees from drought or famine did—because "civil wars force people to walk through unfamiliar rural areas and forests to avoid areas of military operations," as well as because "refugees from war stay in asylum camps for long periods after the war ends, whereas once droughts and famines end refugees can quickly return home."[6]

In assessing the costs of conflict, it is essential to take into account not only battle-related deaths but also indirect costs such as economic losses, civilian deaths from disease and malnutrition, and heightened regional instability.

Conflict is also a major transmission vector for HIV/AIDS. High rates of HIV infection among soldiers and militia groups, along with the prevalence of rape in conflict zones, can have catastrophic effects on civilian populations. The health risks to refugees and IDPs are further aggravated by the disruption of health services and of family and communal ties, and by increased socioeconomic vulnerability among women and youth.

Security-Related Costs

Civil wars can also provide useful cover for large-scale terrorist organizations such as al-Qaeda or al-Shabaab, because the country's government may be unable or unwilling to exercise the rule of law throughout its territory. Before the terrorist attacks of September 11, 2001, al-Qaeda was based successively in two conflict-torn countries, Sudan and Afghanistan. It has since relocated to yet another conflict zone in northwestern Pakistan. Moreover, evidence indicates that before September 11 al-Qaeda garnered some revenue from trafficking in West African conflict diamonds. Al-Shabaab has come to control large swaths of southern and central Somalia, a country lacking any effective central government. The absence of a Somali state means that international actors cannot partner with authorities in the host nation to support counterterrorism initiatives.

Deadly conflict creates favorable conditions for terrorist organizations and international criminal networks. The vast majority of the global supply of opium and coca is produced in countries either currently experiencing or emerging from civil conflict.

Deadly conflict also facilitates the production and trafficking of illegal drugs. Since 1990, about 95 percent of the global supply of opium and virtually 100 percent of the global supply of coca has been produced in countries either currently experiencing or emerging from civil conflict.[7]

Perils of Prediction

It's tough to make predictions, especially about the future.
—Yogi Berra

In 1913, the British journalist Norman Angell published the fourth edition of a critically acclaimed bestseller called *The Great Illusion*. In his book, Angell made a compelling case that the progress of international commerce had rendered war obsolete. He argued that war belonged

> to a stage of development out of which we have passed; that the commerce and industry of a people no longer depend upon the expansion of its political frontiers; that a nation's political and economic frontiers do not now necessarily coincide; that military power is socially and economically futile . . . ; that, in short, war, even when victorious, can no longer achieve those ends for which peoples strive.[8]

By 1913, Europe had indeed entered an era of unprecedented globalization: the value of international trade as a percentage of world GDP had reached a level not matched until the 1990s; the American and German economies were expanding at unheard-of rates; and international communications and travel had been revolutionized by the telegraph, railroad, steamship, and the newly invented automobile and airplane. Nevertheless, it all came crashing down the following year in the global bloodletting of World War I.[9]

Conflict analysts should always maintain a sense of humility about their predictive powers. But a variety of techniques exist for anticipating potential future events in an uncertain environment. One such method is *trend analysis*, which uses historical patterns along with factors currently in play to project future trends. For example, based on historical and current demographic data, the United Nations estimates that the world's population will increase from seven billion in 2012 to nine and a half billion in 2050, and that the vast majority of population growth will occur in the developing world, including India and China.[10]

Trend analysis can also be used to predict future developments for markets in hydrocarbons and other critical resources. The International Energy Agency projects that crude oil production from currently producing and known undeveloped oil fields will decline sharply after 2020. To meet the global level of production needed by 2035—99 million barrels per day (MBD)—the world will need to bring online an additional 47 MBD, twice the current production of all Organization of Petroleum Exporting Countries (OPEC) in the Middle East.[11]

Over the next several decades, global demand is also expected to exceed the global supply of other resources including potable water, food crops, and strategic minerals. According to the U.S. National Intelligence Council, the critical uncertainty is not so much whether such resource shortages will occur, but rather how sudden and traumatic the shortages will be: "In some cases, the surprise element is only a matter of *timing*: an energy transition, for example, is inevitable; the only questions are when and how abruptly such a transition occurs."[12] The more severe the squeeze on critical resources, the greater will be the shocks to global economic and political institutions.

An even more pessimistic scenario is found in a 2008 planning document produced by the United States Joint Forces Command (JFCOM). The analysis begins by pointing out a common sociological dimension of revolutionary violence:

> Serious violence, resulting from economic trends, has almost invariably arisen where economic and political systems have failed to meet rising expectations. A failure of globalization would equate to a failure to meet those rising expectations. Thus, the real danger in a globalized world, where even the poorest have access to pictures and media portrayals of the developed world, lies in a reversal or halt to global prosperity.[13]

The scenario warns that a severe and prolonged global economic crisis could destabilize large swaths of the "arc of instability," particularly those regions that have enjoyed a modicum of economic growth in recent years (see figure 1.2). Even more seriously, such a crisis could potentially destabilize nations such as China, where rapid economic growth may have papered over deep social fault lines. JFCOM warns that

> Real catastrophes may occur if economic growth slows or reverses either on a global scale or within an emerging power. Growing economies and economic hopes disguise a number of social ills and fractures. The results of a dramatic slowdown in China's growth, for example, are unpredictable and could easily lead to internal difficulties or aggressive behavior externally. That is precisely what happened in Japan in the early 1930s with the onset of the Great Depression.[14]

Although most conflict management practitioners have little or no influence over the macro-level trends discussed earlier, a consideration of such factors can be useful in developing long-term strategic plans in conflict-prone regions. For example, practitioners involved in designing agricultural projects for sub-Saharan Africa or the Tigris-Euphrates Basin would be

FIGURE 1.2 State Fragility Index 2011: Arc of Instability

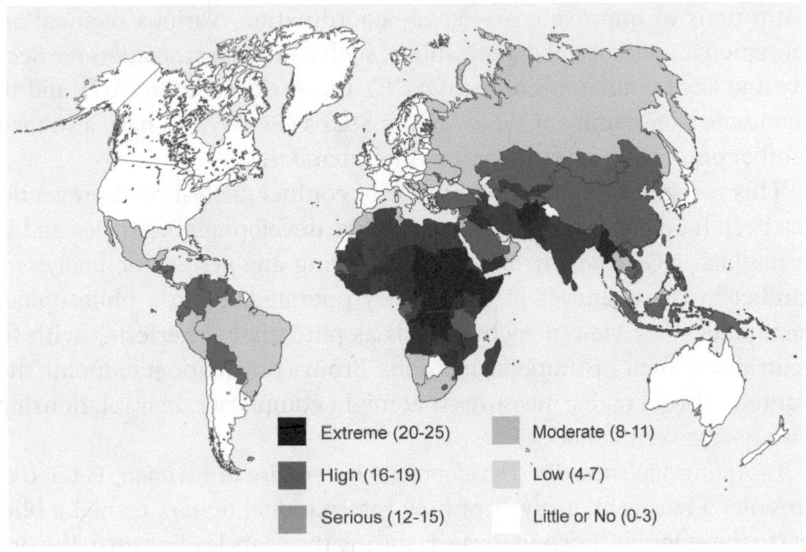

Source: Center for Systemic Peace, www.systemicpeace.org. Reproduced with permission.

wise to consider the rainfall projections produced by computerized global climate models. Likewise, long-term projections of global oil production and prices provide important data concerning the political prospects of energy-producing countries.

Conflict Analysis and Adaptive Leadership

Since I had no textbook for field missions, my approach was to listen and listen again to people, and to look and look again around me in the cities and in the countryside.

—Ahmedou Ould-Abdallah, *Burundi on the Brink*

In the face of these global trends, a wide range of governments, international organizations, and NGOs have over the past decade made conflict analysis and prevention central elements of their institutional missions. The United Nations has established new initiatives such as the Peacebuilding Commission and the UN Special Adviser on The Prevention of Genocide. The World Bank has created several offices charged with responding to intrastate conflict and state failure; and many Western donor governments have reorganized their development assistance and national security institutions to improve cross-agency coordination. Various regional and subregional multilateral organizations, such as the Organization for Security and Cooperation in Europe (OSCE), the African Union (AU), and the Economic Community of West African States (ECOWAS), have also made conflict prevention a central part of their mandates.

This recognition of the importance of conflict analysis and prevention has been hard earned. Until the mid-1990s, development agencies and international NGOs largely avoided conducting any systematic analysis of conflict in the countries in which they operated. From a philosophical standpoint, they viewed such analysis as potentially interfering with the neutrality of their institutional missions. From a pragmatic standpoint, they wanted to avoid taking measures that might complicate their relationships with host governments.

In *Aiding Violence: The Development Enterprise in Rwanda*, Peter Uvin presents a masterful analysis of how international donors turned a blind eye to the emerging crisis in Rwanda during the years leading up to the 1994 genocide. For example, he notes that a hundred-page World Bank historical and policy analysis on Rwanda written in 1987 did not once mention ethnicity and that it contained only a single line about "widespread disturbances in the countryside" at the time of independence. A series of other World Bank reports produced between 1984 and 1991 described Rwanda as "politically stable" (1984, 1986, 1989), possessing a "sound administration" (1989, 1991), noteworthy for the "cultural and social adhesion of its people" (1986), and characterized by "ethnic and socioeconomic homogeneity" (1991). This "rosy image of Rwanda was shared by NGOs as well as bilateral and multilateral aid agencies." Most damning of all, "No aid agency ever denounced the official racism or the quota system or the ethnic IDs—not even in the 1990s, when it was clear that they were being used to prepare for mass killings."[15]

Father William Headley of Catholic Relief Services (CRS), which had operated in Rwanda since before the country's independence in 1962, describes the profound effect of the genocide on CRS program priorities:

> In truth, Rwanda was not a case of a mysteriously appearing genocide. There had been major societal and ethnic rifts as well as related injustices for years. These were not hidden. They were considered to be outside CRS' development mandate. Our traditional programming improved socioeconomic life. It did not touch the country's latent conflict. CRS' projects were wiped out in minutes; the people we served became "the well-fed dead."[16]

Development agencies and NGOs were not the only international actors that avoided putting too sharp a point on their analyses of the Rwandan conflict. Official diplomatic cable traffic from Rwanda sometimes adopted a tone of studied vagueness regarding the emerging crisis. For example, on December 16, 1992, the U.S. State Department's Bureau of Human Rights and Humanitarian Affairs transmitted a draft of the 1992 Country Report on Human Rights Practices for Rwanda to the American embassy in Kigali. The report charged that "in 1992 there were significant human rights abuses, many related to the conflict with the RPF [Rwandan Patriotic Front]," and that "credible reports allege that local officials were involved in widespread ethnic violence in March in which 300 died and 15,000 were displaced."[17] A week later, Embassy Kigali cabled back to protest these allegations:

> We contest the claim of "significant human rights abuses." War, ethnic violence, political violence, terrorism and unchecked assaults are abominations and cause immense human suffering. Can they, however, be classified as human rights abuses when their links to government actions or agents are tenuous, unproven and, indeed, seem to be perpetrated by all sides and not necessarily orchestrated or organized? In Rwanda, all sides are suspect but conclusive evidence is either lacking or ambiguous. We propose [instead]: "In 1992 there were human rights abuses in Rwanda, many related to the conflict with the RPF."[18]

As these examples illustrate, international donors' policy failures toward Rwanda in the years leading up to the genocide were aggravated by analytical failures as well as by bureaucratic unwillingness to get involved.

One international actor who did perceive the potential for genocidal violence was Lieutenant General Romeo Dallaire, commander of the twenty-five-hundred-man UN peacekeeping force in Rwanda. In January 1994, three months before the outbreak of the genocide, Dallaire sent a cable to UN Headquarters in New York reporting that an extremist militia affiliated with the Rwandan government was allegedly planning to massacre Tutsi civilians on a massive scale. He informed his superiors that he intended to raid an arms cache the militia had assembled for this purpose. The director of the UN Department of Peacekeeping Operations in New York sent back an urgent reply, ordering Dallaire to take no action against the arms cache, but simply to report its existence to the Rwandan government. In this case, UN officials' institutional concerns about the future of UN peacekeeping operations trumped their concern about the potential for atrocities in Rwanda. In October 1993, eighteen U.S. Army Rangers involved in the UN

BOX 1.1 Rwanda 1994: Contributors to Strategic Failure

- **Problematic and conflicting mandates.** The policies of international actors failed to alleviate, and in some cases may have exacerbated, the profound ethnic tensions in Rwanda during the period leading up to the genocide. By insisting on taking an apolitical stance in development assistance programming, the World Bank and Western development agencies strengthened the hand of Rwanda's discriminatory Hutu regime. Conversely, Western diplomats pushed aggressively for the implementation of the 1993 Arusha Peace Accords, which frightened many Hutus by granting disproportionate power to the regime's Tutsi opponents. None of the many governments, NGOs, or international organizations operating programs in Rwanda before the genocide focused systematically on alleviating tensions among the country's rival ethnic groups.
- **Operational constraints.** Political fallout from the Black Hawk Down disaster in Somalia in October 1993 placed enormous pressure on the UN Mission in Rwanda (UNAMIR) to avoid any actions that might jeopardize the future of UN peacekeeping. UN headquarters refused to allow UNAMIR's commander to act decisively against preparations for the genocide. Likewise, U.S. diplomats knew that Rwanda was a low priority for the U.S. government, and that the United States was unprepared to back any course of action beyond calling for the implementation of the Arusha Accords.
- **Organizational blinders.** The operational constraints limited not only what international actors in Rwanda were prepared to do but also what they were prepared to *see*. The World Bank and most international NGOs ignored the ethnic and political tensions in Rwanda, considering them outside the development mandate. U.S. and other international diplomats were deeply concerned that Rwanda might revert to civil war, and they worked indefatigably to support the implementation of the Arusha power-sharing agreement. But most Western diplomats and intelligence analysts overlooked the possibility that Hutu extremists might seek to annihilate the Rwandan Tutsi population.
- **Lesson for conflict analysts.** It is essential to remain alert to inconvenient truths that may be incompatible with an organization's programmatic objectives but that could have disastrous effects if ignored.

peacekeeping operation in Somalia had been killed in the Black Hawk Down incident in Mogadishu. UN officials feared that, if a similar disaster were to occur in Rwanda, the political backlash might cause UN member states to abandon multilateral peacekeeping operations altogether (see box 1.1).[19]

The international response to the crisis in the neighboring state of Burundi in 1993 and 1994 offers a striking contrast to the Rwandan case. Burundi had a similar ethnic composition as Rwanda—roughly 80 to 85 percent Hutu and 15 to 20 percent Tutsi—and, like Rwanda, it had experienced several episodes of catastrophic violence since its independence in the early 1960s. In October 1993, when Burundi's first democratically elected Hutu president was assassinated in an attempted coup, a wave of reprisals and counter-reprisals erupted that killed at least thirty-thousand civilians, both Tutsi and Hutu, over the subsequent month. The United Nations, which was then in the process of deploying a full-scale peacekeeping force to Rwanda to support the new power-sharing agreement there, responded by dispatching the Mauritanian diplomat Ahmedou Ould-Abdallah as the special representative of the UN secretary-general (SRSG) to Burundi.

When Ould-Abdallah arrived in Burundi, he had a support staff of two and an operating budget of $1,000 per day. Across the border in Rwanda, the United Nations had deployed three hundred and twenty civilians and twenty-six hundred peacekeeping troops with an operating budget of $1.2 million per day. Aware that "resources alone do not solve emergency situations," Ould-Abdallah set out to listen and learn. His approach was straightforward: to demonstrate willingness to engage in dialogue with anyone, but to enter into formal negotiations only with parties that showed genuine interest in a peaceful settlement, to strengthen moderate forces and to marginalize extremists.

Although Ould-Abdallah had little money and no military forces at his disposal, he recruited support for his mission from respected Burundians and the local media and cultivated his knowledge of the various factions to "wield sticks discreetly." He notes that "the stick is not necessarily a big stick," that it may involve exploring "the backgrounds of individual extremists and their organizations for politically compromising material." He recalls, "When I identified the main extremist, I knew that his own group, the political bureau of his party, was more than 80 percent against him. But they were afraid." Ould-Abdallah reached into his bag of tricks to marginalize such extremist leaders:

> If it is found that certain extremists have evaded paying their taxes or accepted bribes, that information could be leaked to the national and international media if those individuals threaten to obstruct the peace process. Warlords and extremists generally work in darkness and by blackmail, and thus are, as it were, natural targets for a judicious dose of intimidation![20]

Ould-Abdallah performed his greatest service to Burundi during the days after April 6, 1994, when an airplane carrying Rwandan president Juvenal Habyarimana and Burundi's new president Cyprien Ntaryamira, a

Hutu, was shot down on approach to Kigali airport in Rwanda. Within hours, the genocide began in Rwanda when Hutu extremists began killing high-level moderate politicians who opposed the regime. From his previous analysis of the conflict, Ould-Abdallah recognized that the violence could quickly spill over the border into Burundi and therefore immediately brought together Burundi's top Hutu and Tutsi leaders. The group made a joint announcement on Burundi's national television network, emphasizing that Burundi's president had not been the intended target of the attack. Then the group went to army headquarters to display the unity of the nation's civilian and military leadership. In a series of telephone calls to Burundi's provincial governors and the commanders of the country's various military bases, this group instructed the civilian and military leaders to work together to quell any violent uprisings. Ould-Abdallah writes, "Less than twelve hours after the assassination the situation was under control throughout the country. . . . The decision that night to let a fearful nation know that someone was in control was a key preventive action."[21]

Some observers have found fault with aspects of Ould-Abdallah's work in Burundi. René Lemarchand, one of the world's foremost scholars on Burundi, praises Ould-Abdallah for his role in preventing the outbreak of mass violence in April 1994. Nonetheless, Lemarchand argues that Ould-Abdallah's power-sharing plan for Burundi reflected a misunderstanding of the conflict and the range of viable solutions. Although Burundi's Tutsi made up only 15 to 20 percent of the population, Ould-Abdallah's proposal for a Convention of Government (CG) mandated a power-sharing arrangement between the Hutu and the Tutsi. Lemarchand writes, "The singular flaw in the CG is that it blissfully ignored the fundamental fact that the [Hutu-led] Frodebu had won the elections. Rather than creating cohesion, the result was to foster paralysis at every level of government."[22]

But in Ould-Abdallah's view, the top priority was to establish a "minimum of stability or peace" in Burundi rather than to create the optimal formula for political representation. Given the history of Tutsi political and economic dominance in Burundi since independence, he believed that any government that excluded the Tutsi would immediately be overthrown. Unfortunately, subsequent events in Burundi proved both men right. As Lemarchand had warned, Hutu rebel groups rejected the legitimacy of the power-sharing agreement and returned to the battlefield. But as Ould-Abdallah had feared, in July 1996 another coup led by Tutsi military officers overthrew Burundi's Hutu president, further intensifying the civil war (see box 1.2).[23]

BOX 1.2 Burundi 1994: Keys to Strategic Success

- **Clear and focused mandate.** The massive intercommunal violence in Burundi in the autumn of 1993 focused the attention of UN leaders on the core mission of preventing a renewed outbreak of mass atrocities. Ahmedou Ould-Abdallah was able to relegate other long-term political priorities, such as constitutional reform, to a position of secondary importance.
- **Operational flexibility.** Because of the tiny size of Ould-Abdallah's mission and the minimal oversight from UN headquarters, he was able to determine his own course of action and adapt rapidly to changing conditions on the ground.
- **Openness and ingenuity.** Ould-Abdallah remained constantly alert to new information from his interlocutors, and forged relationships that enabled him to maximize the leverage of his limited resources.

Skills in conflict analysis and adaptive leadership are essential not only for high-level officials such as UN chiefs of mission, but also for practitioners working at the local level in conflict zones. In 2004, James Nyawo was the coordinator of a humanitarian program supporting public health and community security in northern Uganda. Among other initiatives, the program provided night shelter for women and children who were afraid of night-time abductions by the Lord's Resistance Army (LRA). Nyawo recalls,

> At night women and children used to move from the surrounding camps into the hospital premises where they felt more protected due to the presence of two military tanks and a military post nearby. They slept on verandas of hospital wards and staff accommodation. In order to improve the sleeping conditions for the "night commuters" as they were called, my organization secured a grant and constructed ten blocks to be used as accommodation. The block offered decent accommodation and protected the night commuters from rain and dusty storms.[24]

Unfortunately, says Nyawo, this well-meaning intervention resulted in unanticipated negative consequences for residents of the camps:

> Approximately three months after the opening of the shelters I received reports through local authorities that gender-based violence had increased in the camps. Out of curiosity, together with my team, I conducted a rapid survey to establish the main causes of the sudden increase in the cases of gender-based violence in the camps. We were shocked to see that the main cause was that husbands in the camps were accusing their wives of denying them their conjugal rights as they sought refuge in the newly constructed shelters. From

> the women's point of view the shelters were more than just for protection from the LRA but also a means of escaping having to negotiate not having sex with their husbands on a regular basis. The husbands regarded the shelters as too comfortable for women, to the extent that they never considered spending some nights at home even when the security improved. Some men went as far as threatening to burn down the shelters.

The conflict analysis conducted by Nyawo's team revealed that men in the IDP camps "were feeling insecure and redundant as life in camps had stripped them of their traditional roles. The humanitarian agencies were replacing their role by providing food, water, and then shelter." In response to this finding, Nyawo invited Kampala-based civil society organizations to provide training on gender issues with both male and female residents of the camps, focusing on communication within families and on "negotiating conjugal rights." After these training programs were established, says Nyawo, women became more willing to spend some nights at home with their husbands when the risk of LRA attacks was low, and reports of gender-based violence in the camps subsided.[25]

Conclusion

The disasters in Rwanda and Burundi, along with other mass atrocities in the 1990s, have had a profound effect on international development organizations. Emphasizing that the goal of development assistance is to help establish vibrant and resilient communities, international donors have moved to establish conflict-sensitive development practices. The goal of such practices is, first, to "do no harm," and ideally to help alleviate conflicts in the communities in which they work. Many development organizations have begun to require conflict impact assessments for programs both at the design and implementation stages. But outside the development field—for example, in most foreign ministries, military planning staffs, humanitarian NGOs, and international corporations—conflict analysis remains a more sporadic and ad hoc activity.

Given the high costs of contemporary conflict, and the likelihood of future shocks to the global system, bold and creative leadership is needed to manage intrastate and interstate conflict more effectively. In part, this leadership may require military action by individual states or international coalitions. But military responses are of limited utility in addressing many of the most serious threats: climate change, pandemic disease, food scarcity, economic crisis, ideological or sectarian extremism, population pressures, and natural resource shortages. To respond effectively to these challenges, decision makers and program implementers at every level will need to understand and anticipate the forces that are driving emerging conflicts, and to recognize and adapt to changing conditions on the ground. These essential skills of conflict analysis are the focus of this guide.

Questions for Practitioners

- Does deadly conflict, or the risk of conflict, adversely affect the work of your organization? If so, how? In what ways—if at all—does your organization work to mitigate the potential impact of conflict on its operations?
- How adaptable is your organization in response to new information about conflict risks? Does the organization have a clear and focused mandate? Does it display operational flexibility? Does it encourage alertness and ingenuity among its staff? What can you do to help cultivate these characteristics in your workplace?

Notes

1. World Bank, *World Development Report 2011: Conflict, Security, and Development* (Washington, DC: World Bank, 2011), 1.
2. Ibid., 63–64.
3. Paul Collier, V. L. Elliott, Håvard Hegre, Anke Hoeffler, Marta Reynal-Querol, and Nicholas Sambanis, *Breaking the Conflict Trap: Civil War and Development Policy* (Washington, DC: World Bank, 2003), 13–14, 20–23, 33–36.
4. Ibid., 23–24.
5. United Nations Office of the High Commissioner for Refugees, *UNHCR Statistical Yearbook 2010*, 10th ed. (New York: UNHCR, 2011), 12, www.unhcr.org/4e9c8d10.html (accessed May 8, 2012).
6. Ibid., 39.
7. Ibid., 42–48.
8. Norman Angell, *The Great Illusion: A Study of the Relation of Military Power to National Advantage*, 4th ed. (London: William Heinemann, 1913), x.
9. United States Joint Forces Command (JFCOM), *The Joint Operating Environment 2030: Challenges and Implications for the Future Joint Force* (Suffolk, VA: United States Joint Forces Command Center for Joint Futures, 2008), 13.
10. Ibid., 12.

11. International Energy Agency, *World Energy Outlook 2011*, Executive Summary (Paris: International Energy Agency, 2011), 3, www.worldenergyoutlook.org (accessed May 8, 2012).

12. United States National Intelligence Council, *Global Trends 2025: A Transformed World* (Washington, DC: Government Printing Office, 2008), xii.

13. JFCOM, *Joint Operating Environment 2030*, 14.

14. Ibid., 15.

15. Peter Uvin, *Aiding Violence: The Development Enterprise in Rwanda* (West Hartford, CT: Kumarian Press, 1998), 44–45.

16. William Headley, "CRS' Contributions to International Peacemaking" (paper presented at USIP Workshop on Catholic Peacemaking," Washington DC, February 5, 2001), www.restorativejustice.org/10fulltext/headley/at-download/file (accessed May 5, 2012).

17. U.S. State Department, Bureau of Human Rights and Humanitarian Affairs, "Rwanda: Initial Edit of 1992 Country Report on Human Rights Practices," December 16, 1992 (declassified document obtained by the George Washington University National Security Project), 3, www.rwandadocumentsproject.net/gsdl/collect/usdocs/index/assoc/HASH01aa/f33c150d.dir/0859.pdf (accessed October 2, 2012).

18. Embassy Kigali to Secretary of State Washington, "Comments on Initial Edit of 1992 Human Rights Report: Rwanda," December 23, 1992 (declassified document obtained by the George Washington University National Security Project), 3, www.rwandadocumentsproject.net/gsdl/collect/usdocs/index/assoc/HASH01ed/79ec2b55.dir/0865.pdf (accessed October 2, 2012).

19. Romeo Dallaire, *Shake Hands with the Devil: The Failure of Humanity in Rwanda* (Toronto: Random House Canada, 2003), 135–67.

20. Ahmedou Ould-Abdallah, *Burundi on the Brink 1993–1995: A UN Special Envoy Reflects on Preventive Diplomacy* (Washington, DC: United States Institute of Peace Press, 2000), 40, 135, 142–44; United States Holocaust Memorial Museum, "Maximizing Your Leverage," in *Negotiating with Killers: Expert Insights on Resolving Deadly Conflicts* (Washington, DC: United States Holocaust Memorial Museum, 2007), www.ushmm.org/genocide/analysis/details.php?content=2007-12-04 (accessed May 3, 2012).

21. Ould-Abdallah, *Burundi on the Brink*, 55–58.

22. René Lemarchand, *The Dynamics of Violence in Central Africa* (Philadelphia: University of Pennsylvania Press, 2009), 168.

23. Ibid., 168; Ould-Abdallah, *Burundi on the Brink*, 93–102; Ould-Abdallah, personal communication with the author, October 2009. I thank Frederick Ehrenreich for his helpful analysis of this controversy.

24. James Nyawo, personal communication with the author, March 2012.

25. Ibid.

2

CAUSES OF CONFLICT AND PEACE

Key Points

- Deadly conflict and stable peace are both complex social phenomena. A variety of strategic, political, socioeconomic, psychological, and cultural factors can either exacerbate conflict or contribute to peace.
- Conflicts turn deadly when one or more actors make a strategic decision that the most effective way to achieve their objectives is through violence against another group. Actors base their decisions on whether and how to use violence on their calculations of the relative costs and benefits of nonviolent and violent political strategies. To prevent deadly conflict, it is essential to shift this calculus by increasing the relative costs and decreasing the relative benefits of using violence.
- The risk of deadly conflict is exacerbated when high levels of mutual distrust and fear exist between rival parties. Measures to build mutual trust and establish patterns of cooperation across group lines can help mitigate the risk of violence.

Although conflict is a nearly universal feature of human life, large-scale deadly conflict is relatively rare. Conflict and peacebuilding expert Michael Lund has created a diagram called the curve of conflict to illustrate how violent conflicts begin and end (see figure 2.1). The curve helps organize terms and concepts used by conflict management professionals, showing

FIGURE 2.1 The Curve of Conflict

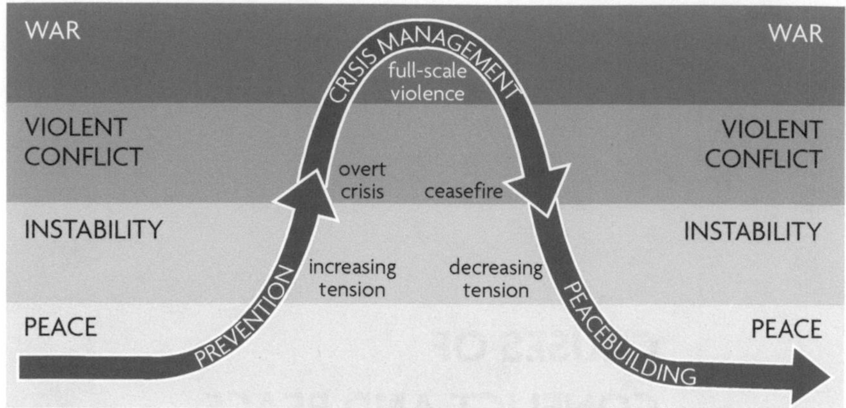

Source: Adapted from the USIP original artwork by Michael Lund.

how the phases of a conflict relate to one another and to various kinds of third-party intervention.

The Curve of Conflict

"The course of disputes that become violent conflicts," Lund explains, "is traced in relation to two dimensions: the intensity of conflict (the vertical axis) and the duration of conflict (the horizontal axis). The line that forms an arc from left to right across the diagram portrays the course of a conflict as it rises and falls in intensity over time." He notes that the "smoothly curving bell shape" of the curve "is oversimplified to characterize an 'ideal type' life history." Actual conflicts, by contrast,

> can exhibit many different long and short life-history trajectories, thresholds, reversals, and durations. Even conflicts that have abated can re-escalate. Nevertheless, the model has heuristic value in allowing us to make certain useful distinctions among the conflict management interventions that relate to different levels of intensity.[1]

The left of the curve describes relations between parties to the dispute. It is divided into various phases of peace or conflict: peace, instability, violent conflict, and war—the lower intensity phases characterized by what Lund calls interactive, mutually accommodative behavior, such as debates

The curve of conflict charts the intensity of a conflict on the vertical axis and the duration of a conflict on the horizontal axis, depicting the ideal type of a conflict's life history. The graph of an actual conflict's life history is likely to be jagged rather than curved, because conflict may escalate abruptly or oscillate between periods of greater and lesser intensity.

and negotiations, and the higher intensity phases characterized by unilateral, coercive behavior, such as ultimatums, sanctions, and physical force. The best way to understand the model is to take a close look at each of these phases.

At the stage labeled *peace*, at the lower left of the curve, parties either avoid fundamental disagreements or manage conflicts between them without resort to large-scale organized violence. Conflict management strategies may take a variety of forms. For example, the parties may develop mutually beneficial reciprocal relationships, or resort either to formal mechanisms for dispute resolution, such as a Western judicial system, or to informal mechanisms, such as a council of elders in an agrarian village. Alternatively, the stronger party may dominate or exploit the weaker, and the weaker may yield to the demands of the stronger. The conflict resolution theorist Johan Galtung distinguishes between *negative peace*, which he defines as "the absence of violence, absence of war," and *positive peace*, which is "the integration of human society."[2] Scholars sometimes use the term *structural violence* to refer to situations in which a dominant power preserves order by coercing the weak.

But when established patterns of nonviolent interaction begin to break down, the relationship between rival parties can move from peace to *instability*. This transformation can happen in a variety of ways. For example, a dominant party may escalate its demands against the subordinate party to the point that members of the subordinate group come to consider the level of exploitation intolerable. Or the dominant party's demands may remain unchanged, but members of the subordinate group may adopt a new ideology that depicts the traditional power relationship as illegitimate. Or changing environmental conditions, such as the expansion of the Sahara Desert as the result of drought in Africa's Sahel region, may sharpen conflicts between agriculturalists and pastoralists who previously were able to coexist in relative harmony. Or large-scale migrations from villages to cities may disrupt traditional social institutions for dispute resolution.

FIGURE 2.2. Curve of Conflict and Rwanda, 1918–94

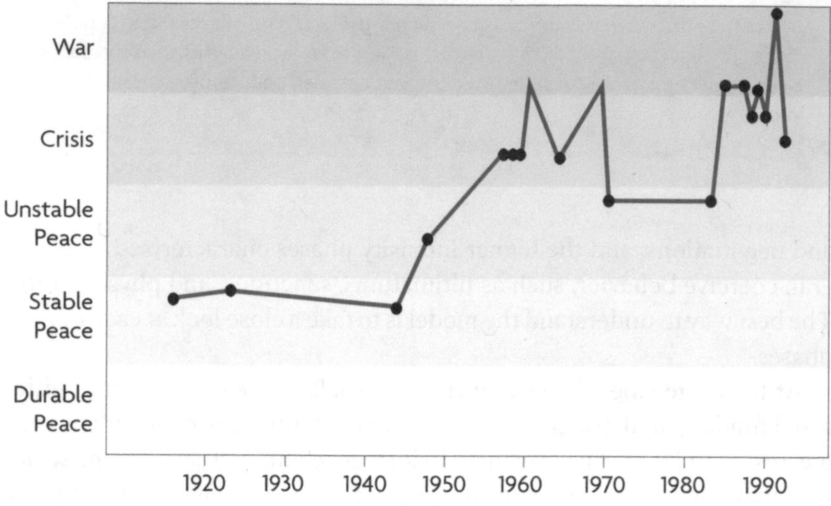

Source: USIP original artwork.

The condition of instability provides the tinder for conflict, which needs only a spark to burst into flame. As rivalries sharpen, and intergroup relations continue to deteriorate, the parties may move toward violent conflict—marked by sporadic acts of violence, such as riots, massacres, extrajudicial killings, and terrorist attacks—or, in extreme cases, to large-scale, systematic organized violence—the phenomenon known as war.

In practice, few conflicts follow this chronological ideal type. Figure 2.2 maps the evolution of intercommunal strife in Rwanda from the end of World War I in 1918 through the genocide of 1994. From 1918 through 1945, Rwanda's Belgian overseers managed to maintain peace in the country by delegating power to the minority Tutsi elite. With the rise of the Rwandan independence movement after World War II, the country's majority Hutu population began to lash out at Tutsi domination, culminating in a series of massacres around the time of Rwandan independence. A military coup in 1973 resulted in a period of lower tensions between Hutu and Tutsi, but intercommunal hostilities escalated sharply again in the late 1980s and early 1990s in response to an economic crisis and a military invasion from Uganda by a force of Tutsi expatriates.

The escalation from peace to instability, and ultimately to violent conflict and war, is never inevitable. Without a spark, or triggering event, an unstable situation may persist without erupting into violence—just as dry and hot conditions in a forest do not always result in a forest fire. So-called intractable conflicts, such as over Northern Ireland, Cyprus, Israel-Palestine, Sri Lanka, and the Mindanao region of the Philippines, can oscillate between instability and violent conflict for decades on end. Intractable conflicts resist attempts at resolution, in part because they typically involve difficult problems such as fundamental value disagreements, high-stakes distributional questions, domination issues, and denied human needs.

Scholarly writings on international conflict typically distinguish between the categories of interstate and intrastate (or civil) war. But, as the World Bank's 2011 *World Development Report* points out, twenty-first-century conflicts often

> do not fit neatly either into "war" or "peace," or into "criminal violence" or "political violence." Many countries and subnational areas now face cycles of *repeated* violence, weak governance, and instability. First, conflicts often are not one-off events, but are ongoing and repeated: 90 percent of the last decade's civil wars occurred in countries that had already had a civil war in the last 30 years. Second, new forms of conflict and violence threaten development: many countries that have successfully negotiated political and peace agreements after violent political conflicts, such as El Salvador, Guatemala, and South Africa, now face high levels of violent crime, constraining their development. Third, different forms of violence are linked to each other. . . . Criminal gangs can support political violence during electoral periods, as in Jamaica and Kenya. International ideological movements make common cause with local grievances, as in Afghanistan and Pakistan. Thus, the large majority of countries currently facing violence face it in multiple forms.[3]

Not only has the nature of organized violence become increasingly ambiguous in recent decades, but the causes of contemporary conflicts are also often multidimensional and complex. In this chapter, we explore five types of factors that can motivate or prevent violence, each of which may be seen as a distinctive dimension of conflict and peace:

- the *strategic* dimension, which involves issues of security and power at the international level;
- the *political* dimension, which concerns the competition for power and the performance of political institutions at the national and subnational level;
- the *socioeconomic* dimension, which relates to the role of economic competition and social institutions in provoking conflict;

- the *psychological* dimension, which reflects the mutual perceptions of rival groups and how they shape intergroup relations; and
- the *cultural* dimension, which involves the ideological and religious dimensions of conflict, as well as issues of group identity such as traditional hierarchies and gender roles.

Certain of these dimensions—particularly the strategic—are more relevant to interstate conflicts. Others—especially the political and the socioeconomic dimensions—are more germane to intrastate conflicts. But most conflicts involve a combination of several of these dimensions. Moreover, different observers may disagree about which of them are most important in motivating a given conflict.

The public debates in the United States during 2002 and 2003 over the decision to invade Iraq demonstrate how competing narratives can emphasize different dimensions of a conflict. During the months leading up to the invasion, proponents of regime change in Iraq stressed the strategic threat that Saddam Hussein's government posed to America's national security, based on the argument that the Iraqi regime might sponsor terrorist attacks using weapons of mass destruction. Opponents of the invasion, by contrast, tended to minimize the Iraqi threat to American security and depicted the rationale largely as a smokescreen for domestic political interests, such as the Bush administration's alleged desire to manipulate the American electorate to strengthen the hand of the Republican Party against the Democratic opposition, and the economic interests of American business elites, such as oil company executives and defense contractors.

Just as conflict has multiple dimensions, so too does peace. Like conflict, peace is a dynamic process involving interactions among diverse actors. In this guide, we use the term *dividers* to describe factors that may be exploited to provoke conflict within or between communities, and the term *connectors* to denote factors that may be used to promote peace. The terms dividers and connectors are drawn from the Do No Harm analytical framework (DNH framework) developed by CDA Collaborative Learning Projects (CDA, formerly Collaborative for Development Action). The DNH framework defines dividers as sources of tension or polarization between groups that may either be "rooted in deep-seated, historical injustice" or "recent, short-lived, or manipulated by subgroup leaders." Connectors, by contrast, are institutions or cultural patterns by which "people, although they are divided by conflict, remain also connected across subgroup lines."[4]

The Strategic Dimension

The strategic dimension of conflict, which concerns issues of power and international security, is a central focus of international relations theory. It is most salient in interstate wars, though it may also play a role in secessionist movements and other civil wars.

During the Cold War, for example, the United States and the Soviet Union supported competing factions in numerous civil wars in Asia, Africa, and Latin America in efforts to enhance their own global influence. Strategic concerns may function as dividers that provoke conflict between states, as in the Great Power rivalries in Europe of the eighteenth and early nineteenth centuries, or as in the Cold War global competition of the later twentieth century. But strategic considerations can also serve as connectors that promote international peace. For example, after the defeat of Napoleon in 1815, the European Great Powers established the Concert of Europe, a grand coalition designed to contain France and preserve continental peace. During the Cold War, the NATO Alliance was successful in preserving internal peace within Western Europe partly because of the external threat posed by the USSR and other Warsaw Pact states.

The various theoretical approaches to international relations place differing emphasis on the roles of dividers and connectors in shaping the relations among states. The realist and neorealist schools depict conflict as largely motivated by the struggle for national power and survival. Realists and neorealists see divisions among rival states as the norm, not the exception—though states may be connected on a provisional basis by mutually advantageous alliances. Other theoretical approaches, such as liberalism and neoliberalism, examine how national and international institutions can either foster connections among states or divide them against one another.

One inspiration for the realist school of international relations is found in the writings of the seventeenth-century political philosopher Thomas Hobbes, who declared the "state of nature" for human beings to be a "state of war," in which there is "continual fear, and danger of violent death; and the life of man [is] solitary, poor, nasty, brutish, and short."[5] The political scientist Hans Morgenthau, an expatriate from Nazi Germany who immigrated to the United States in 1937, is considered the founder of the realist school.

According to realists, modern nation-states exist in the same condition as humans in a Hobbesian state of nature—that is, in a constant state of war against one another. The state of war need not always be violent: at any given time, two or more states may declare a truce; they may even establish opportunistic alliances to help advance their interests. But such alliances are always temporary, and they must never interfere with the state's fundamental imperative, which is self-preservation. Like humans in the state of nature, the nation-state is governed by two impulses: greed and fear. To defend itself against predatory rivals, the state must continually increase its territory and power. Antagonism among states is not the exception but the rule.

Neorealist theory softens the edges of the realists' bleak worldview. Neorealists concur that the international system consists of sovereign states operating in an anarchic environment. They argue, however, that war stems not from the inherently aggressive nature of nation-states, but rather from the structural constraints of the international environment. Some neorealists, such as Kenneth Waltz, emphasize that states may be drawn into war—even against the wishes of their leaders and their people—by the security dilemma. In an anarchic global system of states, anything one state does to enhance its security will necessarily decrease the security of other states. Thus, by taking actions for self-defense, a state may inadvertently provoke aggressive acts by its rivals.[6]

Because neorealist theory attributes states' behavior not to their aggressive nature, but rather to their inherently insecure situation, neorealists argue that global and regional levels of interstate violence depend highly on context. For example, Waltz and other neorealists have argued that a bipolar international system, such as that during the Cold War, is likely to be relatively stable because of the high level of predictability on both sides. A multipolar system, by contrast, is likely to be less stable and more prone to outbreaks of warfare, given the multiple potential combinations of alliances, which aggravate leaders' uncertainties and their perceptions of risk.

Other theorists, such as Raymond Aron and Stanley Hoffmann, have questioned the validity of this claim, that bipolar systems are more stable than multipolar ones. Although the bipolar system of the Cold War remained stable, notes Hoffmann, the bipolar rivalry of Sparta and Athens in ancient Greece led to the devastating Peloponnesian War. Hoffmann contends that any constellation of power relations in the international system "can lead either to peace or to war; it depends on the domestic characteristics of the main actors, on their preferences and goals, as well as on the relations and links among them."[7] According to the neorealist Stephen Walt, states' behavior toward one another is driven less by the absolute balance of power among them than on the "balance of threat" perceived by those states' leaders. In some circumstances, states may seek to balance against a threatening power by forming defensive alignments. In other situations, lesser powers may bandwagon by making asymmetrical concessions to a dominant power and accepting a subordinate role in an alliance, the case in both the Warsaw Pact and the NATO alliance during the Cold War.[8]

According to the **security dilemma,** actions taken by one state to enhance its security will necessarily decrease the security of other states. By acting to defend itself, a state may inadvertently provoke aggressive reactions from its rivals.

The liberal and neoliberal schools of international relations theory emphasize the role of political, economic, and social institutions in influencing the conduct of states toward one another. For example, some scholars argue that democratic states are less prone to wage war against one another than autocratic ones are. Other theorists stress the role of international institutions—the United Nations, the World Trade Organization, and the International Criminal Court, for example—in creating a connective tissue among nation-states that can help manage conflicts and mitigate the risks of war. The liberal and neoliberal schools are closer in spirit to John Locke, another seventeenth-century English political philosopher, who argued that "the end of law is not to abolish or restrain, but to preserve and enlarge freedom."[9] They contend that healthy political and legal institutions, both at the national and international level, can, in Locke's words, "enlarge freedom" and help sustain lasting peace.

Liberal and neoliberal theorists emphasize the importance of international institutions as foundational agreements among states that facilitate cooperation and mitigate the risks of disruptive actions that would jeopardize mutual interests. Institutions can also solve problems in the international system by reducing uncertainty and transaction costs, as well as by facilitating more effective collective actions.

John Ikenberry's theory of strategic restraint incorporates elements of both the liberal and the realist traditions. Ikenberry points out that, since the end of the Napoleonic wars,

> Leading states have increasingly used institutions after wars to "lock in" a favorable postwar position and to establish sufficient "strategic restraint" on their own power as to gain the acquiescence of weaker and secondary states. Leading postwar states might ideally want to tie other states down to fixed and predictable policy orientations and leave themselves institutionally un-

> encumbered. But in seeking the institutional commitment of less powerful states—locking them into the postwar order—the leading state has to offer them something in return: some measure of credible and institutionalized restraint on its own exercise of power.

In Ikenberry's view, binding international institutions can play a vital role in enabling dominant states to transform power into "stable and legitimate order."[10] Such a rules-based order can create a security reciprocity or security incentive that is as powerful as the security dilemma.

The Political Dimension

The political dimension of conflict and peace is related to the exercise of power within individual states rather than among them. In civil wars involving secessionist or revolutionary movements, the political dimension is particularly salient. Domestic political considerations may also influence the conduct of national leaders on the international stage. For example, in national election campaigns in the United States, foreign policy hawks often seek to portray less aggressive doves as untrustworthy stewards of American national security.

Political factors have the potential either to foster cohesion within nation-states or to provoke divisions. Democratic political institutions can serve as powerful connectors within a country because they provide established and legitimate procedures for balancing competing interests and managing dissent. Conversely, authoritarian regimes can also maintain cohesion within a society—at least temporarily—by forcibly suppressing opposition and by rewarding supporters through patronage. For these reasons, intrastate war is rare both in consolidated democracies and in extreme authoritarian regimes.

Although intrastate wars are rare in established democracies, the transition from autocratic to democratic rule is fraught with peril. Civil wars, coups, and other disruptive political events are far more common in transitional regimes than in either democratic or autocratic ones. Unlike consolidated democracies, transitional governments often lack effective checks on executive power and may hold sham elections that simply ratify and perpetuate the political monopoly of a particular clan or ethnic group—aggravating social grievances and diminishing the legitimacy of the regime. Three other political and institutional factors are important in creating conditions for civil war.

One such factor is *winner-take-all politics*. Many countries around the world—including developed nations such as Switzerland, Belgium, and Canada, as well as developing nations such as Nigeria, India, Bolivia, Cambodia, and Malaysia—have established constitutional formulas that seek to limit (with mixed success) the capacity of a single ethnic group to dominate the others. These formulas include a variety of approaches:

- Power sharing within the central government might entail having multiple presidents or prime ministers (Bosnia-Herzegovina and Cambodia), creating proportional representation systems to increase the power of political minorities (South Africa and Brazil), or reserving parliamentary seats for members of particular groups (India and Iraq).
- Federalism or decentralization of power can allow minority groups to exercise political power at the provincial or local level (Nigeria, Bolivia, Belgium, Switzerland, the United States).
- Constraints on majority power are numerous, such as requiring a two-thirds vote or granting veto powers to particular groups on certain issues, or ensuring the protection of minorities' human rights.[11]

In the absence of effective mechanisms for constraining the ruling party and protecting minority groups, a regime is more likely to abuse its power by serving the interests of its narrow constituency, and excluded groups are more likely to believe that violent resistance offers the only viable hope for redressing their grievances.

Another factor is *ethnic favoritism*. Intrastate conflict is particularly likely in countries whose leaders are able to control the state for the exclusive benefit of their clan or ethnic group, as in postindependence Rwanda and Burundi, Iraq under Saddam Hussein, and contemporary Sudan. The marginalization and persecution of other ethnic groups may provoke insurgent movements to take up arms against the regime, as occurred in Rwanda during the early 1990s. In other situations, the regime may take preemptive action to forestall a potential uprising, as was the case with Saddam Hussein's atrocities against Iraqi Kurds and Shiites (see box 2.1).[12]

The third factor is *weak institutional capacity*. According to the World Bank, "countries and subnational areas with the weakest institutional legitimacy and governance are the most vulnerable to violence and instability and the least able to respond to internal and external stresses."[13] In some areas, such as the Democratic Republic of the Congo, "the state is all but absent from many parts of the country, and violent armed groups dominate

BOX 2.1 Democratic Transition, Ethnic Exclusion, and Civil War: The Case of Côte d'Ivoire

Until the death of President Félix Houphouët-Boigny in 1993, the "Ivoirian Miracle" was hailed as an example of prosperity and stability in postindependence Africa. Houphouët-Boigny ruled Côte d'Ivoire for more than three decades, maintaining his grip on power by balancing representatives of the country's major ethnic groups in leadership positions, as well as by recruiting support from the country's Muslim north by granting citizenship to recent immigrants from Burkina Faso and Mali.

But after Houphouët-Boigny's death, his successor Henri Konan Bédié sought to consolidate power—and exclude his Muslim rival for the presidency, Alassane Ouattara—by promoting the concept of *ivoirité,* which held that ethnic Burkinans and Malians in the north were not true Ivoirian citizens. By the late 1990s, Côte d'Ivoire had entered a downward spiral into xenophobia, ethnic conflict, and political upheavals that culminated in a devastating five-year civil war from 2002 to 2007. In autumn 2010, violence erupted again when the incumbent president, Laurent Gbagbo, attempted to overturn the result of a presidential election won by Ouattara, resulting in a four-month conflict that culminated with Gbagbo's arrest. The civil strife in Côte d'Ivoire offers a cautionary tale of how a fragile democratic transition can be derailed when rival factions manipulate ethnic grievances in an effort to seize or hold onto power.

local contests over power and resources." Many vulnerable regions also "face deficits in their collaborative capacities to mediate conflict peacefully," which means that traditional governing institutions in such areas cannot compensate for the absence of state authority.

The Socioeconomic Dimension

Economic interests often play a central role in both interstate and intrastate wars. National leaders may launch an interstate war to secure control over a vital economic resource, for example, an oil field, watershed, port city, or navigation route. In intrastate wars, a complex web of economic interests may be in play. The economist Frances Stewart identifies three types of social and economic factors that can provoke civil wars: group inequality, private motivation, and failure of the social contract. The political scientist Ashutosh Varshney has pointed out a fourth factor: the absence of cross-cutting bonds linking diverse identity groups together in multiethnic societies.

"Since intra-state wars mainly consist of fighting between groups," Stewart notes in discussing group inequality, "group motives, resentments, and ambitions provide motivation for war. Groups may be divided along cultural or religious lines, by geography, or by class. . . . Resentments inspired by group differences, termed horizontal inequalities, are a major cause of war."[14] According to Stewart, economic research on civil wars shows "consistent evidence of sharp horizontal inequalities between groups in conflict," with economically underprivileged groups denied access to political power. One study of 233 politicized communal groups in ninety-three countries found that "most groups suffering horizontal inequalities had taken some action to assert group interests, ranging from nonviolent protest to rebellion."[15]

Some economists emphasize the role of individual greed, that is, *private motivation,* rather than collective grievances, in motivating the participants in insurgent movements. As Stewart observes,

> Young uneducated men, in particular, may gain employment as soldiers. War also generates opportunities to loot, profiteer from shortages and from aid, trade arms, and carry out illicit production and trade in drugs, diamonds, timber, and other commodities. Where alternative opportunities are few, because of low incomes and poor employment, and the possibilities of enrichment by war are considerable, the incidence and duration of wars are likely to be greater.[16]

The economist Paul Collier argues that the availability of lootable resources (such as diamonds, precious minerals, petroleum, and timber) is a particularly important factor in motivating and sustaining insurgent movements. First, it increases the economic stakes of controlling state institutions, making political conflicts more intense—because rival political groups view the control of the state as the key to their own economic enrichment. Second, it also provides funds for insurgencies to buy armaments and to conduct military operations.

The availability of **lootable resources** in a country can increase the risk of conflict, both by providing funds for insurgent movements and by making control of the state a more attractive prize.

In Collier's view, rebellions should be seen "not as the ultimate protest movements, but as the ultimate manifestation of organized crime." Regardless of whether rebels are motivated primarily by greed, by lust for power, or by genuine perceptions of grievance, Collier asserts, "rebellion occurs only when rebels can do well out of war."[17] Such individuals who "do well out of war" are sometimes referred to as conflict entrepreneurs.

The availability of lootable resources such as "conflict diamonds," however, provides at best a partial explanation for the outbreak of armed conflict. For example, alluvial diamonds played an important role in funding the civil war in Sierra Leone from 1991 to 2002. But other countries with alluvial diamond deposits—South Africa, Tanzania, Venezuela, and Brazil—have not experienced civil war over the past two decades. Maps of the locations of global deposits of other natural resources (petroleum, precious metals, timber, and so forth) likewise show at best a weak correlation between the availability of lootable resources and the outbreak of civil wars.[18]

A third factor is *failure of the social contract*. Impoverished countries with high levels of infant mortality and weak public services are particularly vulnerable to civil war. According to Stewart, "Eight out of ten of the world's poorest countries are suffering, or have recently suffered, from large scale violent conflict."[19] Poor countries have an elevated risk of civil war both because rebel groups can recruit members more easily in areas where alternative economic opportunities are scarce and because the governments of such countries are less able to finance effective counterinsurgency campaigns. Likewise, countries with highly dispersed populations (such as the Democratic Republic of the Congo) face a heightened risk because the government is unable to exert effective control over peripheral regions. Research suggests that absolute levels of poverty in a country are less important in triggering civil wars than economic reversals and other disruptive events. Income shocks in poor countries—such as an economic collapse stemming from a drought in sub-Saharan Africa—can increase the likelihood of conflict.[20]

A comparative study of six Indian communities by Ashutosh Varshney demonstrates the importance of personal and associational connections across ethnic and religious lines in mitigating the risk of violent conflict. Three of these communities, characterized by the *absence of cross-cutting bonds*, erupted into Hindu-Muslim riots after a trigger event, but the three communities that had these bonds did not. Varshney observes that interethnic networks serve as "agents of peace" because they help "build bridges and manage tensions."[21]

> India's repeated encounters with ethnic violence of all kinds (religious, linguistic, caste) and its equally frequent returns from the brink have a great deal to do with the self-regulation that its largely integrated and cross-cutting

> civil society provides. Local structures of resistance and recuperation, as well as local knowledge about how to fix ethnic relations, have ensured that even the worst moments—1947–48 and 1992–93—do not degenerate into an all-out collapse of the country into ethnic warfare. A Rwanda, a Burundi, a Yugoslavia are not possible in India unless the state, for an exogenous reason such as a protracted war, kills all autonomous spaces of citizen activity and organization. A more powerful state in India is likely to make the country more vulnerable to ethnic warfare, not less.

Varshney sounds a note of caution about the potential for centralized state institutions to strangle independent civic organizations and thus to make intrastate war more likely:

> In societies where civic organizations are decimated by the state and no autonomous public space for humanitarian organization and deliberation exists, almost the entire society can go up in flames when the state begins to weaken. Alternatively, the entire state may look very peaceful when the state is strong. A totalitarian polity, normally opposed to autonomous nonstate spaces, is thus typically a clay-footed colossus, as so many states of the former Soviet bloc discovered after the late 1980s. Civil society, if present and especially if vibrant, can provide self-regulating mechanisms, even when the state runs into a crisis.[22]

The Psychological Dimension

Psychological explanations of conflict emphasize the role of factors such as leaders' personal characteristics, perceptions of counterparts, communication patterns, and status competition in contributing to the escalation or de-escalation of conflict. Psychologists also stress the role of collective images of other groups, shared by leaders and their constituents alike, in shaping groups' attitudes and conduct toward their rivals. Psychological factors can serve either as connectors that mitigate conflict or as dividers that provoke it.

Rather than focusing on real differences of interests among states, psychologists focus on perceptions of differences. In the words of one leading textbook on conflict psychology, conflict is rooted in "perceived divergence of interest, a belief that the parties' current aspirations are incompatible."[23] To a great extent, such perceptions reflect the levels of mutual trust between the different parties. For example, during the Cold War, both the United States and the Soviet Union invested massive resources in their conventional and nuclear military forces. In part, their actions were driven by

FIGURE 2.3 Dual Concern Model

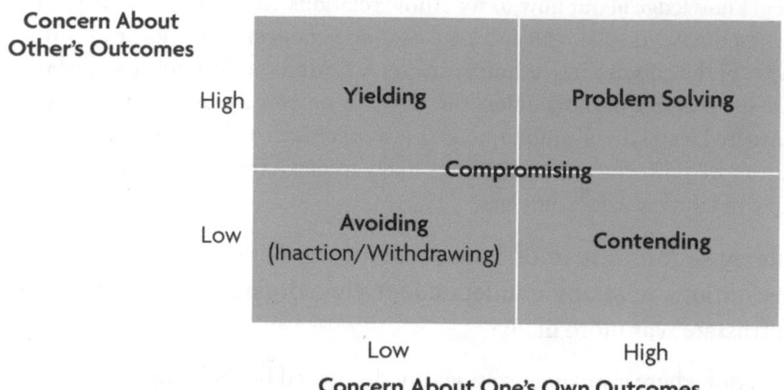

Source: Dean G. Pruitt and Sung Hee Kim, *Social Conflict: Escalation, Stalemate, and Settlement*, 3rd ed. (New York: McGraw-Hill, 2004), 41. Reproduced with permission.

the security dilemma, whereby one nation's defensive moves provoke a corresponding reaction by its rivals. But Canada did not join in this arms race—despite its three-thousand-mile border with the United States. Because Canadian leaders had a high level of trust in their American counterparts, they did not fear an invasion from the south, and thus the American arms buildup did not trigger a security dilemma between the two countries.

Political psychologists use the term *perceived common ground* to describe this sense of shared interests and common purpose among individuals and nations. Figure 2.3 illustrates how the presence or absence of perceived common ground can influence parties' attitudes and behavior toward one another.

The dual concern model identifies five potential strategies that one party may adopt when in conflict with another: avoiding, contending, yielding, compromising, or problem solving. If a party does not care particularly about the outcome of a dispute, it may choose to avoid conflict either by inaction (postponing a discussion) or by withdrawing (physically departing the scene). If a party is concerned about the outcome but only for itself, it may choose a contending strategy, for example, when one nation invades or seeks to intimidate its neighbor. A contending strategy does not necessarily involve the use of violence; it may simply involve an unyielding commitment to a position in a negotiation. Conversely, if a party cares more about the outcome for the other party than for itself, it may decide to yield to the other (when one state gives in to another's demands over a trade dispute).

A fourth option is to seek a compromise that balances the concerns of both parties against one another (for example, by reducing but not eliminating a tariff that seeks to protect a domestic industry from international competition). Finally, if a party is highly concerned for both itself and the other, it may pursue a creative problem-solving approach that seeks to identify a win-win solution (for example, by establishing an international partnership to address an issue of common concern).

As George Levinger and Jeffrey Rubin have shown, several inherent characteristics of international relations can make it more difficult for nations to develop relations based on strong mutual trust than it is for individuals in personal relationships. For example, in international affairs, withdrawal is generally not an option: no parallel exists to the choice of moving to a new neighborhood or suing for divorce, which eliminates one potential path to resolving a conflict. Moreover, power between nations is asymmetrical, which enables strong nations to dominate weak ones, and international agreements are often unenforceable. Given the absence of global authorities, parallel to the police or the courts, for enforcing most international agreements, the most powerful nations can often violate such agreements with impunity.[24]

Conflict management practitioners can use a range of methods to help overcome mutual distrust among nations and expand perceived common ground. One common approach is to establish *confidence-building measures* (CBMs), which are intended to reduce fear and suspicion by increasing the predictability of rival states' behavior. During the Cold War, the United States and the USSR adopted various CBMs to decrease the risk of miscalculations or miscommunications that might inadvertently lead to nuclear war. These included a hotline for direct telephone communications between the White House and the Kremlin, exchanges of information on issues such as troop movements and arms acquisitions, exchanges of military personnel, arms control treaties, and open skies agreements permitting overflight of the other country's territory to verify treaty commitments. As James Macintosh has written, CBMs can do more than simply increase the rival parties' confidence in their existing agreements. "The confidence-building process," he argues, can also "facilitate, focus, and amplify the potential for a significant positive transformation in the security relations of participating states no longer satisfied with status quo security policies."[25]

Another potentially useful approach to building perceived common ground in international relations is *interest-based negotiation* (see chapter 5), in which the parties seek to reframe the conflict by focusing on their underlying interests and needs, rather than on their stated positions. For example, it may be possible to reframe a territorial dispute as motivated by each state's quest to achieve security against attack by its neighbor—a goal that might be achieved through international security guarantees or other measures. As Levinger and Rubin note, "Conflict is driven more by the *perception* of divergence of interest than by the reality of such a divide," and "conflicts at all levels are characterized by mixed motives (by a mix of cooperativeness and competitiveness, in particular)." Thus it may be possible to "modify the experience of conflict" by "framing the way in which parties see the conflict and one another."[26]

> The risk of deadly conflict is exacerbated when high levels of mutual distrust and fear exist between rival parties. By **reframing** the way in which parties see the conflict and each other, it may be possible to open a space for cooperative dispute resolution.

Psychology of Escalation

Social scientists who study the political psychology of conflict have identified two key preconditions for the escalation of conflict: high perceived divergence of interest between the rival parties and instability.[27] For example, during the first half of the twentieth century, a high perceived divergence of interest existed between the political leaders of Germany and France, a fact reflected in the two world wars fought between 1914 and 1945. Levels of stability are determined by a variety of factors, including economic well-being, political institutions, culture and history, leadership behavior, and so forth. At the outset of World War I in 1914, Europe was experiencing relatively high levels of prosperity and economic integration, which led many commentators to dismiss the possibility of a continental war. But imperial rivalries, escalating arms races, erratic leadership behavior, and cultures that glorified warfare all contributed to the destabilization of relations among the European great powers.

The outbreak of violence can be unleashed by a trigger event, such as the assassination of the heir to the Austrian throne in 1914 or the downing of the Rwandan president's airplane in 1994. A trigger event raises the risk of escalation by heightening the parties' perceived divergence of interests, which in turn results in increasing instability.

Psychologists use the term *conflict spiral* to refer to a cycle of escalating hostile actions by rival parties. One type is a *threat spiral*, in which two par-

Potential Trigger Events for Escalation

- a contested election, especially in a state with a winner-take-all political system
- a census that reallocates political representation and resource distribution
- a scandal that calls attention to a collective grievance
- a coup or the assassination of a leading political figure
- electoral violence
- a terrorist attack
- a natural disaster or famine
- economic crisis

ties escalate their threatening actions toward the other, as in an arms race. Another is a *retaliation spiral*, in which Party A's aggressive behavior causes Party B to blame A for harming its interests, which leads B to retaliate, causing A to blame B for harming its interests, which leads A to retaliate, and so forth.

The beginning of the Troubles in Northern Ireland in 1968 to 1969 provides an example of a retaliation spiral that unleashed a bloody and intractable civil conflict. In 1968, young Catholic nationalists began a series of peaceful marches demanding civil rights, which intensified instability by calling attention to political and economic discrimination against Catholics in Northern Ireland. In October 1968, policemen shot several demonstrators, which triggered a conflict spiral of retaliation and counterretaliation. By 1971, the Irish Republican Army (IRA) had fractured into two wings, the militant Provisional IRA committed to waging an armed struggle against British rule. The hardening of positions on both sides resulted in decades of violence and insecurity in Northern Ireland.[28]

Psychology of De-Escalation

Whereas conflict can escalate suddenly and unexpectedly in the wake of a triggering event, de-escalation tends to be a more gradual and halting process. The political psychologists Dean Pruitt and Sung Hee Kim identify four preconditions for de-escalation:

- parties' grudging acceptance of each other as interdependent partners,
- parties' recognition that they are now relatively equal in effective power,
- perceived common ground between the parties, and
- some faith in the chances of success.[29]

De-escalation of conflict becomes possible when rival parties perceive that they have common interests and grudgingly accept each other as necessary and interdependent partners.

As in the escalation of conflict, the perceptions of the situation by the rival parties are all important. For a conflict to escalate, the parties must perceive their interests to be incompatible. Conversely, de-escalation can occur only if the parties perceive some common interests that unite them, and if they acknowledge—however reluctantly—their interdependence.

Closely connected to the parties' recognition of their mutual interdependence is that of the relative equality of their effective power. This may be equivalent even when one side has massive superiority in wealth, firepower, or other resources. For example, in the conflict over Northern Ireland from the 1960s through the 1990s, the British government had overwhelming military superiority over the Provisional IRA and other separatist forces. But because neither side had the capacity to force the other side to yield to their demands, their effective power was essentially equivalent. This was one of the factors that facilitated the negotiation of the Good Friday Agreement of 1998.[30]

Practitioners sometimes use the phrase "window of opportunity" to describe a situation favorable to the de-escalation of conflict. During windows of opportunity, events call attention to commonalities within a society, diminishing the significance of internal fault lines and motivating cooperation across intergroup boundaries. Examples of such events might include a natural disaster, such as the tsunami that struck Indonesia's Aceh Province in late December 2004, or years of devastating conflict that give rise to a universal sense of war weariness within a population, as in Liberia after the ceasefire of 2003.

Certain events—an election or a census, for example—have the potential to either escalate or de-escalate conflict: they can help consolidate peace if they are perceived as legitimate and fair, but can undermine stability if they are perceived as illegitimate. For example, during the months leading up to the 2011 Sudanese referendum on the independence of South Sudan, many observers anticipated the referendum might trigger a renewed North-South civil war in Sudan. Although the pro-independence vote did indeed provoke violence between northern and southern political authorities, it also helped de-escalate tensions among competing factions of southerners. The organization of the referendum triggered a common sense of purpose among the rival southern factions, and international observers strongly emphasized the need to build on those alliances.

Cultural Dimension

The cultural dimension of conflict and peace involves issues of collective identity such as ethnicity, religion, nationality, or language. Cultural differences do not necessarily result in violent conflict. In the vast majority of cases, multiethnic societies remain peaceful. As the anthropologist Abner Cohen writes,

> Men may and do certainly joke about or ridicule the strange and bizarre customs of men from other ethnic groups, because these customs are different from their own. But they do not fight over such differences alone. When men do, on the other hand, fight across ethnic lines it is nearly always the case that they fight over some fundamental issues concerning the distribution and exercise of power, whether economic, political, or both.[31]

But it is equally important to recognize the central role that ethnic and religious identities can play in defining the stakes of a struggle and fueling violence. Humans are motivated not only to advance their economic self-interest, but also by a desire for meaning, which is often provided by communal identities. In the words of conflict-resolution scholar Celia Cook-Huffman, identity "refers to a sense of a self, a way individuals know and understand themselves."[32] Any given individual has multiple identities, such as nation, race, religious community, clan, family, gender, and occupation. But in moments of communal crisis, one of these identities may trump the others. For example, in time of war, a nation-state may conscript its citizens into the armed forces, in which case the draftees' obligations to the nation trump all their other obligations. In these extreme circumstances, when groups or individuals perceive their core identities as threatened, they may act to defend them through violence.

Subsequent chapters of this guide discuss in more detail the nature of communal identities and their role in provoking or mitigating conflict. But one key point is important to emphasize at the outset. More so than economic interests, communal identities can easily become nonnegotiable, which can stymie efforts at conflict resolution. One is unlikely to negotiate away half of one's womanhood or half of one's citizenship. If parties perceive that their rivals are imposing demands that threaten their core identities, the conflict may escalate or become locked into an enduring stalemate.

Because identity-based disagreements can create such profound obstacles to resolving or mitigating deadly conflicts, it is imperative that analysts pay close attention to how all the rival parties understand the cultural and historical dimensions of a dispute, in order to anticipate minefields that could render the conflict intractable and to identify possible new approaches to conflict resolution. Two particular cultural issues warrant further discussion here: first, how to understand the role of traditional elites in managing conflict; and second, how to apply the gender lens to identify potential conflict management resources. Male members of traditional elites and respected women in a community can both play important roles in provoking and perpetuating violent conflict. Conversely, they may also serve as bridges among the rival factions, which can help prevent or resolve episodes of organized violence.

Working with Traditional Elites

Practitioners in international development must often balance their desire to respect local traditions against that to promote modernization. For example, a project to drill wells in a hilltop village may provide clean and abundant drinking water to the residents but impoverish all those villagers who had earned their living by carrying water up the hill.

Conflict management practitioners sometimes encounter a similar dilemma. In many regions of the world, traditional institutions such as councils of elders play an important role in local governance and conflict resolution. But in some cases, such institutions may function at cross purposes with the international actors seeking to promote peace. For example, village elders may sanction certain low-level ritualized violence, such as blood feuds between families, as an acceptable feature of local culture; or youths in a community may be required to lead cattle raids against a neighboring village as a rite of passage to manhood. The edicts of a council of elders may be at odds with international human rights norms—for example, forcing a girl to marry her rapist in order to resolve a conflict between two families. Traditional institutions may also reinforce asymmetries of power between local elites and marginalized groups, potentially perpetuating and exacerbating conflict within a community.

No simple road map exists for navigating these kinds of cross-cultural encounters. Conflict management practitioners often need to find a middle way between cultural imperialism (imposing our values and norms on other societies) and cultural relativism (deferring to local customs even if they are at odds with our core values). On the one hand, it is essential to be attentive to and respectful of local customs and hierarchies. On the other hand, one should avoid idealizing traditional practices as sacrosanct.

Traditional cultures are fluid rather than static, and global historical developments of recent decades have dramatically altered local cultures even in the most remote parts of the world. For example, the widespread availability of small arms and light weapons has empowered young people at the expense of village elders, as has access to cell phones and the Internet. Demographic shifts such as population growth, the so-called youth bulge in developing countries, and increasing urbanization have also destabilized traditional community norms and institutions. In some parts of the world, communities have responded to these radical disruptions by attempting to reestablish traditional forms of governance such as sharia law. But this modern fundamentalism may sanction extreme practices, such as stoning adulterers, that were rarely applied in the premodern era.[33]

Gender Lens

Conflict management practitioners often refrain from insisting that women play a prominent role in peace processes, even though women do bear a disproportionate burden of the suffering in civil wars. Traditionally, formal peace negotiations have brought together the leading combatants—who are almost invariably men—on the theory that the parties who are committing the violence are the only ones who can stop it. This practice results in the exclusion of other actors, such as religious leaders and community organizers, both male and female, whose support may be essential for establishing a lasting peace. Another reason for the exclusion of women is that international interveners have been reluctant to impose Western values of gender equality on traditional patriarchal societies. Of the dozens of UN special envoys dispatched over the past six decades to resolve violent conflicts, not one has been a woman.[34]

One consequence is that gender-related issues tend to be neglected in peace settlements and postconflict reconstruction programs. For example, programs for demobilization, disarmament, and reintegration (DDR) generally focus on male ex-combatants, not on girls and women who served in support roles for militias or as fighters themselves. Moreover, postconflict economic reconstruction programs tend to target economic infrastructure and market reforms, rather than social infrastructure such as schools or health clinics, which offer greater opportunities for female employment. Women are also often excluded from farming assistance and job training programs, and they have suffered from discrimination in postconflict land settlements in countries such as Zimbabwe and El Salvador.[35]

From the standpoint of conflict analysis, it is important to take into account the roles that women can play in either exacerbating or mitigating conflict. Women frequently provide economic and other material support to insurgent movements, and they sometimes participate directly as combatants. They can also contribute to the escalation of conflict by urging the men in their communities to take up arms.

But women's social positions in their communities can sometimes also allow them to play productive roles as peacemakers. For example, during the civil war in Liberia, Christian and Muslim women were able to forge an interfaith peace movement. In 2003, these women prodded Liberian president Charles Taylor to initiate peace talks in Ghana. When the negotiations stalled, Liberian women helped shame the rival factions into reaching a settlement by barricading the negotiators into their conference room and threatening to hold them there until an agreement was signed. One of the leaders of the Liberian women's peace movement, Leymah Gbowee, received the 2011 Nobel Peace Prize for her work.

In some societies, women may occupy positions that enable them to bridge the divides among rival groups. The Algerian diplomat Mohamed Sahnoun was able to capitalize on a feature of Somali marriage customs to prevent violence when he was serving as special representative of the UN secretary-general to Somalia in 1992 (see box 2.2).[36]

To involve women in more robust roles in peace processes does not necessarily mean to impose Western values on non-Western cultures. Just as the authority of tribal elders has been transformed—and often undermined—by contemporary global trends, so too have women's roles been transformed in even the most fundamentalist societies. In some cases, gender-based peacebuilding initiatives may serve not so much to create new roles for women as to restore the authority that women traditionally exercised in their communities, so that they can help heal the connective social tissues that have been torn by civil war.

Violence as a Strategic Choice

This chapter has explored a range of reasons—strategic, political, socioeconomic, psychological, and cultural—why groups may engage in violent conflict. The decision to initiate violence is not predetermined but rather the consequence of human choices. Conflicts turn deadly when one or more

BOX 2.2 Applying the Gender Lens: The Case of Somalia

When serving as UN envoy to Somalia in 1992, Mohamed Sahnoun received intelligence that militias from two rival clans were planning to confront each other the following day at a location near Mogadishu. Because he had no military forces at his disposal, Sahnoun relied on his ingenuity and his knowledge of the Somali clan system to prevent the outbreak of violence.

As Sahnoun recalled in an October 2008 interview, "In Somalia the five clans intermarry, but the clan system follows the father's line, not the mother's. So when there is a confrontation, the Somali woman will find herself caught in a situation where her son will fight her brother, because she is from a different clan than her son. This creates the terrible situation that the women suffer more during a war."

Based on this insight, Sahnoun telephoned the BBC reporter based in Nairobi to request that she interview him for that evening's BBC Somali language news broadcast, which was listened to by "practically every Somali with a transistor radio." In the interview, Sahnoun declared, "We have some very bad news. We would like to prevent a confrontation which is going to happen tomorrow. Two clans are going to confront each other at a specific place near Mogadishu, and that would produce a terrible tragedy. We have to avoid that by all means. So I am calling on the women of Somalia, on the sisters of Somalia, on the mothers of Somalia, to go and stop this fighting." The following day, Sahnoun said, "There were huge demonstrations of women from Mogadishu and around Mogadishu who went to where the two clans were supposed to confront each other. They sat there and stayed there and prevented war between the two clans."

actors make a strategic decision that the most effective way to achieve their objectives is through violence against another group. Actors base their decisions on whether and how to use violence on their calculations of the relative costs and benefits of nonviolent and violent political strategies.

Several factors influence actors' calculations concerning the relative attractiveness of violent versus nonviolent strategies:

- Do they have the capacity to wage a military campaign? In the case of nonstate actors, do they have access to armaments and funding—whether through the theft of lootable resources, narcotrafficking or other criminal activities, donations from diaspora communities, or other strategies? Are they able to recruit fighters and obtain logistical support from their communities, whether through ideological persuasion, individual charisma, bribery, coercion, or some combination of all of these approaches? In the case of government leaders, do they have the authority and resources to wage war, either directly or through the use of proxy forces such as paramilitary groups? Are there constraints on executive power (constitutional restrictions or opposition from political rivals or international patrons) that limit the leader's ability to use military force?

- How strong are the incentives to use violence, and how likely is it that the actors' objectives can be achieved without the use of force? Incentives to use force may be positive (increasing one's power and wealth) or negative (preventing the marginalization or extermination of one's group). Deadly conflict is most likely to occur when high levels of mutual distrust and fear exist between rival parties. When one or more of the parties perceive themselves as existentially threatened by the other, they may resort to extreme violence such as genocide or mass atrocities.
- What are the likely costs of military action relative to a peaceful political strategy? Such costs could include death, defeat, economic losses, or prosecution for war crimes by an international tribunal.

By saying that violence is a strategic choice, we are not asserting that it is a purely rational one. Emotional or moral considerations may also influence leaders' calculations. For example, military historians typically identify the defeat of the German Sixth Army at Stalingrad in 1943 as the turning point of World War II, and they portray Adolf Hitler's obsession with defeating the Soviet army in Stalingrad as a strategic error of catastrophic proportions. Germany's military objective—to halt Soviet shipping traffic on the Volga River—could have been accomplished at a fraction of the cost without seizing the city. But when Hitler decided to destroy the city that bore the name of his nemesis, he became committed to this objective regardless of the consequences for the German army.[37]

The decision to initiate violent conflict may also have structural effects on the competing factions—as was the case with the emergence of the militant Provisional IRA in Northern Ireland in the 1970s. One common consequence of the escalation of a conflict is that political moderates on both sides are marginalized or even physically eliminated. Thus the leadership group that escalated the hostilities becomes increasingly empowered, and any voices that might help resolve the conflict are silenced. This can lead one or both sides to adopt increasingly extreme strategies as the conflict evolves.

For international actors seeking to prevent deadly conflict, it is essential to shift decision makers' strategic calculus by decreasing the relative benefits and increasing the relative costs of resorting to violence. Positive economic or political incentives, such as the promise of development assistance or membership in the European Union, may be made contingent on peaceful political conduct. Conversely, punitive economic sanctions, the deployment of peacekeeping forces, or the threat of international prosecution may be used to increase the risks and reduce the utility of military action.

With respect to formal peace negotiations, practitioners use the term *ripeness* to refer to a situation in which the potential exists for a viable negotiated peace. William Zartman of Johns Hopkins University, a leading scholar of negotiation theory, argues that a conflict typically becomes ripe for settlement only when the competing parties come to perceive themselves as suffering from it and when they lose hope that they can achieve their objectives using armed force. He calls this state of affairs a "mutually hurting stalemate," which contributes to several of the conditions for deescalation identified by political psychologists: the parties grudgingly accept each other as interdependent partners, they recognize that they are now relatively equal in effective power, and they develop perceived common ground because they recognize that the conflict is detrimental to their interests.[38]

Zartman emphasizes that a mutually hurting stalemate is a subjective rather than an objective condition:

> Ripeness is a matter of perception, and as with any subjective perception, there are likely to be objective facts to be perceived. . . . Thus it is the perception of the objective condition, not the condition itself, that makes for a mutually hurting stalemate. If the parties do not recognize "clear evidence" (in someone else's view) that they are at an impasse, a mutually hurting stalemate has not (yet) occurred, and if they do perceive themselves to be in such a situation, no matter how flimsy the "evidence," the mutually hurting stalemate is present.[39]

The other element necessary for a ripe moment is less complex and also perceptional—a way out. Parties do not have to be able to identify a specific solution; they must only have a sense that a negotiated solution is possible and that the other party shares that sense and the willingness to search for a solution too. Without a sense of a way out, the push associated with the mutually hurting stalemate would leave the parties with nowhere to go.[40]

Although mediators and other conflict management practitioners have only limited influence over the parties to a conflict, they can sometimes help the antagonists reframe their perceptions of their interests and each other. If the rival factions begin to see each other as interdependent partners rather than as mortal enemies, they may start to discover openings for cooperative resolution of their disputes.

Conclusion

The perspectives described in this chapter provide complementary rather than contradictory views on the causes of conflict and peace. Each highlights a distinctive aspect that may be of greater relevance to analysts and decision makers in certain situations than in others. International relations theorists emphasize the calculus of strategic threats and opportunities that influence national leaders' decisions. Political scientists analyze how the governing institutions within a nation influence its prospects for peace and stability. Economists and sociologists focus on how competing socioeconomic interests can fan the flames of intrastate and interstate strife. Political psychologists stress the importance of mutual perceptions and patterns of communication among rival groups. Finally, historians and anthropologists of conflict, as well as psychologists, examine the role of identities—defined by ethnicity, religion, nationality, or other characteristics—in provoking and channeling strife among rival groups.

When analyzing the various dividers that can provoke conflict within and among nation-states, it is essential to pay equal attention to the connectors that can promote peace. As the World Bank observes in its 2011 *World Development Report*, the risk of conflict in a given country reflects

> the combination of the exposure to internal and external stresses and the strength of the "immune system," or the social capability for coping with stress embodied in legitimate institutions. Both state and nonstate institutions are important. Institutions include social norms and behaviors—such as the ability of leaders to transcend sectarian and political differences and develop bargains, and of civil society to advocate for greater national and political cohesion—as well as rules, laws, and organizations.[41]

The chapters that follow discuss tools both for analyzing emerging conflict risks and for identifying strategies to enhance the social "immune systems" that enable societies to manage conflicts peacefully.

Questions for Practitioners

- What are the key dividers and connectors in the communities where you work? For example, are there power struggles among rival factions, or political coalitions that reach across group lines? Do economically underprivileged groups express grievances against wealthy elites, or do most people believe that wealth is distributed in a legitimate manner? Are levels of mutual trust and respect across group lines low or high? Do you see any potential flashpoints for identity-based conflicts (such as issues related to ethnicity, religion, language, or history)? What roles are traditional elites and women playing, either in provoking conflict or in helping build and sustain peace?
- Can your organization influence the strategic choices of actors in communities at risk of conflict? Which of the five dimensions of deadly conflict—strategic, political, socioeconomic, psychological, and cultural—are most relevant to your work? Can you take any actions that might help de-escalate conflict by encouraging rival parties to accept each other as necessary and interdependent partners with some common interests?

Notes

1. Michael Lund, *Preventing Deadly Conflicts: A Strategy for Preventive Diplomacy* (Washington, DC: United States Institute of Peace Press, 1996), 38, 40.
2. Johan Galtung, "An Editorial," *Journal of Peace Research* 1, no. 1 (March 1964): 2.
3. World Bank, *World Development Report 2011* (Washington, DC: World Bank, 2011), 2, 5.
4. CDA Collaborative Learning Projects, *The Do No Harm Handbook* (Cambridge, MA: CDA Collaborative Learning Projects, 2004), 3, www.cdainc.com/dnh/docs/DoNoHarmHandbook.pdf.
5. Thomas Hobbes, *Leviathan* (1651; repr., Oxford: Oxford University Press, 1996), 84.
6. Kenneth Neal Waltz, *Theory of International Politics* (Reading, MA: Addison-Wesley, 1979).
7. Stanley Hoffmann, Robert O. Keohane, and John J. Mearsheimer, "Back to the Future, Part II: International Relations Theory and Post-Cold War Europe," *International Security* 15(1990): 192.
8. Stephen M. Walt, *Origins of Alliances* (Ithaca, NY: Cornell University Press, 1987).
9. John Locke, *The Second Treatise of Government* (1690), chap. 6, para. 57.

10. G. John Ikenberry, *After Victory: Institutions, Strategic Restraint, and the Rebuilding of Order after Major Wars* (Princeton, NJ: Princeton University Press, 2001), xi, xiii.

11. Frances Stewart and Graham Brown, "Motivations for Conflict: Groups and Individuals," in *Leashing the Dogs of War: Conflict Management in a Divided World*, eds. Chester A. Crocker, Fen Osler Hampson, and Pamela Aall (Washington, DC: United States Institute of Peace Press, 2007), 231–32.

12. Arnim Langer, "Horizontal Inequalities and Violent Group Mobilisation in Côte d'Ivoire," *Oxford Development Studies* 33, no. 1 (2005): 25–45.

13. World Bank, World Development Report 2011, 7.

14. Frances Stewart, "Root Causes of Violent Conflict in Developing Countries," *British Medical Journal* 324, no. 7333 (February 9, 2002): 343, www.bmj.com/content/324/7333/342.full (accessed May 6, 2012).

15. Frances Stewart, "Development and Security" (*CRISE* working paper no. 3, Centre for Research on Inequality, Human Security, and Ethnicity, Oxford, 2004), 15, www.crise.ox.ac.uk/pubs/workingpaper3.pdf (accessed May 6, 2012).

16. Stewart, "Root Causes," 343.

17. Paul Collier, Economic Causes of Civil Conflict and their Implications for Policy (Washington, DC: World Bank, 2000), 4.

18. Joshua D. Fisher, "The Ecological Correlates of Armed Conflict: A Geospatial and Spatial-Statistical Approach to Conflict Modeling" (PhD dissertation, George Mason University, 2010), 65–105, 150–183.

19. Stewart, "Root Causes," 342.

20. Edward Miguel, Shanker Satyanath, and Ernest Sergenti, "Economic Shocks and Conflict: An Instrumental Variable Approach," *Journal of Political Economy* 112 (2004): 725–53; Ernest Sergenti, "A Probit Model and Other Extension to Miguel, Satyanath, and Sergenti's (2004) 'Economic Shocks and Civil Conflict: An Instrumental Variables Approach" (working paper, New York University, February 2006), https://files.nyu.edu/ejs210/public/Sergenti_Probit_Conflict.pdf (accessed May 7, 2012).

21. Ashutosh Varshney, *Ethnic Conflict and Civic Life: Hindus and Muslims in India* (New Haven, CT: Yale University Press, 2002), 286.

22. Ibid.

23. Dean G. Pruitt and Sung Hee Kim, *Social Conflict: Escalation, Stalemate, and Settlement*, 3rd ed. (New York: McGraw-Hill, 2004), 7–8.

24. George Levinger and Jeffrey Z. Rubin. "Bridges and Barriers to a More General Theory of Conflict," *Negotiation Journal* 10 (1994): 201–15.

25. James MacIntosh, *Confidence Building in the Arms Control Process: A Transformation View* (Ottawa: Department of Foreign Affairs and International Trade, 1996), 1.

26. Levinger and Rubin, "Bridges and Barriers," 10–12.

27. Pruitt and Kim, *Social Conflict*, 35–36, 124–50.

28. Dean G. Pruitt, "Readiness Theory and the Northern Ireland Peace Process," *American Behavioral Scientist* 50, no. 11 (2007): 1520–41.

29. Pruitt and Kim, *Social Conflict*, 177–88.

30. Pruitt, "Readiness Theory."

31. Abner Cohen, *Two-Dimensional Man: An Essay on the Anthropology of Power and Symbolism in Complex Society* (Berkeley: University of California Press, 1974), 94; quoted in Stewart and Brown, "Motivations for Conflict," 221.

32. Celia Cook-Huffman, "The Role of Identity in Conflict," in *Handbook of Conflict Analysis and Resolution*, eds. Dennis J.D. Sandole, Sean Byrne, Ingrid Sandole-Staroste, and Jessica Senehi (London: Routledge, 2009), 19–20.

33. On the transformation of sharia law in the modern era, see Wael B. Hallaq, *Shari'a: Theory, Practice, Transformations* (Cambridge: Cambridge University Press, 2009) and *The Impossible State: Islam, Politics, and Modernity's Moral Predicament* (New York: Columbia University Press, 2012). See also Sadakat Kadri, *Heaven on Earth: A Journey Through Shari'a Law from the Deserts of Ancient Arabia to the Streets of the Modern Muslim World* (New York: Farrar, Straus, and Giroux, 2012).

34. Kathleen Kuehnast, Chantal de Jonge Oudraat, and Helga Hernes, eds., *Women and War: Power and Protection in the 21st Century* (Washington, DC: United States Institute of Peace Press, 2011).

35. Frances Stewart, "Women in Conflict and Post-Conflict Situations" (paper presented at the UN Economic and Social Council's 2010 Thematic Discussion "The Role of Women in Countries in Special Situations," New York, June 30, 2010), www.un.org/en/ecosoc/julyhls/pdf10/frances_stewart.pdf (accessed September 18, 2012).

36. Interview with Mohamed Sahnoun, Washington, DC, October 2008.

37. Ian Kershaw, *Hitler, 1936–1945: Nemesis* (New York: W. W. Norton, 2000), 534–58.

38. I. William Zartman, "Ripeness," *Beyond Intractability*, August 2003, www.beyondintractability.org/bi-essay/ripeness (accessed May 3, 2012).

39. Ibid.

40. Ibid.

41. World Bank, *World Development Report 2011*, 7.

3

RISK ASSESSMENT AND EARLY WARNING

Key Points

- *Watchlists* for conflict early warning and early detection provide an initial screening of global data on conflict risks. They can alert analysts and decision makers to emerging threats and help them establish priority regions for preventive action.
- *Conflict metrics* instruments enable analysts and decision makers to track both risks and sources of social resilience in particular regions on an ongoing basis. Metric instruments can inform the design of programmatic interventions to mitigate threats of violence.
- Environmental degradation, resource shortages, and climate change can be threat multipliers that exacerbate the effects of existing social and political divisions. Environmental conflict risks can be mitigated by institutions that fairly manage access to scarce resources, as well as by national and international systems that increase the resiliency of societies to the effects of resource scarcity and climate change.
- Genocide and mass atrocities typically occur in the context of a broader intrastate or interstate war, and it is often difficult to distinguish the initial stages of genocidal violence from the collateral damage of war. Because campaigns of mass atrocities can involve more explosive and extreme violence than other conflicts, it is vital to remain alert to their distinctive early warning signs.

Effective interventions to prevent or manage deadly conflict depend on the timely identification of emerging threats. This chapter examines two types of analytical instruments that can call attention to vulnerable regions and inform decisions about how best to respond to threats of conflict:

- *watchlists* for early warning and early detection, which identify regions at greatest risk of violence, and
- *conflict metrics* instruments, which identify specific vulnerabilities and resiliencies of regions at risk of violent conflict.

This chapter also discusses two particular types of conflict risks characterized by distinctive warning factors and therefore worthy of special attention: first, conflicts provoked by environmental degradation, resource shortages, or climate change; and, second, genocidal violence that targets civilian groups.

Early Warning Watchlists

A number of nongovernmental organizations (NGOs), think tanks, and private-sector firms publish watchlists on a periodic basis to warn policymakers of threats to peace and international security (see appendix 2). Watchlists produced by NGOs include the annual Fund for Peace's Failed States Index; the Political Instability Task Force Report, produced by a consortium of academic institutions with funding from the U.S. Central Intelligence Agency; the annual Peace and Conflict Instability Ledger, published by the University of Maryland's Center for International Development and Conflict Management; and International Crisis Group's monthly bulletin *CrisisWatch*. In addition, various specialized watchlists such as the Peoples Under Threat list published by the Minority Rights Group International, and the annual ranking Assessing Country Risks of Genocide and Politicide published by the Genocide Prevention Advisory Network, warn of specific threats such as genocide and other gross human rights violations.

A wide range of private-sector firms also provide strategic forecasting of political and business risks, either on a subscription or contract basis. Such entities include the Economist Intelligence Unit, Eurasia Group, Jane's Sentinel Security Assessments, Oxford Analytica, Political Risk Services Group, STRATFOR, and Virtual Research Associates (see appendix 3). In addition, the U.S. government produces classified reports such as the National Intelligence Council's Atrocities Watchlist, a list of countries at risk of genocide and atrocities, as well as classified reports by other intelligence agencies. In this chapter, we focus on publicly available lists produced by nonprofit organizations, excluding sources that are either classified or available only to paying clients.

Although such watchlists are generally described as providing early warning of emerging conflicts and other threats, the term *early detection* may more accurately describe their function. Often the countries identified as being at greatest risk are those that have already suffered protracted and devastating conflicts—Sudan, the Democratic Republic of the Congo, Afghanistan, and Somalia. Only after violence has broken out, at least on a localized scale, are countries typically elevated to a higher risk level on conflict watchlists. Nonetheless, such lists can perform an invaluable function if they focus the attention of analysts and decision makers in a timely manner on the risk of escalation in a volatile region.

To determine which watchlists are most relevant to a particular concern, it is important to distinguish among the objectives of the various lists and what factors these lists measure. For example, private strategic forecasting services typically seek to identify political risks that may adversely affect the operations or profitability of international businesses operating in a given country. Thus, a civil war or a campaign of government-sponsored violence may be of limited relevance to the forecast if the violence is occurring in a region of the country distant from a corporation's facilities and supply lines. Conversely, an analysis of political risks to international businesses may include factors that would be tangential to conflict early warning, such as the threat of default on government debt or expropriation of the assets of international businesses by the national government.

Most of the watchlists discussed in this chapter focus either on risks of state failure or violent conflict. Since the 1990s, a considerable body of social science research has emerged on regions of the world variously termed collapsed states, failed and failing states, fragile states, weak states, ungoverned areas, or low-income countries under stress. These terms are often used interchangeably, though they can refer to a wide range of political conditions. For example, since 1994, the U.S. Central Intelligence Agency has funded an unclassified collaborative academic research project initially called the State Failure Task Force, and subsequently renamed the Political Instability Task Force (PITF). The PITF began its work by compiling a comprehensive list of political instability events that have occurred around the globe since 1955. These events could fall into one of four types: revolutionary wars, ethnic wars, adverse regime changes, and genocides and politicides. Under the

PITF definition, the category of political instability event would include not only an authoritarian coup or a campaign of mass atrocities in a country whose government exercises effective control over its territory and is capable of delivering basic social services, such as Indonesia or Chile, but also a revolutionary or ethnic war in countries whose governments effectively lack the capacity to administer the territory outside their capital cities, such as Afghanistan or the Democratic Republic of Congo.[1]

The terms *fragile states, weak states,* and especially *ungoverned spaces* have been criticized for inflexibly imposing Western political standards on regions with very different political traditions. The phrase *ungoverned spaces* is particularly problematic, because it misleadingly implies that any territory not under the control of a Western-style nation-state lacks any effective institutions for governance. To a lesser extent, the terms *fragile states* and *weak states* also share this defect. Another concern is that many people in the developing world find these terms offensive. As the political scientist Anne Clunan observes,

> The growing prominence of this issue in developed world policy circles, needless to say, provokes concerns in developing countries that the concept of "ungoverned spaces" is merely the latest window dressing for neo-imperialism. Conversely, policy elites in developing states may invoke the presence of ungoverned spaces to solicit western aid and sanction armed intervention, with an eye to marginalizing and suppressing their political opponents out of a desire for personal political survival, rather than genuine security concerns.[2]

Drawing on language from the Fund for Peace's Failed States Index, we define a failed state as one incapable of governing its territory and characterized by

- loss of physical control of its territory, or of the monopoly on the legitimate use of physical force therein;
- an inability to provide public services; and
- erosion of legitimate authority to make collective decisions.[3]

Some authors use the term *collapsed state* to refer to a situation in which national structures have essentially dissolved and left an almost complete vacuum of authority. A weak or fragile state may be on the verge of failure because of instability and weak governance. Although failed and fragile states do not necessarily experience armed conflict, their contested legitimacy and their inability to exercise effective control over their territory make them vulnerable to insurgent movements or civil war.

Quantitative Watchlists

Conflict watchlists use a variety of methodologies. Some, such as the Political Instability Task Force (PITF) reports and the Peace and Conflict Instability Ledger (PCIL), rely on quantitative formulas based on several factors:

- *Regime consistency* (used by both the PITF and the PCIL). Whether the regime is a partial democracy, a full democracy, or a full autocracy. Partial democracies are "semi-democratic regimes in which, typically, electoral processes and legislatures are at the whim of autocratic executives." The greatest risk of instability exists in partial democracies that combine "deeply polarized or factionalized competition with open contestation," in which the ruling elite captures the resources of the state for its exclusive benefit (see chapter 2).
- *Infant mortality* (PITF and PCIL). "A proxy for a country's overall economic development, its level of advancement in social welfare policy, and its capacity to deliver core services to the population." A strong correlation exists between high infant mortality rates and the likelihood of future instability.
- *Neighborhood war* (PITF and PCIL). "When a neighboring state is currently experiencing armed conflict. This risk is especially acute when ethnic or other communal groups span across borders."
- *State-led discrimination* (PITF). The level of repression of minority groups in the country, based on data from the University of Maryland's Minorities at Risk Project.
- *Economic openness* (PCIL). A country's integration into the global economy. Isolated countries with low levels of international trade, such as Burma or North Korea, have a higher risk of conflict or instability.
- *Militarization* (PCIL). The ratio of a country's military personnel to its total population. "Extensive militarization in a country typically implies that a large portion of the society's population has military skill and training, weapons stocks are more widely available, and other pieces of military equipment are more diffused throughout the country," heightening the risk of conflict.[4]

BOX 3.1 Indicators of State Failure (Failed States Index)

Social indicators

- mounting demographic pressures
- massive movement of refugees or internally displaced persons creating complex humanitarian emergencies
- legacy of vengeance-seeking group grievance or group paranoia
- chronic and sustained human flight

Economic indicators

- uneven economic development along group lines
- sharp or severe economic decline

Political indicators

- criminalization or delegitimization of the state
- progressive deterioration of public services
- suspension or arbitrary application of the rule of law and widespread violation of human rights
- security apparatus operates as a state within a state
- rise of factionalized elites
- intervention of other states or external political actors

Other watchlists, including the Fund for Peace's Failed States Index, rely on panels of experts to generate quantitative scores on a series of indicators. The Fund for Peace generates a composite ranking based on twelve indicators of risk for internal conflict and state collapse, each of which is scored on a scale of 1 to 10 (see box 3.1).[5]

To produce its rankings, the Fund for Peace uses a proprietary software program called the Conflict Assessment System Tool (CAST), which uses Boolean logic to analyze tens of thousands of articles and reports from global and regional publications. The CAST software generates a preliminary set of scores. A panel of experts then reviews the preliminary analysis and assigns the final scores.

These and other watchlists provide systematic frameworks for calling attention to regions at risk of violence, and for tracking changes in the level of risk. But these models also have limitations, including the lack of reliable baseline data from conflict zones and the difficulty of distinguishing a real signal from noise. Nor are expert assessments necessarily any better: according to Jack Goldstone, such judgments have often proved unreliable because the "herd consensus" among experts "almost always lagged behind events."[6]

A further shortcoming of conflict watchlists is that they typically identify threats at the national level, whereas deadly conflicts are often subnational or transnational. For example, an intercommunal riot between Hindus and Muslims in Calcutta does not necessarily signal instability throughout India. Conversely, if we identify an insurgency such as the Lord's Resistance Army as a Ugandan problem, we may overlook its potential spillover effects into neighboring countries such as the Central African Republic, South Sudan, and the Democratic Republic of the Congo. Moreover, if a country is experiencing multiple conflicts in different parts of its territory, watchlists organized by countries may not be sensitive enough to detect a new emerging threat. For example, in 2003 Sudan ranked high on various global lists of political instability because it was then still involved in a twenty-year war against a southern secessionist movement. But listing Sudan as a country at risk of instability would not have helped analysts identify the threat of genocide in Sudan's Darfur region. In fact, U.S. government intelligence analysts did not begin to focus on the conflict in Darfur until several months after the mass atrocities against civilians had begun (see box 3.2).

Qualitative Watchlists and Warning Bulletins

Given the limitations of quantitative watchlists, it is important to pay attention to their qualitative counterparts and other reports that provide more nuanced and fine-grained assessments of emerging threats. *CrisisWatch,* a monthly publication of the International Crisis Group (ICG), is particularly valuable.[7] It provides monthly updates of deteriorated, improved, and unchanged situations in countries experiencing or at risk of conflict, along with targeted conflict risk alerts and conflict resolution opportunities. It also provides a summary paragraph on developments regarding the conflict over the past month, along with links to relevant news articles and current ICG research reports. Its value stems both from its timeliness and from the quality of the expert analysis and field reporting by ICG specialists, many of whom are recognized authorities in their field.

Other watchlists provide warnings about particular types of threats. For example, the UN's Humanitarian Early Warning Service (HEWSweb) and its ReliefWeb project provide information about natural disasters and other humanitarian emergencies. The U.S. Agency for International Development's Famine Early Warning System (FEWS) provides news concerning food security crises around the world. Genocide Watch and the

BOX 3.2 Genocide in Darfur: A Failure of Early Warning and Early Detection

From June through October 2003, I served as the atrocities early warning analyst in the U.S. State Department's Bureau of Intelligence and Research as part of a year-long fellowship program for visiting scholars. One of my responsibilities was to represent the State Department in interagency meetings to produce the classified *Atrocities Watchlist*, published quarterly by the U.S. National Intelligence Council, whose purpose was to identify emerging threats of genocide and mass atrocities around the world. During these meetings, neither I nor my counterparts from other U.S. intelligence agencies identified the Sudanese region of Darfur as an area of concern, despite the availability of ample public information about this threat. Only in late autumn 2003 did U.S. analysts begin to focus on the threat of genocide there.

Already on April 27, 2003, Amnesty International had issued a press release calling for an "international commission of inquiry and monitoring" to investigate the "crisis in Darfur." Amnesty asserted that "thousands of villagers have reportedly fled their villages since 11 April after attacks by government forces and government-organized Arab militias." In the "latest tragic incident on 23 April," Amnesty reported, "armed members of nomad groups, some of whom were wearing uniforms and said to be members of a government militia," had massacred fifty-five civilians in a market village in West Darfur.[a] In a June 2003 report, the International Crisis Group declared that the Sudanese government appeared "committed to a military response" to the rebellion in Darfur and that the "current campaign has the potential to trigger intensified ethnic warfare and large-scale forced displacement of the Fur and other African peoples of Darfur."[b]

(Box continued on next page)

Genocide Prevention Advisory Network publish watchlists on emerging risks of genocide and mass atrocities. The University of Maryland's Minorities at Risk project and Minority Rights Group International present detailed reports and chronologies concerning threats to persecuted minority groups around the world. The Enough Project publishes more geographically targeted reports on threats of genocide and mass atrocities in sub-Saharan Africa.

Global watchlists are just one source of information about emerging risks. NGOs such as Amnesty International and Human Rights Watch, as well as think tanks such as the Council on Foreign Relations, the Center for Strategic and International Studies, the Brookings Institution, the United States Institute of Peace, and countless others, publish regular reports by regional experts who offer over-the-horizon thinking about par-

BOX 3.2 Genocide in Darfur: A Failure of Early Warning and Early Detection *Continued*

Why did our group of U.S. government analysts fail to identify the emerging crisis in Darfur? Part of the explanation is the limited analytical bandwidth even of such a vast institutional apparatus as the U.S. intelligence community. The U.S. invasion of Iraq in March 2003 absorbed a large proportion of the resources of U.S. intelligence agencies throughout that year, and analysts working on sub-Saharan Africa were focused on crises in Liberia, Burundi, and other countries, as well as on efforts to resolve Sudan's North-South civil war. Some analysts initially interpreted the violence in Darfur primarily as a conflict between the Sudanese government and a new insurgency, rather than as a government-sponsored campaign of atrocities against civilians.

But institutional prejudices about the relative value of various information sources, as well as gaps in information sharing, may have also played a role in this analytical failure. Intelligence analysts and government policymakers often perceive information labeled top secret as more credible and valuable than open source information such as news accounts, scholarly publications, and reports produced by NGOs—though this prejudice has begun to lessen in recent years. But government intelligence analysts may receive little or no classified reporting from a remote region such as Darfur. It is essential to seek out and cultivate credible sources of open source information to compensate for such information gaps.

a. Amnesty International, "Sudan: Crisis in Darfur—Urgent Need for International Commission of Inquiry and Monitoring," April 27, 2003, www.amnesty.org/en/library/info/AFR54/026/2003/en (accessed May 3, 2012).

b. International Crisis Group, "Sudan's Other Wars, Africa Briefing no. 14 (June 25, 2003): 16, www.crisisgroup.org/-/media/Files/africa/horn-of-africa/sudan/B014%20Sudans%20Other%20Wars.pdf (accessed May 3, 2012).

ticular conflicts and opportunities for productive engagement by international actors.

Conflict Metrics Instruments

The goal of early warning watchlists is to anticipate the outbreak or escalation of deadly conflict. Conflict metrics instruments, by contrast, seek to measure and track current developments in a given region, rather than to predict their outcome. Conflict metrics provide a multifaceted depiction of forces at work within a country. A few notable metrics models are George Mason University's State Fragility Matrix; the World Bank's Country Policy and Institutional Assessment (CPIA) scores; the Global Peace Index published by the Institute for Economics and Peace; and the U.S. government project for Measuring Progress in Conflict Environments (MPICE), funded by the U.S. Army Corps of Engineers and developed as a collaborative effort of the Defense Department, State Department, U.S. Agency for International Development (USAID), and the United States Institute of Peace (see appendix 4).

Like conflict watchlists, metrics instruments may provide global comparisons of macro-level variables, or they may involve more fine-grained and localized assessments of socioeconomic and political factors in vulnerable regions. Over the past several years, organizations including the Brookings Institution, Carleton University, and the UK's Department for International Development have all published (on a one-time basis) rankings of countries around the globe on various measures of social well-being and institutional performance. The State Fragility Matrix, produced by the Center for Systemic Peace, provides a detailed assessment for each of the world's 163 major countries (with populations greater than five hundred thousand). It is organized into a two-by-four matrix of indicators for security, governance, economic, and social dimensions of state performance, each one measured according to the state's effectiveness and legitimacy.

The World Bank's annual Country Policy and Institutional Assessment is another purely quantitative measure of social well-being and institutional performance. The CPIA scores are calculated according to sixteen criteria, organized into four clusters:

- economic management—macroeconomic management, fiscal policy, debt policy;
- structural policies—trade, financial sector, business regulatory environment;
- social inclusion and equity policies—gender equality, equity of public resource use, building human resources, social protection and labor, environmental sustainability; and
- public-sector management and institutions—property rights and rule-based governance, budgetary and financial management, revenue mobilization, quality of public administration, and transparency-accountability-corruption.

The World Bank uses the CPIA scores as a factor in determining the allocation of its development funds. The principal purpose of these rankings has been to inform development assistance programming. Rankings are relevant to conflict analysis to the extent that poverty and poor institutional performance are causative factors for intrastate war.

Another metrics instrument, published annually since 2007 by the Institute for Economics and Peace in partnership with the Economist Intelligence Unit, is the Global Peace Index. This index aggregates data on twenty-three indicators for 158 countries, including such factors as relations with other countries; respect for human rights; potential for terrorist acts; military expenditures; homicides; the percentage of a country's population in jail or prison; ease of access to small arms and light weapons; and number of armed service personnel, internal security officers, and police. The goals of the Global Peace Index are to help national leaders identify areas for institutional improvement, and to help international businesses and donor governments best direct their investments. Its compilers say that their "ambition is to go beyond a crude measure of wars—and systematically explore the texture of peace. The hope is that it will provide a quantitative measure of peacefulness, comparable over time, that will provide a greater understanding of the mechanisms that nurture and sustain peace."[8] As with any quantitative ranking system, the Global Peace Index yields imperfect results and has limited predictive value. For example, in the 2010 index both Egypt and Libya ranked as more peaceful nations than the United States—whose ranking was negatively affected by factors including military spending, homicide rates, ease of access to small arms, and the percentage of the country's population in jail or prison. In the 2011 index, Libya fell eighty-three places and Egypt twenty-four on the list of the world's most peaceful nations.

A more fine-grained metrics instrument is the U.S. government's MPICE. This framework is structured around five sectors:

- political moderation and stable democracy,
- security,
- rule of law,
- economic sustainability, and
- social well-being.

MPICE involves a far more elaborate and labor-intensive inquiry than the indices discussed earlier, including content analysis of media publications, expert opinion surveys, statistical analysis of economic and security data, and survey or polling data obtained through interviews with people living in the conflict zone.

The MPICE survey instrument includes hundreds of questions about aspects of the conflict environment. Under the heading Peace Process, for example, one category of metrics addresses the question, "Do political leaders and elites accept and support the peace settlement?" The indicators include

- percentage of parties to the conflict who have signed the peace settlement;
- number and severity of violations of the peace settlement by faction (including ceasefire, cessation of operations, disarmament, and demobilization of troops);
- faction leaders renouncing use of violence and condemn its use;
- faction leaders implementing power-sharing arrangements without recourse to violence; and
- degree of support for the peace settlement in the mass media.

Under the category Performance of National Security Forces, MPICE lists a series of issues to be investigated either by international staff or by local governing authorities. Among these are the number of checkpoints or roadblocks set up by armed opposition groups; safe and sustainable resettlement in mixed identity group neighborhoods; use of institutions such as schools, banks, and markets; the number of publicly held community-based celebrations; and the amount spent by businesses on private security. It also recommends surveying local residents on whether they feel more secure today than they did six months before, whether they believe that they will be more secure in the months ahead than they are today (by province and identity group), whether they feel they can travel safely within the country (by identity group), and the cost and time required to negotiate checkpoints.

The goal of MPICE is to provide an outcomes- or effects-based instrument for assessing the success or failure of stabilization and reconstruction missions, to supplement the statistics regarding outputs traditionally provided by U.S. government agencies in postconflict environments—for example, the number of schools built, miles of roads paved, or numbers of police trained. Given the complexity and expense of a full-scale MPICE study, however, it is most likely to be used either in a simplified and scaled-back version or in regions where the U.S. government has committed substantial military, economic, and diplomatic resources, such as Iraq or Afghanistan.[9]

The MPICE framework can be helpful in diagnosing progress in post-conflict situations. The challenge for conflict analysts working with the results of an MPICE survey, however, is to translate the thousands of individual data points into an integrated and coherent picture of the evolving conflict environment. As noted in chapter 9 of this guide, it is essential that the selection of metrics be linked to the key hypotheses and conclusions of a comprehensive conflict assessment, and that the metrics be directly relevant to the conflict management objectives and operational approach defined for the mission.

Environmental Degradation and Climate Change

In recent years, both scholars and policymakers have paid increasing attention to the potential for environmental degradation and climate change to provoke or exacerbate deadly conflicts. The U.S. Defense Department declared in 2010 that climate change would play a "significant role in shaping the future security environment." That report asserted that climate change "may act as an accelerant of instability or conflict, placing a burden to respond on civilian institutions and militaries around the world."[10]

A 2008 study by Columbia University's Center for International Earth Science Information Network (CIESIN) found that "climate change is likely to heighten political risks" in historically unstable regions.[11] Particularly vulnerable countries are those that "suffer both high vulnerability to projected temperature changes, and low levels of adaptive capacity based on the strength of state institutions and their histories of instability and conflict." Such nations, according to CIESIN, include South Africa, Nepal, Morocco, Bangladesh, Tunisia, Paraguay, Yemen, Sudan, and Côte d'Ivoire.

But, as Alex Evans of New York University notes, it is important to recognize that climate change and resource scarcity "are rarely, if ever, the sole cause of violent conflict . . . ; instead, they are better understood as 'threat multipliers' that will in practice interact both with other risk drivers, and with diverse sources of vulnerability."[12] Evans observes that "the actual risk of violent conflict posed by climate change or resource scarcity depends as much on the *vulnerability* of populations, ecosystems, economies and institutions as on the strength of climate or scarcity impacts." Scholars disagree both about the degree to which resource conflicts aggravate conflict and about the mechanisms through which they do so. For example, although disputes over water from rivers that cross international borders can be a source of conflict, shared water resources can also stimulate international cooperation. One study found that only thirty-seven violent international conflicts over water occurred during the second half of the twentieth century (of which thirty involved Israel and its neighbors), whereas 295 international water agreements were negotiated and signed during this period.[13]

Whether conflicts over scarce resources provoke deadly conflict or stimulate cooperative solutions is determined in large part by the nature of the political and economic institutions in the affected societies. Patterns of ownership, consumption, and distribution of scarce resources, as well as institutions of governance for adjudicating disputes, can either mitigate or exacerbate resource conflicts.[14] Several characteristic dynamics can result in acute social stress and the potential for violence: resource capture and ecological marginalization, acute shocks, and large-cale unplanned migrations.

Resource capture and ecological marginalization. The increasing scarcity of a critical resource such as arable land or water can deprive marginalized groups of their livelihoods, either inadvertently or as the result of deliberate government policy. An example of inadvertent marginalization occurred in the Senegal River Valley in 1989, where population pressure and land degradation resulted in declining harvests. The Mauritanian government responded by planning a new dam to provide hydropower and expanded irrigation. However, anticipation of the dam led to a sharp increase in land values along the riverbank. According to Thomas Homer-Dixon, "The elite in Mauritania, which consists mainly of white Moors, then rewrote legislation governing land ownership, effectively abrogating the rights of black Africans to continue farming, herding, and fishing along the Mauritanian riverbank," which sparked ethnic conflict in both Mauritania and Senegal.[15]

In Sudan, by contrast, the Arab elite in the Nile River Valley has a long history of deliberately excluding ethnic groups on the country's periphery from access to oil wealth and other resources. In 2003, as Sudan's North-South civil war was moving toward settlement, the Sudanese regime moved to consolidate its control over the Darfur region of western Sudan by increasing its military support to Arab militias in Darfur. As an incentive to fight, the government promised members of the Arab militias title to the lands that they seized from the sedentary "African" tribes of Darfur (see box 3.3).

BOX 3.3 How Environmental Conflicts Become Politicized: The Case of Darfur

In a 2003 report, the International Crisis Group examined how the Sudanese government had politicized land conflicts in the country's Darfur region, which had been exacerbated by advancing desertification on the southern margins of the Sahara. The report concluded that

> government policies were instrumental in transforming "traditional" tribal conflicts over access to receding grazing land and water into a new type of conflict driven by a broader ethnic agenda. The old competition over natural resources was considerably aggravated by Khartoum's deliberate policy of co-opting Arab nomadic tribes in its war against the Sudan People's Liberation Army (SPLA) and against other disgruntled elements within Darfur. The contribution of Arab tribesmen of Darfur in defeating the 1991–92 incursion of the SPLA increased their leverage with the government. They immediately received direct dividends, with creation of new local administrative units including councils, provinces and sub-states that gave them a tribal platform for the first time. The new units were created at the expense of the African groups, further alienating them from the government.
>
> The policy of arming Arab militiamen also led to an open race for small arms and triggered a dramatic increase of violence. In an effort to defend themselves, the African groups who found themselves at the receiving end of the virulent militarism of their Arab neighbors increasingly resorted to the black market and to smuggling firearms from Chad and Libya. Over the past few years the situation of the sedentary Fur, Massaleit and Zaghawa tribes, all dependent on subsistence farming, has been exacerbated by repeated and deadly raids on their villages by government-backed Arab nomadic tribesmen. . . .
>
> The victims of these raids suspect that they have been specifically targeted in a government-backed effort to gain control of fertile areas in their traditional domain, so that Khartoum can reward the nomadic communities that have served as its de facto militias. The lands of many of these nomadic communities are increasingly threatened by desertification. The fact that other tribes in Darfur have come under similar attacks has led to a growing sense of ethnic solidarity among "African" tribes in the region.[a]

a. International Crisis Group, "Sudan's Other Wars," *Africa Briefing* no. 14, June 25, 2003, 11.

Acute shocks. Natural disasters such as droughts, which have become endemic in much of the Sahel, or widespread flooding, as in Pakistan and Australia in 2010, or sudden increases in the prices of food and other commodities, cause severe hardship and stress among marginalized populations. During the 2008 spike in global food and fuel prices, for example, at least sixty-one countries experienced unrest as a result of price inflation; in thirty-eight countries, these protests were violent.[16] One study of civil conflict in Africa found a strong correlation between drought and civil war. The study showed that a 5 percent decline in annual economic growth due to harvest failures increased the risk of civil conflict the following year by more than half.[17] In some cases, the perceptions of resource scarcity can be as damaging as the conditions, because such perceptions can drive a cycle of panic. For example, an aggravating factor in the global food crisis of 2008 was the imposition of export restrictions on food by more than thirty countries when prices were at their peak.[18]

Large-scale unplanned migration. Persistent drought conditions or rising sea levels could force millions of people in affected countries to flee their homes. Among nations with large populations, China, the Philippines, Egypt, Indonesia, and Bangladesh are particularly vulnerable to rising sea levels. China and the Philippines alone have sixty-four million people living within one meter of sea level.[19] As is the case for the other shocks discussed, poor countries with weak state capacity are least likely to be able to manage the burden of climate refugees.

Not only can environmental degradation cause political instability, but vicious cycles can also emerge, whereby a political crisis results in environmental damage, which in turn aggravates economic and political conditions in the society. For example, a postconflict environmental assessment of Afghanistan conducted in 2003 by the UN Environmental Program found that more than 50 percent of natural pistachio woodlands had been destroyed to sell wood for income, or to stockpile it out of fear that access to the forests would be lost. In this case, people's efforts to cope with hardship and political uncertainty resulted in ecological damage that undermined their long-term economic security.[20]

The journalist Christian Parenti has coined the term *catastrophic convergence* to depict the "collision of political, economic, and environmental disasters" that is emerging as the "current and impending dislocations of climate change intersect with the already-existing crises of poverty and violence." Parenti observes that "damaged societies, like damaged people, often respond to new crises in ways that are irrational, short-sighted, and self-destructive." He warns that

> in much of the world, it seems that the only solidarity forthcoming in the case of climate change is an exclusionary tribalism, and the only state policy available is police repression. This is not "natural" and inevitable but rather the

result of a history—particularly the history of the Global North's use and abuse of the Global South—that has destroyed the institutions and social practices that would allow a different, more productive response.[21]

Genocide and Mass Atrocities

The UN Convention on the Prevention and Punishment of the Crime of Genocide, adopted in 1948, defines genocide as

> any of the following acts committed with intent to destroy, in whole or in part, a national, ethnical, racial or religious group, as such: killing members of the group; causing serious bodily or mental harm to members of the group; deliberately inflicting on the group conditions of life, calculated to bring about its physical destruction in whole or in part; imposing measures intended to prevent births within the group; [and] forcibly transferring children of the group to another group.[22]

Although the Genocide Convention has been ratified by 142 countries, genocide has proven to be a difficult crime to prosecute under international law. Two aspects of the legal definition are particularly problematic. First, the victims must be members of either a "national, ethnical, racial, or religious group." Other categories of victims, for example, political or economic groups, or the educated elite (a group targeted for destruction in Cambodia in the 1970s), are excluded from the definition. Second, the definition of genocide requires prosecutors to prove a level of "specific intent" that is difficult to establish in practice. Not only must perpetrators intentionally commit acts of mass violence against a particular target group, but they must carry out those acts with the intent to bring about the "physical destruction in whole or in part" of the target group "as such."[23]

The difficulty of determining the subjective intentions of the perpetrators of mass atrocities often results in protracted and fruitless conversations about whether a given case "rises to the level of genocide." For example, in September 2004, U.S. secretary of state Colin Powell concluded that the government of Sudan was perpetrating genocide against the Fur, Massaleit, and Zaghawa ethnic groups in Darfur. But a subsequent investigation ordered by the UN Security Council denied that the Sudanese government was sponsoring a campaign of genocide in Darfur, even though the "crimes against humanity and war crimes that have been committed in Darfur may be no less serious and heinous than genocide," and even though "in some instances individuals, including Government officials, may commit acts with genocidal intent."[24] The UN report asserted that the Sudanese government's principal objective was "to drive the victims from their homes, primarily for purposes of counter-insurgency warfare," rather than to liquidate the ethnic groups "as such." Thus, the government's crimes did not qualify as genocide.

One way to avoid the definitional minefields surrounding the word *genocide* is to focus more broadly on atrocity crimes or genocide and mass atrocities—categories of crimes that include genocide but do not require proof of specific intent to destroy a target group as such. This approach has been adopted increasingly by both scholars and practitioners. For example, the 2008 report of the Genocide Prevention Task Force, chaired by Madeleine Albright and William Cohen, focused on strategies to prevent genocide and mass atrocities. In 2010, the handbook *Mass Atrocities Response Operations*, designed for military planners, was jointly published by the U.S. Army Peacekeeping and Stability Operations Institute and the Carr Center for Human Rights Policy at Harvard University's John F. Kennedy School.[25] In 2012, these two institutions released a follow-on publication titled *Mass Atrocity Prevention and Response Options*, intended to provide guidelines for integrated civil-military planning by the U.S. government and its international partners.[26]

The term *responsibility to protect* (R2P) focuses on four categories of violent conflict: genocide, war crimes, crimes against humanity, and ethnic cleansing. A recently developed concept, R2P asserts that states have an ethical and legal responsibility to protect their people from these crimes. But if a state is unable or unwilling to do so, that responsibility falls to the international community, which may intervene militarily in extreme cases. The R2P doctrine bridges all phases of the conflict management cycle: it includes the responsibility to prevent, the responsibility to react, and the responsibility to help rebuild communities that have been devastated by these crimes.

Genocide and mass atrocities typically occur in the context of a broader intrastate or interstate war, and it is often difficult to distinguish the initial stages of genocidal violence from the collateral damage of war. As we have seen in both chapter 1 and this chapter, many observers of Rwanda in 1994 and Darfur in 2003 were initially more concerned about the threat of civil war than the threat of genocide in those countries and were unprepared for the scope and suddenness of the violence against civilians.

It is vital to remain alert to the distinctive early warning signs of genocide and mass atrocities, because genocidal violence can be more explosive and extreme than other conflicts. For example, in Burundi in 1972, between one hundred and fifty thousand and three hundred thousand civilians were killed over several months. In Cambodia under the Pol Pot regime, about two million people—one-quarter of the country's population—died by execution, hunger, or disease between 1975 and 1979. In Rwanda, between one half and one million civilians were murdered during one hundred days in 1994. Genocidal violence can result in far higher death tolls than civil wars because it targets unarmed civilians, who are often concentrated in cities and towns, rather than armed insurgents in inaccessible locations. Moreover, genocidal regimes typically make extreme claims about the existential threat to the nation posed by members of the target groups. They often assert that the survival of their nation requires the displacement or total extermination of the target groups, rather than just the defeat of an armed insurgency.

Gregory Stanton, a leading genocide scholar, has identified an eight-stage political process that genocidal violence typically follows: classification, symbolization, dehumanization, organization, polarization, preparation, extermination, and denial. Although "all cultures have categories to distinguish people into 'us and them' by ethnicity, race, religion, or nationality," Stanton notes that such classifications only come to motivate genocide when one group "denies the humanity of the other group," equating its members with "animals, vermin, insects or diseases." Extremist groups broadcast "polarizing propaganda," and the state may reinforce discriminatory patterns through laws that "forbid intermarriage or social interaction" and through sanctioning the intimidation of political moderates. Along with this ideological polarization, genocidal regimes take logistical steps to prepare for mass killing operations. They may organize special military units or paramilitary proxy groups to carry out the killing. They may draw up lists of prospective victims, expropriate the property of members of target groups, and confine them to detention camps or "protected zones." Only at the conclusion of these first six stages, writes Stanton, do systematic killing operations begin.[27]

Among younger genocide scholars, two of the leading experts are Benjamin Valentino and Scott Straus. Valentino argues that mass killings of civilians should be viewed literally as "final solutions" to existential political challenges, which are pursued by regimes when other less extreme approaches have failed. Straus points out an additional risk factor: to perpetrate genocide or mass atrocities, a regime must exercise some degree of political control over the regions inhabited by the target groups, but it must perceive this control as imperiled in the absence of drastic "defensive" measures including mass killings.[28]

Early Warning at the Local Level

Most of the watchlists and indices discussed in this chapter have analytical value primarily at the broad strategic level—as tools for informing decision makers in governments, international organizations, and NGOs about vulnerable regions around the world. For practitioners working in conflict-prone regions, it is also essential to pay attention to more subtle indicators of emerging risks. In eastern Kenya, for example, one community-based early warning network monitors activity in local marketplaces. When female merchants in the markets refuse to sell to women from rival clans or tribes, the observers interpret it as a sign of rising intercommunal tensions that may erupt into violence. Another monitoring network in the Horn of Africa keeps track of local cigarette sales, because young men often buy up all the cigarettes in the village markets before heading out to the bush to wage cattle raids against neighboring communities.

In many cases, the indicators of rising tensions may be less tangible. Mary Hope Schwoebel, who taught international conflict management programs for the U.S. Institute of Peace, points to the significance of rumors as a sign of intensifying conflict (see box 3.4):

> I think that the proliferation of rumors, particularly of a certain nature, can be an indicator that a conflict is escalating, particularly rumors that tend to reinforce people's stereotypes of each other. They may be true, they may be false, it's almost irrelevant because what's important is the perception that they're generating. In particular, anything that plays on ethnic stereotypes is a particular indicator that conflict is in an escalatory phase."[29]

The hate-radio broadcasts in Rwanda on the eve of the 1994 genocide, which identified Rwandan Tutsis as "cockroaches" who threatened the safety of the majority Hutu population, are a notorious example of state-supported rumor-mongering. Joyce Leader, who was then serving as deputy chief of mission in the U.S. Embassy to Rwanda, recalls that Tutsi staff members at the embassy were too exhausted to work effectively in the fall of 1993. They reported that their families were so terrified of being attacked that they were coming together with their neighbors to sleep in the same house, and parents were standing watch throughout the night.[30]

BOX 3.4 Early Warning Signs of Civil War in Somalia

In the late 1980s and early 1990s, Mary Hope Schwoebel lived in Mogadishu, Somalia, during the collapse of the Siad Barre regime and the outbreak of civil war. In a February 2012 interview, she recounted some of the ominous signs she observed as the country spiraled into conflict:

> One of the things I noticed, as a woman, was that fashions began changing. When I had first arrived in Somalia in 1988 women wore a lot of gold—they flaunted their gold. Little by little women were wearing less gold, and not only that, they were covering more and more of their bodies, trying to call less and less attention to themselves. The population of the city was growing; there were increasing numbers of squatters and internally displaced persons (IDPs) coming from the regions outside of the capital and setting up squatter camps on the perimeter of the city. Everything just became more and more crowded. You started hearing dialects from parts of Somalia that had not commonly been heard in Mogadishu. Because many people were desperately poor, crime started increasing. People would just climb over fences to steal a package of Omo, the laundry detergent, if you left it out. You couldn't leave anything out, nobody left anything out.
>
> You started hearing horrible rumors, terrible rumors about women who had their arms cut off for their bracelets or their fingers cut off for their rings or had their earrings yanked out. I myself had my glasses yanked off my face, presumably to be sold in the black market. There were awful stories, for example, that thieves had entered a woman's house and they had started cutting off bits and pieces of her baby to try to get her to reveal where her gold and money were hidden.
>
> You also heard about kidnappings of foreigners, and there was a case of a European man and woman who were killed in their home. Pretty soon the foreigners started leaving, and Somali people who could afford to were also leaving the country, or sending their children overseas. There were a lot of lines outside the ministers' offices to get scholarships for people's kids overseas, to get visas for travel overseas or passports so people could leave the country.

Conclusion

Each quantitative and qualitative tool for risk assessment and conflict early warning is suited for a distinctive analytical objective. For example, development NGOs might use the Fund for Peace's Failed States Index or George Mason University's State Fragility Matrix to make a first cut in establishing priorities for future development assistance, or in assessing the potential of their existing programs to be derailed by violence. Some of the qualitative analytical tools described here, such as International Crisis Group's *CrisisWatch* bulletin, provide more fine-grained information about conflict zones that can be helpful for those involved in planning and implementing missions in the field. The analytical value of *CrisisWatch* and other early warning bulletins derives from their timeliness, the quality of their field reporting, and the authority and credibility of the individual analysts who write and edit the reports.

Metrics instruments such as MPICE can provide nuanced and detailed information for tracking the evolution of a conflict or postconflict situation. But the value of an MPICE survey depends heavily on the quality of the process used to select questions, collect data, and analyze the findings to provide relevant information for program planning, implementation, and assessment.

The discussion in this chapter of environmental causes of conflict and of genocide and mass atrocities has sought to illuminate the distinctive dynamics and early warning signs for each. For example, environmental crises and resource shortages typically result in violence only in situations where institutions for adjudicating access to resources and for cushioning humanitarian suffering are missing or inadequate. Genocide and mass atrocities tend to occur in highly polarized ideological climates in which members of the ruling elite portray the target groups as a threat to the very survival of the nation.

In the next section, we discuss various analytical approaches that can help illuminate the forces at work in a given conflict and facilitate the development of effective conflict management strategies. We also discuss how to

Questions for Practitioners

- What procedures does your organization use for risk assessment and early warning? Do you systematically survey your operating environment for emerging risks and opportunities, or do you rely mainly on the experience and intuition of your organization's leaders? Do you use external consultants or other experts to help identify emerging trends? Do you discuss risks and opportunities on a regular basis with your colleagues in staff meetings or other settings?
- Could your organization benefit by using any of the analytical tools discussed in this chapter? Which analytical methods or instruments are relevant to your work, and how could your organization use them? How could you work with your colleagues in order to implement these techniques?

frame the insights derived from an analysis to make them relevant and persuasive to both policymakers and program implementers in the field.

Notes

1. Political Instability Task Force, "Internal Wars and Failures of Governance, 1955–Most Recent Year," http://globalpolicy.gmu.edu/pitf/ (accessed May 3, 2012).
2. Anne L. Clunan and Harold A. Trinkunas, *Ungoverned Spaces: Alternatives to State Authority in an Era of Softened Sovereignty* (Palo Alto: Stanford University Press, 2010), 5.
3. Fund for Peace, "What Does State Failure Mean?" *Failed States Index*, www.fundforpeace.org/global/?q=fsi-faq#5 (accessed May 3, 2012).
4. All quotes in this summary of risk factors are from J. Joseph Hewitt, Jonathon Wilkenfeld, and Ted Robert Gurr, *Peace and Conflict 2010, Executive Summary* (College Park: University of Maryland Center for International Development and Conflict Management, 2010).
5. Fund for Peace, "Conflict Indicators," *Failed States Index*.
6. Jack A. Goldstone, "Using Quantitative and Qualitative Models to Forecast Instability," Special Report 204 (Washington, DC: United States Institute of Peace, 2008), 15.
7. "About CrisisWatch," *International Crisis Group*, www.crisisgroup.org/en/publication-type/crisiswatch/about-crisiswatch.aspx.
8. Vision of Humanity, "About the Global Peace Index," www.visionofhumanity.org/about (accessed May 3, 2012).
9. John Agoglia, Michael Dziedzic, and Barbara Sotirin, eds., *Measuring Progress in Conflict Environments (MPICE): A Metrics Framework* (Washington, DC: United States Institute of Peace, 2010), 22, 10–11, xii.
10. U.S. Department of Defense, *Quadrennial Defense Review Report*, February 2010, 84–85, www.defense.gov/qdr/qdr%20as%20of%2029jan10%201600.PDF (accessed May 9, 2012).
11. Marc Levy et al., "Assessment of Select Climate Change Impacts on U.S. National Security" (CIESIN working paper, Columbia University, July 2008), iii; www.ciesin.columbia.edu/documents/Climate_Security_CIESIN_July_2008_v1_0.ed.pdf (accessed May 3, 2012); The Earth Institute of Columbia University, "Climate Change May Challenge National Security, Classified Report Warns," July 2, 2008, www.earth.columbia.edu/articles/view/2202 (accessed May 3, 2012).
12. Alex Evans, "Resource Scarcity, Climate Change and the Risk of Violent Conflict," (Washington, DC: World Bank, 2010), 6.
13. Ibid., 11.
14. Ibid., 10.

15. T. Homer-Dixon, "Environmental Scarcities and Violent Conflict: Evidence from Cases," *International Security* 19, no. 1 (Summer 1994): 8, www.library.utoronto.ca/pcs/evidence/evid1.htm (accessed September 10, 2012); quoted in Evans, "Resource Scarcity," 8.
16. Evans, "Resource Scarcity," 13.
17. Edward Miguel, Shanker Satyanath, and Ernest Sergenti, "Economic Shocks and Civil Conflict: An Instrumental Variables Approach," *Journal of Political Economy* 112, no. 4 (2004): 725–53.
18. Evans, "Resource Scarcity," 4.
19. The Earth Institute at Columbia University, "Climate Change May Challenge National Security, Classified Report Warns," *Science Daily*, June 25, 2008, www.sciencedaily.com/releases/2008/06/080625090302.htm (accessed May 3, 2012).
20. United Nations Environmental Programme, *Post-Conflict Environmental Assessment: Afghanistan* (Geneva: UNEP, 2003), 11, http://postconflict.unep.ch/publications/afghanistanpcajanuary2003.pdf (accessed May 3, 2012).
21. Christian Parenti, Tropic of Chaos: Climate Change and the New Geography of Violence (New York: Nation Books, 2011), 7–8.
22. United Nations Convention on the Prevention and Punishment of the Crimes of Genocide, adopted December 9, 1948, Article II.
23. Ibid.
24. "Report of the International Commission of Inquiry on Darfur to the United Nations Secretary-General, Pursuant to Security Council Resolution 1564 of 18 September 2004" (Geneva: United Nations, January 25, 2005), 4, www.un.org/news/dh/sudan/com_inq_darfur.pdf (accessed October 2, 2012).
25. Sarah Sewall, Sally Chin, and A. Dwight Raymond, *MARO: Mass Atrocity Response Operations, A Military Planning Handbook* (Boston, MA: Carr Center for Human Rights Policy and U.S. Army Peacekeeping and Stability Operations Institute, 2010).
26. A. Dwight Raymond, Cliff Bernath, Don Braum, and Ken Zurcher, *MAPRO: Mass Atrocity Prevention and Response Options, A Policy Planning Handbook* (Carlisle, PA: Carr Center for Human Rights Policy and U.S. Army Peacekeeping and Stability Operations Institute, 2012).
27. Gregory Stanton, "The Eight Stages of Genocide," www.genocidewatch.org/genocide/8stagesofgenocide.html (accessed May 3, 2012).
28. Benjamin Valentino, *Final Solutions: Mass Killing and Genocide in the 20th Century* (Ithaca, NY: Cornell University Press, 2004); Scott Straus, "Identifying Genocide and Related Forms of Mass Atrocity" (working paper, United States Holocaust Memorial Museum, Washington, DC, 2011), www.ushmm.org/genocide/pdf/indentifying-genocide.pdf (accessed May 3, 2012).
29. Mary Hope Schwoebel, interview by the author, Washington, DC, February 2012.
30. Joyce Leader, interview with PBS Frontline, September 30, 2003, www.sciencedaily.com/releases/2008/06/080625090302.htm (accessed May 10, 2012); *Rwanda's Struggle for Democracy and Peace, 1991–1994* (Washington, DC: The Fund for Peace, 2001), 21–30, 48–60.

PART II

TOOLS FOR THE TRADE

4

CONFLICT ASSESSMENT FRAMEWORKS

Key Points

- Conflict assessment frameworks are qualitative analytical tools to help forge a shared set of questions about the nature and potential trajectory of a conflict and a shared vocabulary with which to discuss opportunities for preventive actions.
- Use of a conflict assessment framework can foster structured and holistic conversations about a conflict among multiple stakeholder groups or the staff of a single organization, helping identify areas of consensus and key disagreements.
- Self-assessment is critical to any conflict assessment. It is essential for analysts to clarify their objectives and perspective on the conflict to effectively frame their questions and recognize potential biases and blind spots.
- Although different frameworks use a wide range of terminology and deliberative processes, most center around four issues: dividers and connectors, actors, drivers of conflict and peace, and indicators of the conflict's future trajectory.
- Some conflict assessment frameworks also explicitly address the transition from analysis to planning, using the findings of the assessment as the basis for program design and evaluation activities.

Part I of this guide explores the complex nature of conflict in the contemporary world and discusses various macro-level analytical tools for identifying socioeconomic and institutional vulnerabilities that heighten the risks of violent conflict. Part II discusses analytical approaches for moving from the global level of risk assessment to the national and subnational levels at which conflict management strategies are designed and implemented.

The four chapters of part II present a menu of complementary tools practitioners can use to enrich their understanding of the factors driving a conflict, and of potential opportunities for managing or resolving it. This chapter addresses conflict assessment frameworks that can help facilitate more effective communication and joint program planning among diverse institutional stakeholders. Conflict assessment frameworks differ from quantitative watchlists and metrics instruments (discussed in chapter 3) in that they seek to provide a more organic and holistic portrait of a conflict-prone region, and rely primarily on qualitative rather than quantitative data. Moreover, they are intended to be used collaboratively by individuals and organizations charged with making policy decisions, rather than by professional analysts alone.

Some practitioners use the terms *conflict assessment* and *conflict analysis* interchangeably. This guide depicts conflict assessment as a distinctive stage within a larger analytical process. Conflict assessment is primarily a descriptive rather than a predictive or prescriptive process. It provides a portrait of the context, the actors, and the driving forces behind a conflict to provide decision makers and program implementers with the information necessary to operate effectively in a conflict zone.

Conflict assessment should be seen as the essential first step of a conflict analysis process; it can also set the stage for program planning and evaluation processes. The assessment offers a snapshot of a given conflict at a particular moment in time. The subsequent chapters of this book discuss various analytical tools that can complement and enrich a conflict assessment. These include

- narrative analysis, which permits deeper insight into the motives and intentions of key actors;
- conflict mapping and systems mapping, which permit a more dynamic view of the forces promoting stability or instability;
- scenario analysis, a valuable tool for over-the-horizon thinking; and
- situation analysis, which can help identify the potential strengths and weaknesses of one's organization in responding to a conflict.

Conflict assessment frameworks are intended as tools for structuring productive conversation and facilitating common understanding of a conflict among diverse institutional stakeholders. An important function of conflict assessment is to provide both questions for practitioners and policymakers about the nature and potential trajectory of a conflict, and terms in which to discuss opportunities for preventive actions. For a particular conflict, some questions will be more useful than others, and the probing analyst will continually find new questions to ask.

Participants in conflict assessment processes should recognize that all conflict analysis is partial and provisional. Conflict assessments inevitably and invariably reflect the analyst's institutional and personal perspectives. Moreover, given the volatile nature of deadly conflict, political alignments and constellations of forces can quickly change. It is thus essential to revisit and reevaluate one's assessment on a regular basis, and to cross-check conclusions with colleagues both inside and outside the organization.

A wide range of governmental and nongovernmental institutions have developed conflict assessment frameworks for use as part of their policymaking processes, particularly in the development field (see appendix 5). These include

- the U.S. government's Interagency Conflict Assessment Framework (ICAF);
- the Post-Conflict Needs Assessment (PCNA) tool created by the UN Development Group, European Commission, World Bank, and other partners;
- the UN Development Program (UNDP)'s Conflict-Related Development Analysis;
- the Conflict Prevention and Post-Conflict Reconstruction Network's Peace and Conflict Impact Assessment (PCIA); and
- the Netherlands Institute of International Relations' Stability Assessment Framework.

Various conflict assessment frameworks have also been developed by the World Bank, the UN Peacebuilding Support Office, the British Department for International Development (DFID), the German Gesellschaft für Technische Zusammenarbeit (GTZ), and the Swedish International Development Cooperation Agency (SIDA).

These frameworks vary widely in their objectives and methodology. Many—those created by the World Bank, UNDP, DFID, GTZ, and SIDA, for example—are intended for use primarily by development organizations. Others, such as the ICAF, PCNA, and PCIA, are designed for conflict prevention or postconflict reconstruction missions. In terms of methodology, some frameworks can be used by practitioners working outside the conflict zone, either individually or in a workshop format. Others require extensive field-based research and interaction with local actors. The frameworks also range widely in the level of their complexity, and in the time and effort required to conduct an assessment. For example, the PCIA requires analysts to complete an elaborate eleven-page questionnaire on a variety of topics: conflict profile; peace profile; stakeholder profile; rights, responsibilities, and underlying causes; and scenarios and objectives. By contrast, USAID's Tactical Conflict Assessment and Planning Framework (TCAPF), which was originally developed for use by U.S. government civil-military teams deployed to Afghanistan and Iraq, uses a list of just four questions that field staff should ask local residents:

- Have there been changes in the village population in the last year?
- What are the most important problems facing the village?
- Who do you believe can solve your problems?
- What should be done first to help the village?

Whatever framework is adopted, analysts should be attentive to their preconceptions and the limits of their expertise. In the words of Lisa Schirch, a leading scholar-practitioner of conflict analysis, "The process for conducting conflict assessment is as important as the quality of the framework. If the people conducting a conflict assessment are not deeply knowledgeable about local languages, cultures and complex political and economic dynamics in a context, the output of the assessment may not enable the planning process. In gruff terms, this is often referred to as the 'garbage in, garbage out' problem."[1]

The remainder of this chapter synthesizes elements from a number of the identified frameworks and maps out a four-step process that examines dividers and connectors, actors, drivers of conflict and peace, and indicators.

It also addresses three activities that bracket the assessment process: self-assessment; information gathering in conflict zones; and transition to planning, in which the conclusions of the assessment guide the design, implementation, or evaluation of programs in a region at risk of conflict.

Self-Assessment

Conflict is intrinsically complex and multidimensional, reflecting the competing perspectives and interests of the parties either directly or indirectly involved. Before undertaking any systematic assessment, analysts must articulate their objectives and point of view. The key question is simple: "Why am I analyzing this conflict now?"

For practitioners working for governments or other large organizations, the answer will give rise to further questions: What is my organization's stake in this conflict? How are our own interests implicated? How is the history of my country or organization intertwined with the history of this conflict? Why is my organization interested in this issue at this particular time? How will the findings of the assessment be used (see box 4.1)?

BOX 4.1 Questions for Self-Assessment

Institutional and logistical issues

- Who is requesting the assessment, and how strong is the institutional buy-in from other key stakeholders and participants?
- How much time and how many resources do you have to carry out this assessment? Who needs to be involved? Will it be conducted in the field or in your organization's home office?
- Is the assessment connected to other institutional processes such as policy planning, budgeting, program evaluation, or interagency coordination efforts?

Scope

- Will the scope of the assessment be local, national, or transnational?
- Will the assessment focus on short-, medium-, or long-term issues (the next six months or the next five to ten years)?
- Will the assessment focus on a particular sector (such as economic development or rule of law), or will it be a more comprehensive and holistic review of the conflict?

Objectives and interests

- What is your personal or institutional stake in this conflict? Are you an insider or an outsider? An interested party or an impartial observer?
- Who are the intended audiences for the assessment? What are the desired outcomes?
- Is the primary objective of the assessment to inform decision making by international actors or to empower host-country nationals to better understand and resolve their conflicts? To what extent will local organizations and individuals have ownership over the design and conclusions of the assessment?

The self-assessment process serves multiple ends. From a pragmatic standpoint, it helps clarify the scope and the logistical requirements of the conflict assessment and ensure a realistic fit between the available resources and the desired outcomes. For example, if the goal is to assess the potential impact of a development project on communities in a conflict-prone region, the assessment process should include field surveys in the target communities. An assessment on this topic carried out solely by analysts in Brussels or Washington is unlikely to offer much insight into local conflict dynamics.

Equally important, the self-assessment can help focus the inquiry by clarifying the analytical needs of the requesting organization. Because human knowledge is inevitably partial and imperfect, no assessment process can achieve a comprehensive and objective understanding of a conflict situation. The method and conclusions of the analysis will inevitably reflect the analyst's point of view. The goal of conflict assessment should not be to produce a single homogenized understanding across all organizations, but rather to identify potential synergies and points of friction among diverse stakeholder groups.

Koenraad Van Brabant is head of Reflective Practice at Interpeace, an international peacebuilding organization with offices in Geneva, Nairobi, and Guatemala. He stresses the vital importance of robust and diverse participation by members of the affected society in the conflict assessment process.[2] In the absence of such participation, he notes, conflict assessments may devolve into "external actors chattering among themselves." Lisa Schirch reinforces this point:

> It is natural for people with different backgrounds to view a conflict in different ways. The best conflict assessment is produced by a diverse range of people from within a community or region complemented by outsiders who bring inter-disciplinary and comparative insights from outside the region. Assessment processes that rely only on outsiders with limited or token participation by elite local representatives are likely to miss a wide array of cultural and contextual insights.[3]

Van Brabant points to a further danger of approaching conflict analysis as a technical exercise that seeks to forge a consensus about a conflict among a range of international actors. The attempt to reduce the conclusions of a conflict assessment to "one objective position," he notes, inevitably means "throwing out other perspectives." This is typically done by either privileging the narrative of one group over that of others, or by imposing the external actors' superior "expert" analysis on that of the "local" actors. In both cases a critical driver of the conflict dynamics gets obscured, that is, the different perspectives of competing groups.[4]

Privileging the analysis of one group over that of another, or one's external analysis over that of internal actors, carries another risk—that you as external actor are taking sides or coming with an agenda. As Van Brabant points out, such suspicions seriously undermine your ability to be an effective external peacebuilder.

Interpeace and its local partners have conducted broad-based inclusive conflict and peace assessments in many countries, typically covering people across the territory, but also from the village level to the president's office, and resources permitting, even parts of the diaspora. Such consultations, which can take several months, simultaneously provide both a participatory analysis of a conflict and a space for facilitated public debate and discussion. The conclusions are consolidated in a written report and sometimes also in a video documentary, which is then presented back to a national conference event, with participants from all sectors and levels of society. Somalilanders called their report a self-portrait. In Van Brabant's words, such a participatory assessment is a process in which "a society comes to look in the mirror at itself. The mirror is cracked, but everybody together can see the fragmented picture and identify where the fault lines run and what some of the more divisive and difficult issues are."[5]

Gathering Information

Information for a conflict assessment can be obtained from a wide range of sources: news accounts, scholarly publications, reports by NGOs and advocacy groups working in a conflict zone, Web-based platforms for crowdsourced reporting such as Ushahidi.com, and polling data collected by organizations such as World Public Opinion, Afrobarometer, and the Latin American Public Opinion Project (LAPOP). Analysts working in government positions may also have access to classified materials such as intelligence assessments and diplomatic reporting cables.

Whenever possible, a conflict assessment process should include a field survey component, which enables the assessment team to gather information directly from residents of a conflict zone. Some organizations mandate the use of specific methodologies or templates for collecting information in the field. Regardless of the interview methodology, researchers should keep several principles in mind.

First, be curious. It is important for outside observers to take the time to seek out very different groups of people: women as well as men, young people as well as village elders, people who may be marginalized socially as well as those who occupy positions of power. Mary Hope Schwoebel stresses that information gathering need not involve any specialized expertise or survey methodology:

> It's very, very simple actually: you just ask people, "Has life changed here? How has it changed? When did it start to change? What do you attribute the change to? What specific factors seem to have played a part in the change?" These are questions that anybody can answer, they don't have to be literate, they don't have to speak English if you have an interpreter. This is the stuff of kitchen talk as it were, the stuff that in a conflict context people are talking about in the kitchens there just like we do in the U.S. So, you talk to your taxi driver, you talk to the guy you buy your stuff from, your laundry soap from down at the local kiosk, you talk to anybody and everybody. They will all be able to tell these stories.[6]

It is useful to ask interviewees not only what they think is driving the conflict but also what has been tried as a solution. Why has this approach not worked in the past? How have things changed? Open-ended questions can offer insight into the various parties' perspectives on the conflict.

Second, be humble. An outsider going into a conflict zone inevitably has only limited knowledge of the conflict dynamics and broader social dynamics. Avoid jumping to conclusions or aligning consciously or unconsciously with either faction's narrative of the conflict. Remain open to the perspectives from various sides and try to understand why those intimately involved see the conflicts as they do. By remaining humble, we can be conscious of the limits of our knowledge and not jump to inappropriate conclusions.

Third, do no harm. Practitioners of conflict analysis must recognize that, when conducting field interviews, one is never only an observer; one is also an actor in the conflict. No matter how impartially questions are framed, an interviewer will inevitably influence the dynamics in that community. One will inevitably talk to certain people and not to other people, and one will experience greater empathy with certain interlocutors than with others. Sometimes, simply by asking questions about the nature of a conflict, one may call attention to things the residents of that community haven't yet considered. Thus, the very process of asking questions can influence the way people see their conflict.

A further complicating factor, especially for representatives of large and powerful organizations like the U.S. government or UN agencies, is the possibility of inadvertently raising expectations for external assistance by posing open-ended questions such as "What important needs are not being met in this community?" Interviewers must take care to avoid creating expectations they are not prepared or able to fulfill.

Andrew Blum, who has administered grant programs in the two Sudans for the U.S. Institute of Peace, points out an additional imperative for interviewers conducting field surveys in conflict zones: the need to adapt one's research methodology to local cultures. In many rural areas of South Sudan, notes Blum, it is difficult to conduct surveys of individual respondents, because villagers will gather around any outsider who shows up asking questions. Moreover, residents are likely to be cautious about volunteering information unless they know that local authorities have given their blessing to the survey process. Thus, when operating in South Sudan and other similar environments, an interview team should budget time for visiting relevant local authorities to explain the research process. The team should also consider adapting survey methodology to rely on focus groups rather than individual respondents (see also box 4.2).[7]

Four-Step Assessment Process

A wide range of governmental, intergovernmental, and nongovernmental organizations have developed conflict assessment instruments for use as part of institutional planning and decision-making processes. Here we synthesize elements found in many of these frameworks to identify points of synergy among them, as well as to facilitate better coordination of assessment processes among diverse organizations. The four-step assessment process described here draws most heavily on the concepts and terminology of the U.S. Interagency Conflict Assessment Framework (ICAF) and the Do No Harm (DNH) Framework.

Step 1. Dividers and Connectors

- What divides the people of the region against each other? What connects them?

The terms dividers and connectors were introduced in chapter 2. The DNH Framework defines dividers as sources of tension or polarization between groups that may be either "rooted in deep-seated, historical injustice" or "recent, short-lived, or manipulated by subgroup leaders." Connectors, by contrast, are institutions or cultural patterns by which "people, although they are divided by conflict, remain also connected across sub-group lines."[8]

BOX 4.2 Conflict-Sensitive Interview Techniques

Veronica Eragu Bichetero is a lawyer who has documented human rights abuses as a commissioner at the Uganda Human Rights Commission. Interviewed by the author in early 2012, she offered advice for conducting interviews in volatile conflict environments:

> When you are gathering information concerning conflict you're dealing with people who have been affected, people who are traumatized. You don't have to be overly sympathetic. The most important thing is, first of all, to briefly say you are sorry about the conflict and tell them you share their pain. After that, you should walk around without rushing to ask them exactly what happened. You must always find time to walk around, see the damage, touch one or two people, mainly children. People tend to feel you belong to them when you pick up a child here and there or shake hands with an old woman. You have to be careful not to go and shake hands with young girls lest you be misunderstood.
>
> In most African countries, and maybe with all fragile people, people want body contact. If you're going to greet them, you should give a handshake and after the handshake then you start talking about the conflict. It's best to walk around with a member of the community. You can ask the elders to identify someone. If you are a man, I would recommend a young man to walk with you and interpret, because some of those things are better recounted in the language of the people of the community where it happened. If you are a woman, you look for a young woman—or maybe it's better to have both a man and a woman take you around.
>
> The other thing is never to be in a hurry, always have time to talk to groups, elders on their own, women on their own, and hear their problems and then those of the youth. The youth are always eager to participate; sometimes they will want to accompany you to the next village or to where there is better evidence. It's also good to not restrict yourself to one group or to tie yourself to government agents even if they brought you there, because you don't know: maybe the conflict more than anything else includes the government agents.

The meaning of both of these terms overlaps with certain concepts used in other conflict analysis frameworks. For example, the concept of dividers is associated with such concepts as issues, grievances, tensions, root causes, and proximate causes. The concept of connectors is associated with sources of social and institutional resilience and local capacities for peace.

- A **divider** is a potential source of polarization within or between groups.
- A **connector** is a potential source of cohesion within or between groups.

But the two terms are more neutral and analytically specific than the associated concepts. Terms such as *grievances* and *root causes* are generally perceived as having negative connotations, whereas sources of resilience and local capacities for peace carry positive ones. But a divider should not be seen as intrinsically bad, nor should a connector be seen as intrinsically good. For example, a popular protest movement against an authoritarian state or the emancipation of women from strict patriarchal authority could be interpreted as divisive events because they diminish—at least in the short term—the social and political cohesion of a society in transition. Just as conflict can be a beneficial phenomenon, provided that it is channeled productively, certain types of divisive forces can serve positive social functions. Conversely, endemic corruption or warlord rule in rural Afghanistan might be interpreted as connectors to the extent that these practices help stabilize and preserve a fragile social order. In such circumstances, the forces that maintain cohesion may hurt rather than help a community because they reinforce patterns of structural violence.

In this guide, not using terms such as root causes and proximate causes is a deliberate decision made to emphasize that conflict is always a human phenomenon that results from decisions by human actors. For example, endemic poverty is sometimes described as a root cause that has motivated political violence in countries such as Burundi and Nepal. But poor countries such as Tanzania and Bangladesh have avoided civil war in recent decades—in large part because key political actors there have decided to pursue peaceful rather than violent political strategies. Likewise, political leaders in Sudan have exploited environmental conflicts stemming from global climate change to provoke violence between pastoralists and farmers (see box 3.3). But in other parts of the Sahel, resource conflicts between pastoralists and farmers have been managed more peacefully. Thus, a source of social or political stress (such as poverty, global climate change, resource competition, or ethnic divisions) becomes a cause of conflict—or *driver of conflict,* as we will call it here—only when political actors mobilize around this issue.

Table 4.1 provides some examples of dividers and connectors along each of the five dimensions of conflict and peace discussed in chapter 2: the strategic, political, socioeconomic, psychological, and cultural. Dividers and connectors may include both objective conditions, such as demographic shifts, and subjective perceptions, such as mutual distrust or perceptions of group victimization (see box 4.3). But they are merely potential sources of polarization or social cohesion, rather than actual ones, because they exclude the dynamic interaction whereby political leaders seek to persuade and mobilize their constituents either to escalate or de-escalate conflict.

TABLE 4.1 Dividers and Connectors

	Dividers	Connectors
Strategic	Persistent rivalries with neighboring states	Peaceful relations with neighboring states
	Interstate or intrastate wars involving neighboring states	Peace and stability within and between neighboring states
	Global or regional powers seek to dominate or destabilize the country	Global or regional powers seek to stabilize the country
	Nonstate actors (for example, terrorist organizations) seek to destabilize the country	International or regional organizations (such as the UN, AU, ECOWAS) seek to stabilize the country
Political	Partial democracy with limited checks on executive authority and winner-take-all system of government	Consolidated democracy with checks on executive authority
	Exclusion of certain ethnic, religious, or geographical groups from power	Consolidated autocracy that can buy off potential opponents through patronage or suppress dissent
	Pervasive corruption favoring entrenched elites	Effective rule of law and controls on corruption
	Limited institutional capacity for managing conflict; weak rule of law	Coalitions across ethnic and religious lines
Socioeconomic	Economic stagnation or contraction	Sustained economic growth
	Horizontal inequality along ethnic or geographic lines, with certain groups facing systematic marginalization	Equitable distribution of wealth across group lines
		Economic cooperation (such as trade) across group lines
	Availability of lootable resources (such as oil, minerals, timber), which enrich certain groups	Existence of cross-cutting bonds within or between communities, transcending ethnic and religious differences
	Rapid urbanization and/or population growth; youth bulge	Demographic stability
	Failure of the social contract due to poverty, weak public services, and the like	Effective delivery of public services
Psychological	Perceptions that different groups have opposing interests	Existence of perceived common ground among groups
	Mutual distrust across group lines	Mutual trust across group lines
	Inflammatory rhetoric and actions by political and cultural leaders	Conciliatory rhetoric and actions by political and cultural leaders
Cultural	History of discrimination or violence against certain groups	History of cooperation across group lines
	Historical narratives of victimization and collective trauma	Historical narratives emphasizing unity and shared values

BOX 4.3 The Nigerian Election of 2011: Dividers and Connectors

In April 2011, President Goodluck Jonathan, a Christian from southeastern Nigeria who had succeeded to the presidency after his Muslim predecessor died in office, prevailed by a decisive margin in a national election that was declared to be largely free and fair by both Nigerian and international observers. In the words of David Smock, a Nigeria expert at the U.S. Institute of Peace, this represented "a remarkable step toward giving democratic processes real roots in Nigeria," a country with a long history of vote-rigging and military coups. Unfortunately, however, the declaration of Jonathan's victory sparked intercommunal violence in Nigeria's primarily Muslim North.[a]

The key provocation for the violence, Smock notes, was that Jonathan's reelection disrupted "the established pattern in Nigeria that the presidency should rotate between a Christian and a Muslim." Because Jonathan's Muslim predecessor had died before completing a full presidential term, "many Muslims from the North argued that a Muslim should have been elected in this election because the Muslims did not get their deserved opportunity to have a Muslim president for a full term."

This postelectoral violence in Nigeria illustrated the ambiguous and subjective nature of connectors and dividers. From the standpoint of international observers, Nigeria's success in holding a free and fair presidential election was a connector, because it reinforced the legitimacy and effectiveness of democratic institutions in Nigeria. Yet many Nigerian Muslims perceived the election result as a divider, because it violated an implicit power-sharing compact between the country's majority Christian South and its majority Muslim North.

As Smock observes, these competing perspectives on the outcome of the presidential election were symptomatic of deeper socioeconomic and cultural fault lines in Nigeria: "The overarching long-term challenge is to achieve greater reconciliation between Muslims and Christians, which also reflects a division between the North and the South. High levels of poverty and unemployment, particularly among youth in the North, must also be addressed since it is this segment of the population that has instigated most of the violence."

The "discontent of the people in the Niger Delta" in southeast Nigeria represented another significant divider in the country, according to Smock: "Most of Nigeria's oil comes from the Niger Delta, but that region is particularly undeveloped." Here again, the 2011 presidential election result had the potential to serve as a connector: President Jonathan was "well positioned to address" the alienation of residents of the Niger Delta, because he himself was a native of that region.

a. David Smock, "Post-Election Violence Erupts in Nigeria," On the Issues (Washington, DC: United States Institute of Peace, April 19, 2011), www.usip.org/publications/post-election-violence-erupts-in-nigeria (accessed May 10, 2012).

Step 2. Actors

- Who contributes to conflict among the people of the region? Who helps build peace?

Actors may be thought of as the cast of characters that drive the drama of conflict—each one with its own histories, motives, resources, and relationships with other members of the cast. Actors can include not only individuals who play a key role in promoting or mitigating conflict, but also public or private institutions, as well as informal groups defined on the basis of identities or shared interests.

Analyzing Actors and Their Relationships

- Who are the primary actors in the conflict?
- Who are the secondary actors?
- Who else has influence over events?
- What are the resources and capacities of each actor?
- What are the existing relationships and channels of communication within and among the rival groups?

Primary actors are the principal players in a conflict who can influence its outcome. These are the characters without whom the drama would be impossible—for example, Hamlet and his uncle Claudius in the Shakespearean tragedy. Primary actors might include

- national or local leaders (depending on the scale of the conflict),
- insurgents and paramilitary groups,
- religious and civil society leaders, or
- criminal networks.

Secondary actors are internal or external stakeholders who have a significant interest in the conflict but are less centrally involved—minor players such as Polonius or Ophelia in *Hamlet*. Secondary actors could include

- neighboring states,
- global superpowers with an interest in the conflict,
- multilateral organizations such as the United Nations and World Bank,
- international businesses with investments in the region,

- NGOs, or
- diaspora populations.

In practice, the distinction between primary and secondary actors is not always clear. For example, in some cases a neighboring state or global superpower may decisively influence the course of a conflict.

The *two-level game model*, developed by the political scientist Robert Putnam, is a useful framework for thinking about relationships among parties to a conflict.[9] The premise behind the model is that any conflict has to be understood on multiple levels. Not only are leaders involved in waging a conflict with each other, or trying to reach a settlement with each other, but each leader has one or more constituencies whose wishes must be considered. Those constituencies have relationships with their leaders, and they also have direct relationships with each other, independent of those between the leaders. The two-level game model offers a simplified depiction of these multifaceted relationships (see figure 4.1).

Of course, real intergroup conflicts are more complex and multilayered than the two-level game model. In decoding messages by particular lead-

FIGURE 4.1 Two-Level Game Model

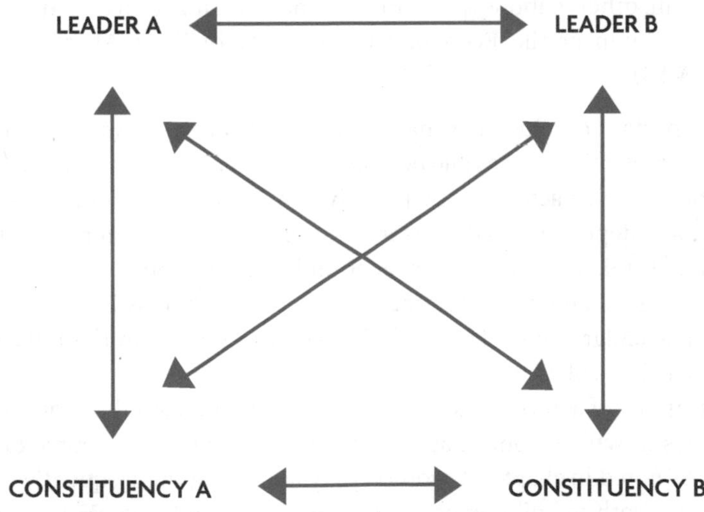

Source: Adapted from Andrew Moravcsik, "Integrating International and Domestic Theories of International Bargaining," in *Double-edged Diplomacy: International Bargaining and Domestic Politics*, eds. Peter B. Evans, Harold K. Jacobson, and Robert Putnam (Berkeley: University of California Press, 1993), 32.

ers, it is essential to recognize that they must simultaneously address multiple constituencies, not only leaders of rival states, but also their domestic constituents, international patrons and clients, their political competitors, and so on. In this sense, political speech is a multidimensional chess game. One reason political leaders often speak ambiguously is that they are seeking to respond to the demands of one constituency without alienating the others.

The analyst should pay close attention to two categories of actors:

- *Spoilers* benefit from the continuation of the conflict, either economically or politically, and therefore seek to block its resolution. Spoilers can include extremists whose power would be diminished in a peaceful society or criminal networks that are able to operate more easily in a chaotic environment. Spoilers whose profits depend on conditions that promote conflict are sometimes referred to as conflict entrepreneurs, especially if they are engaging in illegal economic activity.[10]

- *Peacebuilders* seek to mitigate or resolve a conflict. They might include journalists, religious and civic leaders, or members of traditional elites with an interest in promoting peace. Peacebuilders may be indigenous to a society, or they may be outsiders such as representatives of international humanitarian NGOs, members of diaspora populations, or mediators from other nations or from regional organizations such as the African Union or the Economic Community of West African States (ECOWAS).

It is important to remember that the words *spoiler* and *peacebuilder* are inherently subjective. Just as one person's terrorist is another person's freedom fighter, a given actor may be perceived as either a spoiler or a champion of peace, depending on the observer's perspective and interests. It may be useful to think of spoiling and peacebuilding as functions performed by various actors in a conflict at various times, rather than as intrinsic attributes of particular actors. This issue is explored further in the following section on drivers of conflict and peace.

One's survey of actors in the conflict environment should pay attention to the ways in which women, as well as men, influence the course of the conflict. As noted in chapter 2, women play important but frequently overlooked roles both in building peace and in fueling violence. Women have been active in building peace networks that have helped bridge the divide between warring parties, such as the Mano River Women's Peace Network

(MARWOPNET) in Guinea, Liberia, and Sierra Leone. Women have also forged coalitions across factional lines in Northern Ireland, Burundi, Liberia, and both southeastern and northern Nigeria. Conversely, women have provided both material and ideological support to violent insurgencies around the world. A survey of conflicts in fifty-five countries found that women were active in thirty-eight of them, forming between one-tenth and one-third of the fighting forces. Most frequently, women perform support roles or are "army wives," but women have also been active combatants in conflicts such as those in Algeria, El Salvador, Eritrea, Mozambique, Namibia, Nepal, Nicaragua, South Africa, and Sri Lanka.[11]

Step 3. Drivers of Conflict and Peace

- How do actors use dividers to provoke conflict? How do actors use connectors to promote peace?

In step 3 of the assessment process, the team synthesizes the findings of the previous two steps. Taking into account the contextual factors that create both vulnerabilities to conflict and opportunities for peacebuilding, the team analyzes the dynamic interactions by which leaders mobilize their constituents to provoke conflict or promote peace. In analyzing the behavior of both leadership and constituent groups, the assessment team should keep in mind two questions: What are the motivations of these actors? What resources do they have at their disposal that could enable them to achieve their objectives?

Figure 4.2 illustrates how leaders use dividers to mobilize constituents as a means of escalating conflict. Indicators of escalation might include

- signs that leaders are attempting to mobilize their constituents (either through words or deeds) by emphasizing divisions in the society,
- signs that constituents are receptive to these appeals (such as political rallies or acts of violence against members of target groups), or
- signs that constituents are pressuring their leaders to further escalate the conflict (for example, by questioning the courage or patriotism of any leader who is contemplating compromises).

In the case of the 2011 Nigerian presidential election, certain key actors (Muslim leaders in northern Nigeria) sought to mobilize their constituents (Nigerian Muslims) around a divider (the perception that Nigeria's

FIGURE 4.2 Drivers of Conflict

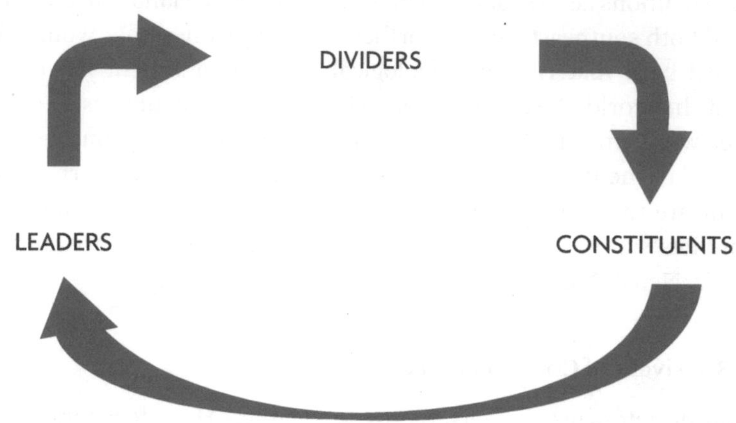

Christians had stolen the presidency from the country's disadvantaged Muslim population) to incite sectarian violence. As figure 4.2 indicates, the divisive tactics employed by leaders to mobilize their constituents may create a reinforcing feedback loop whereby constituents demand that their leaders further escalate the conflict rather than agree to a negotiated settlement.

> **Drivers of conflict**
>
> - How are key actors using dividers to escalate conflict?
> - What are the motivations of these actors?
> - What resources do they have at their disposal?
>
> **Drivers of peace**
>
> - How are key actors using connectors to resolve or de-escalate conflict?
> - What are the motivations of these actors?
> - What resources do they have at their disposal?

Figure 4.3 illustrates the converse phenomenon: how leaders use connectors to mobilize constituents as a means of de-escalating conflict. For example, in Nigeria after the 2011 election, some leaders sought to use a connector (national pride in the free and fair election process) to promote peaceful coexistence among Nigeria's Christians and Muslims. In some cases, conciliatory moves by the leaders of a group may create a positive feedback loop by contributing to a more trusting and less antagonistic relationship between the rival groups, creating a space for further peacebuilding efforts.

FIGURE 4.3 Drivers of Peace

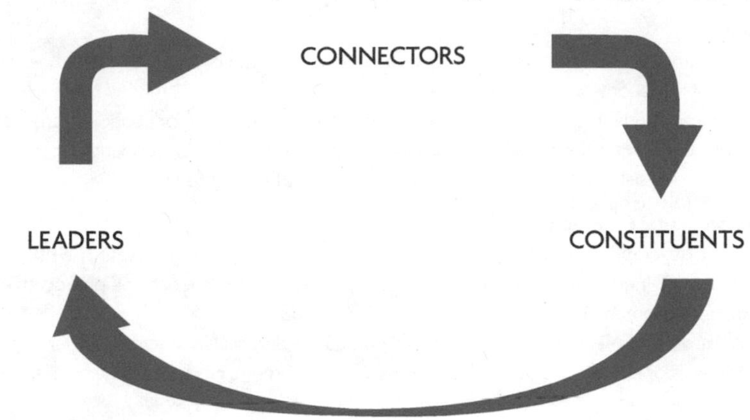

Step 4. Windows of Vulnerability and Opportunity

- What events or conditions in the conflict environment could elevate the risk of escalation, or create opportunities for de-escalation?

A *window of vulnerability* is a moment at which the escalation of conflict becomes more likely, whether because of a trigger event, such as an assassination or a contested election (see chapter 2), or because of more gradual developments in the conflict environment such as food shortages or rising unemployment. Conversely, a *window of opportunity* is a moment when conditions are favorable for the de-escalation of conflict, such as during the aftermath of the tsunami that struck Indonesia's Aceh Province in December 2004. During windows of opportunity, events call attention to overarching commonalities within a society, diminishing the significance of internal fault lines and motivating cooperation across intergroup boundaries.[12]

In assessing the potential future trajectory of a conflict, it is useful to begin by creating a list of possible events that could create windows of vulnerability or windows of opportunity for conflict management efforts. Building on the Nigeria example, the death of President Goodluck Jonathan's predecessor (an unanticipated event) and the April 2011 presidential election (an anticipated event) were both potential windows of vulnerability for violent conflict. But the integrity of the election process also created a window of opportunity for mitigating conflicts in Nigeria. Because a given event, such as the Nigerian election, may create both vulnerabilities and

Analyzing Windows of Vulnerability and Opportunity

Events

- What anticipated future events (such as a national election or a census) have the potential to become a flashpoint for violence?
- How might unanticipated events (a natural disaster, a crop failure or economic crisis, a civil war in a neighboring state, an assassination, a terrorist attack, a political scandal, a controversial court decision or legislative action) influence the conflict?

Environmental conditions

- What developments or trends in the conflict environment could elevate the risk of escalation (pervasive human rights abuses, pervasive hate speech, or provocative troop movements)?
- What developments could create opportunities for de-escalation (cross-border economic cooperation or peacebuilding initiatives by women's groups or other civil society organizations)?

opportunities, some practitioners prefer to use the term *windows of uncertainty* to discuss transitional moments at which either positive or negative changes in the conflict are more likely.

As well as listing potential transformative events, it is important to explore the dynamic interactions that could escalate the conflict or de-escalate it. Are key actors perpetrating human rights abuses or inciting violence through hate speech? Are they importing weapons, training paramilitary groups, or moving troops to the border of a rival country? Conversely, are initiatives under way that have the potential to mitigate or resolve conflict—the establishment of confidence-building measures among rival states, cross-border economic cooperation, interfaith dialogues, or peacebuilding initiatives by women's groups or other civil society organizations?

That a window opens does not necessarily mean that anyone climbs through it. A window of opportunity or vulnerability is a potential turning point, but not an inevitable one. For example, the 2004 Asian tsunami provided a catalyst for resolving the violent insurgency in Indonesia's Aceh Province. But in Sri Lanka, which was also devastated by the tsunami, the violent struggle between the Tamil insurgency and the Sri Lankan government resumed shortly after the disaster.

Transition to Planning

In some organizations, such as governmental intelligence agencies, a clear division exists between the roles of analyst and policymaker. Analysts are responsible for providing impartial reporting on a given conflict, leaving to other officials all decisions concerning program planning and implementation. An increasing number of organizations, however, are seeking to integrate conflict analysis into program planning and program evaluation activities. For example, the World Bank and USAID both mandate conflict assessment processes as part of the planning phase for certain development assistance programs. In this section, we discuss the integration of analysis and planning on the basis of two examples, the UN's Post-Conflict Needs Assessment (PCNA) tool and Mary Anderson's Do No Harm (DNH) Framework.

Postconflict Needs Assessment

The PCNA is used as "an entry point for conceptualizing, negotiating and financing a common shared strategy for recovery and development in fragile, post-conflict settings." According to the UN Development Group, the primary value of a PCNA lies in "the collective effort to assist national partners to develop a vision for the future and, on that basis, analyze which priority needs are to be addressed first, based on a clear understanding of why and how such interventions are most likely to contribute to the larger peacebuilding and recovery process, and the analysis of absorption and implementation capacity."[13]

The PCNA has been used for a range of joint assessment and planning projects in recent years, and has been helpful in identifying priority needs and program gaps. For example, a PCNA on Zimbabwe highlighted the destabilizing impact of youth militias in the country, which led international donors to emphasize youth-related programming in their development assistance strategy for that country. Likewise, a PCNA conducted on the Republic of Georgia after the 2008 war with Russia found that assistance programs for internally displaced persons needed to target not only IDPs from the 2008 conflict but also the residual needs of IDPs from the Georgian civil war of 1991–93. Based on this finding, the UN designed its resettlement programs for Georgia to address the needs of all IDPs, not just those from the 2008 war.[14]

Do No Harm Framework

The DNH Analytical Framework was created through a participatory process conducted by CDA Collaborative Learning Projects (CDA, formerly Collaborative for Development Action). The framework is descriptive rather than prescriptive; its purpose is to help development practitioners identify and avoid unintended negative consequences of their programs. It also seeks to call attention to unrecognized opportunities for a given program to help mitigate conflict. The DNH assessment tool involves seven steps, some of which are discussed earlier in this chapter:

1: Understanding the context of conflict

2: Analyzing dividers and tensions

3: Analyzing connectors and local capacities for peace

4: Analyzing the assistance program

5: Analyzing the assistance program's impact on dividers and connectors

6: Considering (and generating) programming options

7: Test programming options and redesign project

The DNH Framework is intended to encourage "reflective practice" by development assistance professionals, helping to integrate conflict assessment into day-to-day programming decisions. As the instruction book to the framework emphasizes, "It is not enough, when analyzing a program, to ask these questions once. It is necessary to ask them again and again, until the whole structure of the program has been made explicit and clear."[15]

Conclusion

The four-step conflict assessment process presented here synthesizes elements of frameworks developed by a wide range of governments, international organizations, and NGOs (see appendix 5):

- *Dividers and connectors:* What divides the people of the region against each other? What connects them?
- *Actors:* Who contributes to conflict among the people of the region? Who helps build peace?
- *Drivers of conflict and peace:* How do actors use dividers to provoke conflict? How do actors use connectors to promote peace?

- *Windows of vulnerability and opportunity:* What events or conditions in the conflict environment could elevate the risk of escalation? What events or conditions could create opportunities for de-escalation?

Many organizations mandate the use of their assessment frameworks as part of larger analytical and planning processes. Our goal is not to substitute the assessment process described here for those frameworks, but rather to identify points of synergy among a wide range of conflict assessment instruments, and thus to enable better coordination of assessment processes among diverse organizations.

Conflict assessment is not a stand-alone activity, but a process that must reflect and respond to the objectives and analytical needs of one's organization. Self-assessment is a critical preparatory task for any conflict assessment because it is essential to develop an explicit understanding of the scope of inquiry, the logistical and institutional constraints one will face, and the objectives and interests that motivated the decision to conduct the assessment. When designing and conducting the assessment, it is also important to keep in mind any follow-on activities. Is the goal simply to provide a snapshot or baseline understanding of a conflict-prone region, or to contribute to institutional processes for program planning, implementation, or evaluation?

Collaborative processes, particularly when they involve participants from a diverse range of organizations, can help serve three valuable functions:

- provide a common set of questions about the nature and trajectory of a conflict,
- establish shared concepts and a shared lexicon for discussing opportunities for preventive actions, and
- facilitate coordinated decision making on conflict mitigation strategies by local actors and third-party interveners.

As Koenraad Van Brabant of Interpeace observes, it is essential to keep in mind that conflict assessment is not a technical process but a human one. Rather than seeking to arrive at a single comprehensive consensus about the nature of a given conflict, a collaborative assessment should help bring to light and evaluate the diverse perspectives of stakeholder groups. This deliberative process can help participants test the validity of their assumptions and identify potential synergies and frictions among the various perspectives. In many cases, the interpersonal relationships and the delibera-

Questions for Practitioners

- Does your organization use any formal process or framework for conflict assessment? If so, has this process given practitioners new insights into the conflict? Has it helped define a common set of questions and a shared lexicon for discussing the conflict?
- Which—if any—of the conflict assessment tools discussed here might be useful for your organization? What would be the best way to structure a collaborative conflict assessment exercise in your workplace? Who should participate? What steps would you take to maximize the likelihood that the findings of the assessment would have a positive impact on your organization's operational activities?

tive process established during the conflict assessment will be more valuable than any specific conclusions arrived at by the group.

The next three chapters discuss several collaborative analytical techniques—narrative analysis, conflict mapping, and scenario analysis—that can be used either in conjunction with a conflict assessment framework or on a stand-alone basis. Each of these tools can help sharpen the focus of a conflict analysis process and enrich one's understanding of the conflict dynamics.

Notes

1. Lisa Schirch, *Conflict Assessment and Peacebuilding Planning: A Strategic, Participatory, Systems-Based Handbook on Human Security* (Bloomfield, CT: Kumarian Press, 2013), chap. 1.
2. Koenraad Van Brabant, personal communication with the author, May 2011.
3. Schirch, Conflict Assessment and Peacebuilding Planning, chap. 2.
4. Van Brabant, personal communication, 2011.
5. Ibid.
6. Mary Hope Schwoebel, interview by the author, Washington, DC, March 2012.
7. Andrew Blum, personal communication with the author, Washington, DC, April 2012; Veronica Eragu Bichetero, interview by the author, Washington, DC, March 2012.
8. CDA Collaborative Learning Projects, *The Do No Harm Handbook* (Cambridge, MA: CDA Collaborative Learning Projects, 2004), 3, www.cdainc.com/cdawww/default.
9. Robert D. Putnam, "Diplomacy and Domestic Politics: The Logic of Two-Level Games," *International Organization* 42, no. 3 (1988): 427–60. I thank Gabriella Blum for tutoring me on this model.

10. See Stephen J. Stedman, "Spoiler Problems in Peace Processes," *International Security* 22, no. 2 (Fall 1997): 5–53, http://cisac.stanford.edu/publications/spoiler_problems_in_peace_processes (accessed May 10, 2012).

11. Frances Stewart, "Women in Conflict and Post-Conflict Situations" (paper presented at the UN Economic and Social Council's Thematic Discussion of the Role of Women in Countries in Special Situations, June 30, 2010), www.peacewomen.org/assets/file/Resources/UN/remarks_by_frances_stewart_2.pdf (accessed May 10, 2012).

12. Office of the Coordinator for Reconstruction and Stabilization, U.S. Department of State, "Interagency Conflict Assessment Framework," 14, www.state.gov/organization/161781.pdf (accessed May 10, 2012).

13. United Nations Development Group, "Post-Conflict Needs Assessments," 2012, www.undg.org/index.cfm?P=144 (accessed May 10, 2012). I thank Kristoffer Nilaus Tarp for his assistance with this section.

14. Ibid.

15. CDA, *Do No Harm Handbook*, 14–15.

5 NARRATIVE ANALYSIS

Key Points

- Narrative analysis is a method for illuminating the multiple dimensions of a conflict by examining the stories that rival parties tell about their grievances and their desires.
- The goal of narrative analysis is not to grasp the objective truth of a conflict, but rather to gain insight into the subjective perspectives that shape the parties' decisions and actions.
- It is important to examine the perspectives not only of the primary actors in a conflict, but also of secondary actors and influential third parties.
- Narrative analysis is an efficient way to develop a more empathic and intuitive understanding of the dynamics of a conflict. It can help analysts identify potential vulnerabilities and flashpoints, as well as potential openings for conflict resolution efforts.

"The single most significant strategic strength that an organization can have is not a good strategic plan, but a commitment to strategic listening on the part of every member of the organization."

—Tom Peters, "Leadership: Listening"

The behavior of parties to a conflict is often determined not so much by their objective situation as by their subjective perceptions. A simple and intuitive approach called *narrative analysis* can help newcomers to a conflict zone understand the stakes of the struggle, and can help experts refine and enrich their knowledge of the conflict's dynamics. The analyst seeks to learn the subjective truths articulated by the various parties about the conflict to gain insight into the actors' motives and potential courses of action. This analytical approach can also be useful for lifelong residents of the conflict zones, including the parties to the conflict. By telling their stories about the conflict, and by listening openly to the stories told by members of other groups, the parties may begin to acknowledge that other groups' perceptions of the conflict may differ from their own.

Narrative analysis is closely related to a skill known as *strategic listening*, a business management term. Strategic listening involves paying attention to all of the messages people are conveying through both verbal and nonverbal cues. Any given sentence may express not only a factual meaning, but also an underlying intention or feeling not explicitly stated. By recognizing and understanding these various messages, an astute listener can acquire additional information that supports effective decision making.[1] In conflict situations, the act of listening to multiple stakeholders may be a first step toward conflict resolution.[2]

Narrative analysis encompasses the art of strategic listening but may also include reading, watching, and observing with all the senses—not just hearing. It might be used, for example, to analyze the imagery and symbolism in a campaign poster or television ad, or the rhetoric of a political speech. Narrative analysis involves paying attention to stories people tell about their conflict and trying to unpack all the information about the speaker and the conflict that these stories reveal. It also involves examining one's stories about a conflict and how they may shape one's objectives and decisions. We must recognize that third-party actors inevitably become participants in, as well as observers of, a conflict. By asking questions, by conversing with people on the ground, a third-party observer will shape the way local actors perceive themselves and their conflicts. And because most people go to conflict zones as members of larger organizations, it is important to examine the objectives, perspectives, and interests of one's own organization. The decisions of third-party actors can have a significant impact on the course of a conflict, either for good or for ill.

Listening as a Peacebuilding Technique

According to Koenraad Van Brabant, head of reflective practice at Interpeace, it is essential for peacebuilders to listen carefully to the various narratives about a given conflict told by diverse actors. Listening is a central element of a conflict resolution approach called *narrative mediation*. As Van Brabant observes,

> Hearing the conflict analysis from a diversity of "local" actors is important because every side has their story. There will be different narratives, narratives that shape the perceptions, mindsets and behaviors of those who believe them. The different narratives therefore are part of the dynamic, and understanding a particular group's narrative is highly relevant for the peace activist. If for example a group sees itself overwhelmingly as "victim," while it has also on occasion been "perpetrator," the peace actor will have to find ways and means of this group recognizing and acknowledging a more complex reality.
>
> From a peacebuilding perspective, active engagement of a diversity of people from the conflict-affected society is central and part of the peacebuilding process. There is no one-size-fits-all rule about how to conduct such participatory conflict analysis. Sometimes it will be advisable to listen to different actors and their different narratives/analysis separately; at least initially while the situation is not ready for them to come together and listen to each other. In other instances, some actors or some individuals from different groups are willing and able to sit together and listen to each other's analysis.
>
> Reflecting on the origins, nature and dynamics of their own conflict is a first step for people to start taking some analytical distance from what they are living, a precondition for being able to consider more options for action and intervention. Different actors will also have different perspectives about what the conflict is about, what caused it, what is driving it today, who the "perpetrators" and who the "victims" are, and what needs to change to reduce the violence. Being able to listen—in a well facilitated encounter—to the conflict narratives of different members of the same society, especially those seen as on the other side of a divide, can be a first step towards more constructive dialogue.[3]

In a narrative analysis exercise, one listens for the answers to six questions, the same six that journalists learn to address in a news story: who, what, why, when, where, and how.

BOX 5.1 How to Use Narrative Analysis

Narrative analysis is a flexible and adaptable technique that can be used in a wide range of settings by analysts, decision makers, and conflict-resolution practitioners. Three particularly useful applications are to help scan the environment in a conflict zone, to inform an organization's decision makers by enriching their knowledge of key actors in a conflict, and to support narrative mediation processes for conflict resolution.

- **Scanning the environment.** It takes minimal effort to use narrative analysis during the daily routine, while reading newspaper articles, listening to political speeches, conversing with members of competing factions in a conflict, or talking with colleagues about the conflict. In such contexts, narrative analysis may involve nothing more than heightened sensitivity to the attitudes, beliefs, motives, and world views of others.
- **Informing decision makers.** Narrative analysis can be used, on a more structured basis, as part of a collaborative exercise involving organization staff members. In such an exercise, several small groups are each assigned to analyze the narratives told by a particular faction in the conflict, using the U.S. Institute of Peace Narrative Analysis Framework (see appendix 6). The participants then convene in plenary session to identify key points of friction and potential areas of compatibility among the various narratives. Such an exercise, which typically requires two to three hours, can help decision makers identify not only potential flashpoints in a conflict zone, but also potential opportunities for mitigating or resolving the conflict. An alternative, less formal, and time-consuming approach is to assign each group to analyze the content and implications of the mythic histories told by one of the competing factions and to compare these histories in plenary session.
- **Supporting narrative mediation processes.** Narrative mediation is an emerging conflict resolution technique that seeks to foster trust and mutual understanding among rival groups by recognizing the importance of the stories that different sides tell about the conflict in shaping both their attitudes and those of their rivals. A note of caution: narrative mediation requires extensive preparation and a carefully structured environment for conversation. If a mediator tries to use narrative mediation methods in a casual or ad hoc manner, it is more likely to aggravate than to resolve differences among the parties to a conflict.

Who: Leaders and Constituents

Chapter 4 discusses how actors may be thought of as the cast of characters that drive the drama of conflict—each one having its own history, motives, resources, and relationships with other members of the cast. *Primary actors* are the principal players in a conflict—either individuals or institutions—who can influence its outcome. *Secondary actors* are internal or external stakeholders who have a significant interest in the conflict but are less centrally involved (see "Anwar Sadat and the Two-Level Game").[4]

Narrative analysis examines the ways in which various parties depict the key actors in a conflict and the relationships among them. In particular, it focuses on the relationships between *leaders* and *constituents* (as visualized in the two-level game model discussed in chapter 4, p. 101) , exploring the rhetorical strategies leaders use to advance their agendas. Three questions are central to this inquiry:

- How do leaders attempt to influence and balance their own multiple constituencies?
- How do leaders attempt to position themselves advantageously against their rivals?
- How do constituent groups constrain and motivate the behavior of their leaders?

Anwar Sadat and the Two-Level Game Model

In October 1981, Egyptian president Anwar Sadat was assassinated by members of his presidential guard while observing a military parade. This event marked the tragic failure of Sadat's efforts to reconcile his competing political constituencies to a strategic realignment of Egyptian foreign policy.

In the wake of two embarrassing military defeats by Israel in 1967 and 1973, Sadat had begun searching for ways of breaking the stalemate in the Middle East, which he considered disadvantageous for Egypt's national interests. Under his predecessor, Gamal Abdel Nasser, Egypt had aligned itself with the Soviet Union and the other states of the Arab League, and had rejected Israel's right to exist. Sadat calculated that, by shifting Egypt's strategic alignments, he might be able to broker deals with Israel and the United States that would benefit Egypt and potentially also help solve the Israeli-Palestinian conflict.

In carrying out this realignment, Sadat's most dramatic gesture was his 1977 trip to Jerusalem, where he spoke to a session of the Israeli Knesset. The two-level game model provides a useful means of illustrating this gambit. Sadat (leader A) had no relationship with the newly elected Israeli prime minister Menachem Begin (leader B), who had a reputation as a hard-liner.

Likewise, most Egyptians (constituency A) and most Israelis (constituency B) were hostile toward each other. By traveling to Jerusalem, Sadat sought to maneuver around Begin by appealing directly to the Israeli public and thus to create pressure on the Israeli government to make peace with Egypt. He also wanted to empower Knesset members who were more amenable than Begin to a peace deal, such as Israeli foreign minister Moshe Dayan.

Unfortunately for Sadat, his trip to Jerusalem had a strong negative effect on his relationship with other Arab leaders and with his constituents. Egypt's allies in the Arab League were enraged by Sadat's conciliatory gesture toward Israel, as were domestic groups such as the Egyptian Islamic Jihad, which would carry out his assassination four years later. (It is difficult to map all these domestic and international actors onto the two-model game diagram, an indication of its limits as an analytical device.) But the visit had at least one salutary effect: it persuaded U.S. president Jimmy Carter that Sadat had a genuine desire for peace and thus helped open the path to the Camp David Peace Accords between Egypt and Israel the following year.

What and Why: Positions Versus Interests and Needs

According to the theory of *interest-based negotiation,* conflicts frequently remain stalemated because rival parties cling to positions based on a zero-sum calculus, believing that one party's gain necessarily entails the other's loss. In such circumstances, a mediator can sometimes help move the conflict toward resolution by shifting the focus of the conversation away from the stated positions and toward the underlying interests and needs that motivate them. The process of interest-based negotiation may be compared to peeling an onion (see figure 5.1). The mediator seeks to move from the outer layer of positions (what the parties say they want) to the layer of interests (what the parties really want) and finally to the innermost layer of needs (what the parties must have).[5]

As the discussion of the escalation and de-escalation of conflict in chapter 2 revealed, the mediator's efforts to identify shared interests and needs are unlikely to be successful unless the parties to the conflict have established a certain degree of mutual trust and concern. To understand the challenges involved in peeling the conflict onion, practitioners must be alert to the various types of positions, interests, and needs that may manifest themselves in a conflict.

FIGURE 5.1 The Conflict Onion

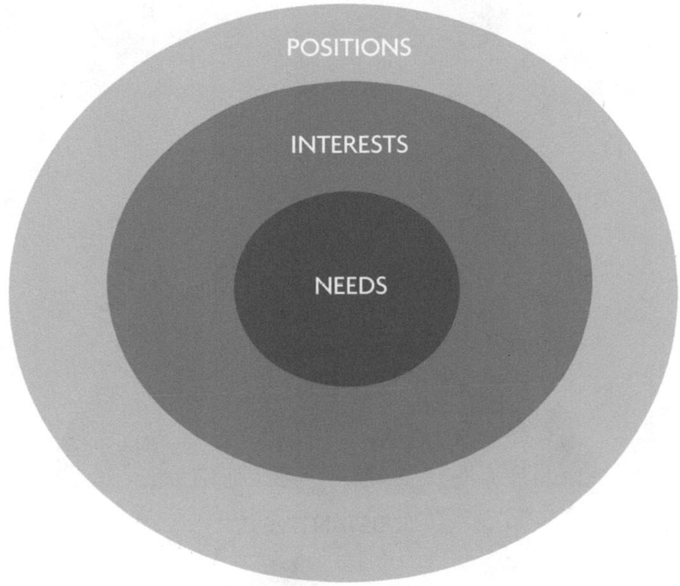

Positions

To identify the positions of the rival parties, the analyst should start by asking two questions: What do the actors say the conflict is about? What do they say they want?

In general, the positions in a conflict are expressed openly by the rival parties. In certain situations, however, the parties may refrain from announcing all their positions at the outset of a negotiation process. In some cases, the positions may be maximalist versions of the parties' actual needs. In other cases, the position may reflect an entirely different interest. For example, a negotiation may become deadlocked not only because of objections to the terms of the proposed settlement, but also because the parties are compelled to demonstrate their toughness to domestic political rivals.

Interests and Needs

Interests are typically the unstated motives behind the parties' positions. One of the objectives of an interest-based negotiation process is therefore to make the parties' interests more transparent to each other and in some

FIGURE 5.2 Substantive, Procedural, and Relationship Interests

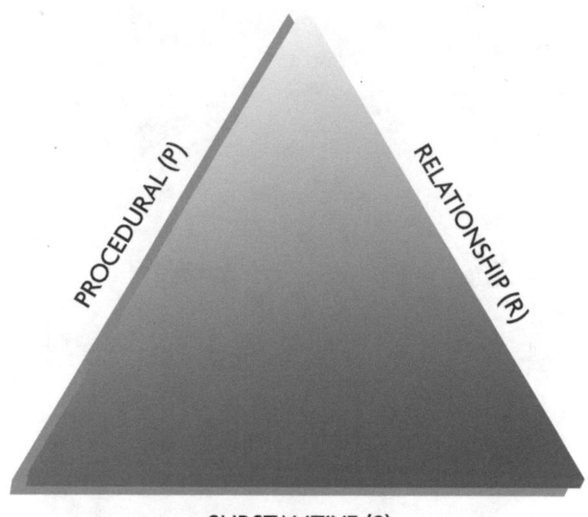

cases to increase the parties' awareness of their own underlying interests and needs.

Interests may involve material desires: control over economic wealth, natural resources, or land. They may involve the desire for power or status: political or military might. They may also involve concerns over identity: the desire for an independent nation-state for one's ethnic group, or for the redress of a historical grievance. Conflicts involving material interests are often more amenable to a negotiated settlement than conflicts involving identity interests. Whereas the parties may be able to arrive at compromises over territorial boundaries, power sharing, or control of natural resources, it can be more difficult to find a mutually acceptable middle ground where issues of identity, such as religion or ethnicity, are at stake.

Some negotiation theorists distinguish among three types of interests: substantive (S), procedural (P), and relationship (R) interests (see figure 5.2).[6] *Substantive* interests include each of the types of interests discussed in the previous paragraph: they involve the core issues over which the rival parties are contending.

Procedural interests relate to the question of whether the substantive issues are perceived as being decided in a fair and proper manner. For example, in northern Iraq since the U.S. invasion of 2003, Kurdish and Arab inhabitants have argued over the status of the city and province of Kirkuk. The substantive issue in this dispute is whether Kirkuk should be governed by the autonomous Kurdish Regional Government (KRG) or by the Iraqi central state. But this issue is connected to a series of procedural disputes about how the issue will be resolved. Article 140 of the Iraqi constitution called for a referendum to determine the status of Kirkuk by the end of 2007, which in turn required a census to determine the relative proportions of various ethnic groups on the voter rolls. But the census was delayed, in part by allegations that the KRG was forcing non-Kurdish residents out of Kirkuk to increase the proportion of Kurdish voters.

Relationship interests involve perceptions of status, dignity, respect, and mutual trust. One reason the conflict over Kirkuk has been so intractable is that, during the 1980s and early 1990s, Saddam Hussein's regime committed mass atrocities against the Kurds and attempted to Arabize Kirkuk by expelling its Kurdish residents. Thus, many Kurds have remained suspicious of the motives of the Iraqi central government, even after the overthrow of Saddam Hussein and the establishment of a Shia-led regime. In a negotiation process, perceived slights or insults can derail the deliberations. During the 1978 Camp David negotiations, Israeli prime minister Menachem Begin and Egyptian president Anwar Sadat disliked each other so intensely that President Carter's negotiating team engaged in shuttle diplomacy between the two parties' cabins, which were just steps away from each other, to decrease this risk.

Needs include not only basic physiological requirements for survival (food, water, physical safety, economic livelihoods) but also higher-level needs including community, dignity, and spiritual fulfillment. According to the psychologist Abraham Maslow, humans have a *hierarchy of needs*, and it becomes possible to focus on the higher-level needs only after one's most fundamental needs have been satisfied.[7]

Conflict resolution theorist John Burton has developed the theory of *basic human needs*, which departs from Maslow's logic by arguing that some of Maslow's higher-level needs are equally as basic as the physiological ones. Burton argues that humans have a universal need for identity, recognition, security, and personal development, which do not lend themselves to compromise. Moreover, when such needs are at stake, intergroup conflict cannot be solved unless these needs are addressed. Burton declares, "Needs and values are not for trading."[8]

1978 Camp David Accords

In the 1967 Arab-Israeli War, Israel seized control of the Sinai Peninsula from Egypt. Six years later, in the war known in the Arab world as the Ramadan War and in Israel as the Yom Kippur War, Egypt attempted unsuccessfully to recapture the Sinai. For Egypt's leaders, the Sinai Peninsula was an integral part of the historical Egyptian nation. But Israel's leaders saw this territory as an essential security buffer against any future Egyptian attack. Moreover, by the late 1970s, some forty-five hundred Israeli settlers had moved into the Sinai, and the Israeli government faced the prospect of domestic opposition if it were to order their displacement.

The Egyptian and Israeli positions on this territorial question appeared to preclude the possibility of any mutually acceptable negotiated solution: neither side was willing to compromise its claim to the Sinai Peninsula. But U.S. president Jimmy Carter's negotiating team was able to find a way forward by focusing not on the two sides' positions, but instead on their underlying interests and needs.

Although both Egypt and Israel staked a claim to the same territory, they did so for different reasons. Egypt's claim was based on its interest in the territorial integrity of the Egyptian nation, which reflected a deeper need for communal dignity and respect. Israel had an interest in maintaining a security buffer against any future Egyptian attack, which reflected its need for the physical safety of its people.

The Camp David Accord addressed both sides' interests and needs by returning the Sinai Peninsula to Egypt but establishing a demilitarized zone, to be guaranteed by an international monitoring mission, in the portion of the Sinai adjoining the Israeli border. A U.S. pledge of bilateral aid to both Egypt and Israel—which has averaged about $3 billion to Israel and $1.5 billion to Egypt ever since 1978—was a sweetener that helped seal the deal.

When: Mythic Histories

In a typical journalistic story, the questions of who, what, where, and when can usually be answered simply, whereas the why and the how can be more complex. But, in a narrative analysis exercise, the when and the where are often the most controversial questions, because they play a key role in defining the identities of the rival parties and the stakes of the struggle.

In chapter 4, we discussed several conflict assessment frameworks that also use a version of the six Ws to structure the analysis. These frameworks instruct analysts to seek objective answers to questions such as "When did the conflict break out?" and "Where are the battles being fought?" In narrative analysis, by contrast, the analyst seeks to understand the rival parties' subjective answers to questions about history and geography. For example,

- What mythic histories do the various parties tell?
- When do they say the conflict broke out, and what events do they focus on?
- When and how do they believe the conflict will end?

The phrase *mythic histories* is not meant to imply that the stories about the conflict told by the rival parties are false, but rather that they convey culturally significant meanings as well as historical information, whether true or false. The anthropologist Benedict Anderson depicts nations as "imagined communities." He observes that, although nationalist leaders typically describe their nations as primordial communities originating in the mists of time, in fact nationalism is a much more recent phenomenon, dating roughly to the era of the French Revolution of 1789.[9]

Leaders of nationalist movements often tell their nations' histories according to a three-part plot that includes descriptions of a glorious past, a degraded present, and a utopian future. They assert that the nation has fallen from an original state of grace as a result of external blows or internal flaws but that it still has the potential to redeem itself and to achieve a utopian future condition. This type of story performs several important functions for those seeking to mobilize a cadre of activists for nationalist or other mass political movements. First, it defines the criteria for membership in the national community, based on its idealized descriptions of the nation's past and future conditions. Second, it provides a diagnosis that explains why the community fell from the glorious past to the degraded present. Third, it provides an implicit or explicit prescription that identifies a potential path to the utopian future. Finally, by presenting highly stylized and exaggerated visions of the nation's past, present, and future conditions, it creates emotional tension that can be used to mobilize the participants in the movement to avenge the nation's suffering (see figure 5.3).[10]

The psychiatrist Vamik Volkan uses the term *chosen trauma* to describe such mythic histories. He notes that members of ethnic or national com-

FIGURE 5.3 Triad of Nationalist Rhetoric

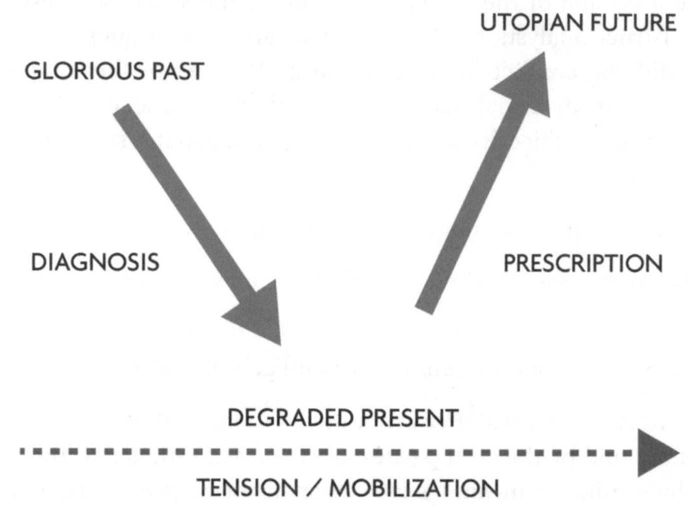

Source: Adapted from Matthew Levinger and Paula Franklin Lytle, "Myth and Mobilization: The Triadic Structure of Nationalist Rhetoric," *Nations and Nationalism* 7 (2001): 186. Reproduced with permission.

munities may transmit memories of humiliating historical events across generational lines:

> The chosen trauma becomes a significant marker for the large-group identity. Furthermore, it may create a foundation for the society's development of an exaggerated entitlement ideology that, under new historical situations such as a threat to group's identity, can be manipulated by political leaders to develop new political programs and/or take new actions supported by this ideology. Exaggerated "entitlement" provides a belief system that asserts that the group has a right to own what they wish to have.[11]

The triadic narrative pattern is by no means universal in the rhetoric of nationalist and other mass political movements. In some cases, political leaders may not speak at all about their community's past or future. In other cases—for example, in a presidential speech given the day after a World Cup victory—the nation's past may be portrayed as degraded and its present as glorious.

More commonly, the leader of a nationalist movement may speak in great detail about the causes of the nation's suffering but remain silent on the subject of how to respond to these grievances. Slobodan Milošević's speech on the Battle of Kosovo is an apt example (see following section).[12]

In such instances, it is useful to keep the following rule of thumb in mind: "The prescription is the inverse of the diagnosis." In other words, if the speaker depicts the nation's suffering as resulting from the loss of a specific territory, the implicit prescription is that the nation must recover that land to restore its health. If the "pollution" of a nation's ethnic or racial stock has led to its decline, the cure is ethnic or racial "cleansing."

A political leader may want to preserve a degree of ambiguity about the prescription for how to heal the nation for several reasons. As noted in the discussion of the two-level game model, political speech is typically addressed to multiple audiences with diverse interests and concerns. A leader may wish to mobilize a group of extremists without alienating more moderate constituents. Moreover, such rhetoric would also potentially alarm international audiences such as donors of military aid or development assistance funds, the UN Security Council, or even the International Criminal Court. Finally, a leader may want to test the waters of political extremism, assessing the potential level of support, as well as the responses of domestic and international audiences, before committing irrevocably to a campaign of political violence.

Slobodan Milošević's Speech on the Battle of Kosovo

On June 28, 1989, Serbian president Slobodan Milošević gave a speech on the site of the Field of Blackbirds in Kosovo, where the Ottoman Empire had defeated Serbia six hundred years earlier. Milošević had spent his career until then as a Communist Party apparatchik, but as socialist governments throughout Eastern Europe became increasingly imperiled, he reinvented himself as a Serbian nationalist.

Addressing a crowd of two hundred thousand ethnic Serbs gathered on the field, Milošević declared, "[The Serbs'] national and historical being has been liberational throughout the whole of history and through two world wars, as it is today. They liberated themselves, and when they could they also helped others to liberate themselves."[13]

The defeat of 1389 had dealt a profound and lasting blow to the Serbian national community, Milošević claimed:

> What has been certain through all the centuries until our time today is that disharmony struck Kosovo six hundred years ago. If we lost the battle, then this was not only the result of social superiority and the armed advantage of the Ottoman Empire but also of the tragic disunity in the leadership of the Serbian state at that time. In the memory of the Serbian people, this disunity

BOX 5.2 Punctuation of Mythic Histories

One important feature of mythic histories is an aspect of communication known as *punctuation*. Even when rival factions agree on the sequence of events in a conflict, they may disagree about the causal relationships among these events. If Party A and Party B are locked in a conflict spiral, they may engage in hostile actions in the following sequence:

A→B→A→B→A→B→A→B→A→B

The conflict narratives told by the two parties may blame the other party for the outbreak of each new conflict episode. Party A may discount the provocative nature of its own actions, punctuating the history of the conflict as follows:

[A], B→A, B→A, B→A, B→A, B

Party B, by contrast, may punctuate its narrative as follows:

A→B, A→B, A→B, A→B, A→B

In Party A's narrative, B is always the aggressor and A is always the victim. In Party B's narrative, the situation is the reversed: A is the aggressor and B is the victim. Such patterns of biased punctuation make conflicts difficult to resolve because they reinforce each party's perception that the rival side is intrinsically hostile and untrustworthy.[a]

a. On biased punctuation, see Roderick M. Kramer, "The 'Dark Side' of Social Context: The Role of Intergroup Paranoia in Intergroup Negotiations," in *The Handbook of Negotiation and Culture*, eds. Michele J. Gelfand and Jeanne M. Brett (Palo Alto, CA: Stanford University Press, 2004).

> was decisive in causing the loss of the battle and in bringing about the fate which Serbia suffered for a full six centuries.[14]

But Milošević saw a hopeful sign in the current reawakening of Serbs' historical consciousness: "This year, the Serbian people became aware of the necessity of their mutual harmony as the indispensable condition for their present life and further development." He concluded the speech with a ringing call to the barricades—while insisting that those barricades were still only figurative: "Six centuries later, now, we are being again engaged in battles and are facing battles. They are not armed battles, although such things cannot be excluded yet. . . . Let the memory of Kosovo heroism live forever! Long live Serbia! Long live Yugoslavia! Long live peace and brotherhood among peoples!"[15]

To an outside observer, Milošević's rhetoric might have appeared innocuous, given his emphasis on the "liberational" character of the Serbian people, the need for "mutual harmony," and his desire for "peace and brotherhood among peoples." But Milošević had established himself over the previous two years as an advocate for ethnic Serbs within the predominantly Albanian Yugoslav province of Kosovo—famously telling a group of Serbian protesters confronted by Kosovar riot police in April 1987, "You shall not be beaten!" Milošević's references to unity and harmony must be understood in the context of his support for reforms to the Yugoslav constitution limiting Kosovo's autonomy, which were violently opposed by many ethnic Albanians.

Most ominous were Milošević's references to the disharmony that had "struck Kosovo six hundred years ago," which had been "decisive in causing the loss of the battle and in bringing about the fate which Serbia suffered for a full six centuries." According to a legend propagated in Serbian folktales, the Serb nobleman Vuk Branković had defected to the Ottoman side on the eve of the Battle of Kosovo of 1389. Milošević thus diagnosed the cause of Serbia's six centuries of suffering as the fault of those who had converted to Islam to curry favor with the Ottoman oppressors. Milošević's implicit message was that all Muslims are traitors to the Serbian nation.

Given the rule of thumb that the prescription is the inverse of the diagnosis, Milošević could be—and was in fact—understood by his followers to mean that the Muslims deserved to suffer in return for the suffering they caused the Serbs. Thus, even though Milošević told his listeners that the Serbian people were not yet engaged in armed battles, his speech initiated the work of defining membership in the Serbian nation and mobilizing Serb extremists for the struggle that lay ahead.

Where: Territorial Narratives

Like nationalist histories, territorial narratives have a strong mythic component. The questions about where that one asks in a strategic listening exercise are simple: Do the factions disagree about the identity of the contested territory? How do such disagreements influence the conflict?

But the answers can be enormously complex and contentious, as the naming of the State of Israel makes clear (see following section).[16] Peter Weinberger of the U.S. Institute of Peace uses the metaphor of the palimpsest to describe territorial narratives about political communities. A palimpsest is a page written on many times, where each new layer obscures but does not erase the previous one.

Territory may be seen, both figuratively and literally, as a palimpsest. The architecture of an ancient city such as Rome or Jerusalem combines traces of both the present and the past. An archaeological dig in such a city strips away the accretions of recent history to reveal progressively older layers of human experience. But an archaeological excavation cannot determine which layers are true and which are false. Indeed, most archaeologists would argue that each of the layers is equally true.

Leaders of nationalist and other mass political movements often assert, however, that certain layers of historical experience are more authentic than others. Thus, for example, the territory now called the West Bank has been known at various times, and by various parties, as Palestine, the occupied territories, occupied Jordan, the British Mandate, the land of the Philistines, the land of the Canaanites, or Judea and Samaria, among other names. One of the thorniest obstacles to achieving a settlement of the Israeli-Palestinian conflict is that partisans on all sides of this conflict assert the authenticity of their own territorial narratives and deny the validity of the narratives told by the opposing sides.

The Naming of Israel

In November 1947, the United Nations General Assembly approved a resolution to partition the territory of the British Mandate for Palestine into two states—one Jewish and the other Arab. The ensuing debate over what name to give the new Jewish state, which was resolved only on the eve of Israel's declaration of independence in May 1948, highlighted the conflicting views within the Jewish community of Palestine concerning its own political identity and its relations with the Arab inhabitants of the region.

The writer Aharon Reuveni, who is credited with coining the term State of Israel (Medinat Yisrael), noted various alternative names in a letter of December 1947: "Why not Land of Israel (Eretz Yisrael)? Or Judea? Or Zion? Or Yeshurun? Or State of the Jews? Or State of the Hebrews? Or Ever? (one of the sons of Shem, whose name was transliterated into Latin as Ebreo)."[17] Reuveni considered, and rejected, each of these alternatives: "It cannot be called 'Land of Israel,' because it will not occupy the whole land, or most of it, or even half of it." As for Judea, "How shall we give the name Judea to a state that does not include Jerusalem and Hebron, and leaves the Judean Hills outside its border?" He found the name Zion equally problematic, because Mount Zion in Jerusalem lay outside the territory designated for the new Jewish state. Reuveni concluded that the name State of Israel was most appropriate, in part because it highlighted the parallels between the ancient Jews and the modern Jews who were returning to the Holy Land from the Diaspora.

But the name of the new state was not decided until May 12, 1948—two days before Israel's declaration of independence—and even then the question of how this name should be translated into Arabic was left unresolved. The name Medinat Yisrael was approved by a 7–3 vote of the People's Administration at its meeting of May 12. One of the dissenters, Aaron Zisling, declared, "I am against a name that will compel every Arab to bear a name against which he should rise up." A proposal had been made to name the state Israel in Hebrew but to translate it into Arabic as Palestine, but this was rejected, partly on the grounds that "It is possible that the Arab state in the Land of Israel will continue to be called 'Palestine' in the future, and this is liable to cause confusion."[18] This debate over the naming of Israel reveals the fluidity and uncertainty of political conditions in the British Mandate in 1947 and 1948. For example, it shows that a number of Jewish leaders at that time accepted the inevitability of an Arab Palestinian state adjoining Israel. It also shows that Jewish leaders were acutely aware of the political significance of geographical names. Delegates such as Zisling, who hoped to avoid war between Arabs and Jews, did not want to give the new state a name that would signal the exclusion of its Arab residents.

But in Reuveni's view, this concern was misplaced. He later recalled that, during the autumn of 1947, "Of one thing I was certain: The days of the Mandate were numbered, and after it an open life-and-death struggle would erupt with the Arabs. . . . If our strength fails us, we will not escape extinction. If we overcome, a Jewish state will arise."[19] Thus, Reuveni embraced a name for the new state that excluded the historical identity of its non-Jewish residents in part because he believed that the Arab residents of the British Mandate sought to annihilate the Jews.

Some Palestinian leaders have depicted this belief as a self-fulfilling prophecy. Writing on the occasion of the sixtieth anniversary of Israel's founding in 2008, Elias Khoury declared of the Palestinian Arabs, "These peasant farmers, who made up the majority of the Arab population of Palestine in 1948, did not discover that they had had a 'nation' of their own until they lost it. They had been living in a historical continuity for hundreds of years, as a succession of invaders of different nationalities and ethnicities took control of their lands and communities. But they were astonished to discover that these new invaders did not wish to control the land in the manner of the former invaders; instead they wanted it emptied of its inhabitants."[20]

How: Strategy and Tactics

The questions about how relate to the strategic objectives and the tactics employed by the rival parties to a conflict:

- What is each side's game plan?
- How does it hope to prevail in the conflict?
- What weapons, organization, and methods (both violent and nonviolent) does it use? What is the scope of the battlefield? The competing parties may see this in different ways.
- What would victory look like? What would defeat or failure look like?
- Is victory feasible? Do the parties believe it is feasible?

It is important to recognize that the rival parties may envision the stakes of the conflict, and the scope and locations of the spaces in which the battles are fought, in very different ways. Not only may different parties utilize asymmetric tactics, but their overarching strategic objectives may be defined in asymmetric ways as well (see following section).

In addition to examining the strategies and tactics of the primary actors in a conflict, analysts should study the motives and means of potential third-party interveners—including their own organizations. Often a given third party may have a range of motives for becoming involved in a conflict, both altruistic and self-serving. For example, the leaders of a global hegemon such as the United States may wish to alleviate humanitarian suffering in a given conflict zone, but may also be concerned about preventing terrorist threats, securing access to strategic resources, and maintaining the international prestige of the United States. Likewise, a humanitarian NGO may be focused on promoting peace and economic development, but also needs to compete with other NGOs to secure charitable donations to support its work.

It is important to explore not only the actual motives of potential third-party interveners, but also how their motivations are perceived by people living in the conflict zone. When a foreign power takes an interest in events in one of its former colonies (for example, France in Côte d'Ivoire or Britain in Kenya), it may be perceived as attempting to reassert its imperial power over the country. This popular perception, even if false, may undermine the legitimacy and effectiveness of the intervention.

Asymmetric Strategies: "War" Between al-Qaeda and the United States

The term *asymmetric warfare* has gained wide currency since September 11, 2001, when nineteen hijackers armed only with box cutters succeeded in killing thousands of people and causing tens of billions of dollars of property damage in New York and Washington, DC. The word *asymmetric* has typically been used to describe either the nature of the parties to the conflict (a relatively small terrorist organization versus the largest superpower in the world) or the tactics they employ (hijackings and bombings of civilian targets versus large-scale conventional military campaigns).

But the asymmetries in the so-called global war on terror (or, more recently, the war against al-Qaeda) have extended to the ways in which the parties define their strategic objectives, as well as to the tactics they employ. Osama bin Laden's infamous 1996 "Declaration of War Against the Americans Occupying the Land of the Two Holy Places" justified attacks on American military and civilian targets on the basis of the "occupation of the land of the two Holy Places . . . by the armies of the American Crusaders and their allies."[21]

Bin Laden declared that the Saudi regime had "torn off its legitimacy" through its support for "the infidels" and the "corruption, repression, and the intimidation taking place in the country." The "situation cannot be rectified," bin Laden asserted, "unless the root of the problem is tackled. Hence it is essential to hit the main enemy who divided the Ummah into small and little countries and pushed it, for the last few decades, into a state of confusion. . . . Clearly after Belief (*Imaan*) there is no more important duty than pushing the American enemy out of the holy land."[22] For al-Qaeda's leaders, at least initially, the overthrow of westernized Arab regimes was the ultimate objective of the struggle. They saw terrorist attacks against the United States and other countries primarily as a means toward this end.

For U.S. political leaders in the post–September 11 era, by contrast, defending the American homeland was the principal strategic objective. To achieve this goal, President George W. Bush authorized invasions of countries deemed to be state sponsors of terrorism: first Afghanistan and then Iraq, despite the fact that the Iraqi regime had played no role in planning or executing the 9/11 attacks.

Only at the highest level of abstraction could the "war aims" of al-Qaeda and the U.S. government be seen as symmetrical. Al-Qaeda's leaders hoped that, by striking against American targets, they could force the United

Questions for Practitioners

- How might you use narrative analysis methods in your own work? Could you use any of the techniques discussed here to enrich your understanding of the attitudes and motivations of key actors in a conflict? Might your organization be interested in holding a two-hour workshop using the USIP Narrative Analysis Framework (see appendix 6) to inform your organization's decision-making processes?
- How do the conflict narratives told by the various factions align with your own organization's narrative of the conflict? Koenraad Van Brabant, head of reflective practice at Interpeace, points out that it is crucial for an organization's staff to pay attention to their own stories about a conflict: "It may be that your own narrative is fairly close to the narrative of one of the parties to the conflict, which means that the parties will associate you with one of the parties or interest groups. So you undermine your ability to be accepted as an impartial actor by all of the parties" (see chapter 4). What steps can you take to avert this danger?

States out of the Middle East and thus pave the way to establishing a unified, authoritarian, fundamentalist regime in the Arab world. Some senior officials within the U.S. government believed that, by invading Iraq and overthrowing Saddam Hussein, the United States could create the conditions for the establishment of democratic, secular regimes in Iraq and elsewhere in the Middle East that would hold more benign attitudes toward the United States and its allies. In this sense, the theories behind al-Qaeda's war against the Americans and the U.S. government's war on terror could be seen as opposites—or inverse images—of each other.[23]

Conclusion

The method of narrative analysis discussed in this chapter provides a simple framework for unpacking the hidden meanings of the stories that parties tell about their conflicts. The method involves *listening strategically* to the competing stories told by the different sides in order to understand how the parties' worldviews shape their behavior in a conflict.

In conducting a narrative analysis, we must take everything we hear or read with a grain of salt. Any given story about a conflict will convey at best a partial understanding of a situation. Moreover, given the volatility of conflict environments, it is essential to revisit our analysis on a regular basis.

But this analytical approach can help us understand the reasons behind behavior that initially may appear opaque or even irrational to us. At best, it may help us identify potential openings for conflict resolution efforts, or potential minefields that we may have overlooked. In sum, it is an essential first step of conflict assessment and a precondition for engaging productively in efforts to prevent, resolve, and recover from deadly strife.

Notes

1. See, for example, Jeannine S. Tate and Dennis R. Dunklee, *Strategic Listening for School Leaders* (Thousand Oaks, CA: Corwin, 2005); Bernard T. Ferrari, *Power Listening: The Most Critical Business Skill of All* (New York: Penguin, 2012); Mark Brady, *The Wisdom of Listening* (Somerville, MA: Wisdom Publications, 2003).
2. Koenraad Van Brabant, e-mail message to the author, October 3, 2011.
3. Ibid.
4. On the history of the Egyptian-Israeli peace process, see Harold Saunders, *The Other Walls: The Arab-Israeli Peace Process in a Global Perspective,* rev. ed. (Princeton, NJ: Princeton University Press, 1991).
5. On the conflict onion, see Simon Fisher, Dekha Ibrahim Abdi, Jawed Ludin, Richard Smith, Steve Williams and Sue Williams, *Working with Conflict: Skills and Strategies for Action* (London: Zed Books, 2000), 27–29. On the principles of interest-based negotiation, see Roger Fisher and William Ury, with Bruce Patton, *Getting to Yes: Negotiating Agreement Without Giving In,* 2nd ed. (New York: Penguin, 1991).
6. On substantive, procedural, and relationship interests, see Christopher Moore, *The Mediation Process: Practical Strategies for Resolving Conflict*, 2nd ed. (San Francisco: Jossey-Bass Publishers, 1996).
7. Abraham H. Maslow, *Motivation and Personality* (New York: Harper, 1954).
8. John Burton, *Conflict: Resolution and Prevention* (New York: St. Martin's, 1990), 39.
9. Benedict Anderson, *Imagined Communities: Reflections on the Origin and Spread of Nationalism*, rev. ed. (London: Verso, 2006).
10. Matthew Levinger and Paula Franklin Lytle, "Myth and Mobilization: The Triadic Structure of Nationalist Rhetoric," *Nations and Nationalism* 7 (2001): 175–94.
11. Vamik D. Volkan, "Chosen Trauma, The Political Ideology of Entitlement and Violence (2004), www.vamikvolkan.com/Chosen-Trauma,-the-Political-Ideology-of-Entitlement-and-Violence.php (accessed May 4, 2012). See also *Blind Trust: Large Groups and Their Leaders in Times of Crisis and Terror* (Charlottesville, VA: Pitchstone Publishing, 2004).
12. See Levinger and Lytle, "Myth and Mobilization."

13. Slobodan Milošević, speech in Gazimestan, the Field of Blackbirds (Kosovo Polje), June 28, 1989, trans. British Broadcasting Corporation, Historical and Investigative Research, www.hirhome.com/yugo/bbc_milosevic.htm (accessed October 1, 2012).
14. Ibid.
15. Ibid.
16. "Why Not Judea? Zion? State of the Hebrews?" *Ha'aretz,* May 9, 2008, www.haaretz.com/hasen/spages/981617.html (accessed May 10, 2012); Elias Khoury, "For Israelis, an Anniversary. For Palestinians, a Nakba," *New York Times*, May 18, 2008, www.nytimes.com/2008/05/18/opinion/18khoury.html?pagewanted=all (accessed May 10, 2012).
17. Quoted in *Ha'aretz*, "Why Not Judea?"
18. Ibid.
19. Ibid.
20. Khoury, "For Israelis, an Anniversary."
21. See Osama bin Laden, "Declaration of War Against the Americans Occupying the Land of the Two Holy Places," August 23, 1996, www.terrorismfiles.org/individuals/declaration_of_jihad1.html (accessed May 4, 2012).
22. Ibid.
23. Ibid.

6

CONFLICT MAPPING AND SYSTEMS MAPPING

Key Points

- A conflict map is a graphical representation of various dimensions of a conflict that seeks to illuminate a conflict's dynamics, evolution, and scope.
- A systems map synthesizes information about patterns of interdependence among actors and institutions in complex social systems.
- By visualizing dynamic interactions and feedback loops within a conflict system, systems maps can help analysts assess the potential consequences of internal disruptions or external interventions. Systems maps can be particularly valuable in helping anticipate unintended consequences and second-order effects of actions by third-party interveners

The narrative analysis method discussed in chapter 5 may be seen as a microanalytic technique for understanding the perspectives of particular actors in a conflict. In this chapter, we discuss two macroanalytic approaches to visualizing the complex dynamics of a conflict system. *Conflict maps* are graphical representations of the geospatial, temporal, or relational dimensions of a conflict. Conflict mapping techniques can be used to depict the relationships among the actors in a conflict and how they shift over time. A *systems map* is a tool for synthesizing information about patterns of interdependence among actors and institutions in complex social systems. Systems mapping can be particularly useful in illuminating the forces that stabilize or destabilize a social system and in helping practitioners anticipate how a system may respond to external interventions or internal disruptions. Each of these types of maps can be valuable in communicating information about a conflict within and across organizational boundaries and for helping analysts and decision makers better understand the factors likely to influence the course of a conflict.

Conflict Mapping

The term conflict mapping is used in a wide range of ways by conflict management practitioners. Some practitioners use it figuratively, referring to a simple list or chart of the key actors, along with their motivations and resources, as a conflict map. In this chapter, we confine our focus to three types of mapping techniques that use graphic representations to illuminate the dimensions of a conflict system. Appendix 7 provides a list of conflict mapping tools and software packages.

Geospatial Mapping

Analysts sometimes literally map incidents of violence, using either paper maps or electronic geographic information systems (GIS) mapping tools such as Google Earth. Conflict mappers are increasingly using interactive software for reporting conflict events in real time. One such project, Ushahidi.com, was created by a group of Kenyans during that country's electoral violence in early 2008. Ushahidi uses a *crowdsourcing* methodology that allows anyone in the world with a computer or mobile phone to report information about conflict-related incidents in several target countries, including Kenya, the Democratic Republic of the Congo (DRC), and Somalia. Other crowdsourcing technologies that have been used for mapping conflicts and humanitarian disasters include OpenStreetMaps, a *wiki-mapping* technology that allows users to use geographical data in a collaborative way from anywhere on Earth, and FrontlineSMS, an open source platform that enables collaborative messaging by large groups of people to collect and share incident reports and other data.

> **Crowdsourcing** technologies can support collaborative conflict mapping efforts by allowing residents in a conflict zone to report information to a central database. But this technology can also be misused to incite violence unless the system's designers create mechanisms to screen and validate reports.

The premise behind the crowdsourcing approach is that, although any individual report may be unreliable, errors can be corrected through the "wisdom of crowds"—the guiding principle behind Wikipedia and other collaborative Internet-based projects. Just as anyone can report an incident, anyone can comment on or dispute a given report, so the potential exists to correct errors and disinformation. A note of caution is in order, however, concerning the potential pitfalls of using crowdsourcing technologies for publicizing reports on violent conflicts. Just as perpetrators used hate radio to incite violence during the Rwandan genocide of 1994, Internet-based communications technologies can be used to provoke as well as to mitigate violence. For example, in Kenya after the disputed election of December 2007, text messages and anonymous chain letters distributed through the Internet were used to incite intercommunal violence. Another danger is that those individuals who report incidents of violence may themselves be targeted either by government security forces or by nonstate combatants. It is important to take these issues into account when designing systems for reporting and mapping data on armed conflicts.

Temporal Mapping

Michael Lund's curve of conflict (discussed in chapter 2) is one tool for mapping the chronological progression of a violent conflict: the bell-shaped curve begins at the left side with peace, then escalates to instability, violent conflict, and finally to war, before descending back to peace on the right side of the curve (see figures 2.2 and 2.3).

The chronological evolution of a conflict may be mapped not only at the macro level, but also in more detail. For example, researchers at the University of London studied nearly fifty-five thousand violent events in nine historical and present-day insurgencies, including those in Iraq and Afghanistan. They found "strikingly regular and similar patterns in the sizes and timings of violent events" across the nine insurgencies: for example, large-scale attacks tended to occur in tight clusters. One practical consequence of this finding is that, when a nation is fighting against a violent insurgency, its "emergency response planning has to have a lot of capacity"—even though "this capacity would be under-utilized almost all of the time."[1] Similarly, a team of scholars at the University of Maryland has developed a framework called Stochastic Opponent Modeling Agents (SOMA) that uses historical data to generate rules assessing the probability that a group will take certain actions under certain conditions. This model has been used to predict the actions, such as kidnappings, bombings, or rocket attacks, of Hezbollah and thirty-five other terrorist groups in the Middle East.[2]

Relational Mapping

Conflict mapping can also refer to figurative maps of relationships among the various parties to a conflict. For example, *social network analysis* involves charting the connections among actors within a system, often using automated algorithms. Social network analysis can help illuminate which actors in a system are pivotal and which are more peripheral, as well as help identify "critical nodes" that might be targeted for conflict management efforts.[3]

Law enforcement and intelligence agencies rely on various commercially available software packages for social network analysis to investigate criminal and extremist organizations; examples include Analyst's Notebook, Centrifuge, Palantir, and Pen-Link. Such programs allow analysts to chart connections among the targets of an investigation, such as financial transactions, face-to-face meetings, and digital communications. The programs visualize these links with tools such as timelines, frequency graphics, and GIS location mapping.

But conflict mapping need not involve such elaborate technology and data acquisition methods. The purpose of a conflict map is to help visualize the dynamics of a given conflict to better understand potential risks and opportunities for engagement. In some situations, a rough diagram scrawled on a paper napkin may serve this function better than the most elaborate computer-generated flow charts.

Conflict mapping exercises are often most productive when conducted as collaborative activities, because the visual iconography of the map provides a focal point for discussion within the assessment team. Figure 6.1 presents a set of graphical elements for conflict mapping developed by the German development agency Gesellschaft für Technische Zusammenarbeit (GTZ) that draws

A **conflict map** can provide a visual focal point for discussion among analysts and decision makers, helping identify areas of consensus and disagreement, along with key knowledge gaps.

FIGURE 6.1 Graphic Elements Used for Conflict Mapping

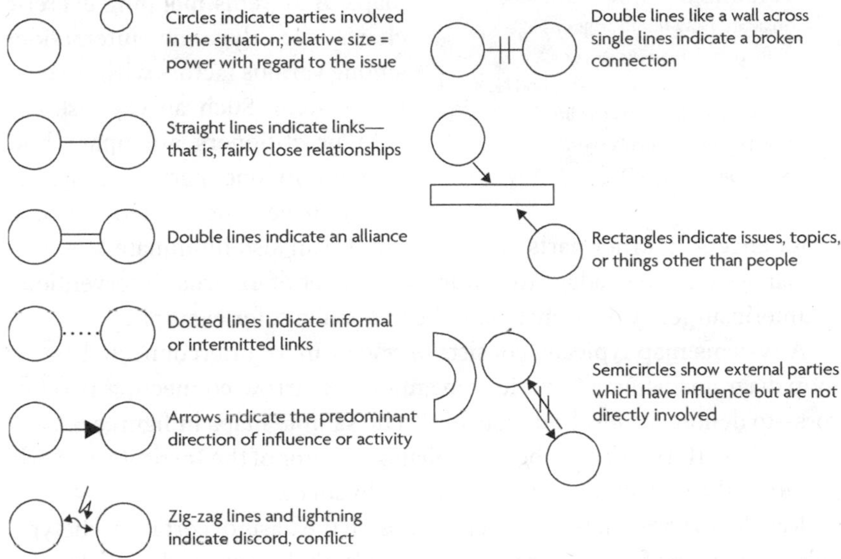

Source: Gesellschaft für Technische Zusammenarbeit, "Conflict Analysis for Project Planning and Management: A Practical Guide" (draft, August 2001), 61; based on Simon Fisher, ed., *Working with Conflict: Skills and Strategies for Action* (London: Zed Books, 2000), 23–24.

on the work of Simon Fisher. Circles indicate the principal parties involved in a situation, larger circles depicting parties with greater relative power regarding the issue at stake. Single lines indicate relationships between two parties, and arrows are used to indicate the predominant direction of influence. Double lines indicate an alliance, whereas zigzag lines indicate conflict between two parties. Semicircles depict external third-party actors with significant influence over the situation.

People learn and process information in diverse ways: some are more attuned to the written word, others to a spoken message or graphic representation. A collaborative conflict mapping exercise can provide a forum for exchanging information in all three of these forms: text, conversation, and pictures. Ideally, such a map can help organize productive conversations about the conflict dynamics.

Systems Mapping

Systems mapping uses graphic representations of conflict dynamics to synthesize the findings of a conflict analysis exercise and may incorporate

Systems maps can help practitioners anticipate how their programs in a conflict zone may produce unexpected second-order effects and how systems may adapt to thwart the impact of external interventions.

elements of temporal and relational maps. A systems mapping exercise charts the dynamic interactions among various factors within a conflict system. Such an exercise can help practitioners anticipate how changes in one part of a system might have unexpected second-order effects on other parts of the system. It can also illuminate how particular systems may adapt to thwart the impact of external interventions, counterinsurgency or counternarcotics campaigns, for example.

A systems map typically consists of one or more interconnected causal loop diagrams using a "simple convention—an arrow connecting two factors—to denote a causal relationship." The sample maps in figures 6.2 and 6.3 are from the work of Robert Ricigliano, director of the Institute of World Affairs at the University of Wisconsin–Milwaukee.[4]

Ricigliano constructs his systems maps on the basis of certain archetypal subsystems. The first of these is what he calls a balancing cycle or balancing loop—exemplified by the operation of a thermostat (see figure 6.2). In a balancing loop, a destabilizing event is counteracted by an opposing force that restores the equilibrium in the system. For example, if one opens the windows in one's house on a cold winter day, the thermostat will trigger the furnace in the house to produce hot air, compensating for the loss of heat through the windows.

In politics, balancing loops may be found in the relationship between a political elite that controls the apparatus of the state and an opposition movement that seeks to challenge that monopoly on power. As an opposition movement becomes increasingly effective, the elite may seek to maintain stability by increasing the intensity of its efforts to preserve control, for example, by banning political demonstration and jailing opponents of the regime.

The second key system archetype is a *reinforcing* or *action-reaction cycle*. In a reinforcing cycle, a relatively minor initial event can escalate into something of much greater magnitude. The security dilemma, discussed in chapter 2, is an example of a reinforcing cycle in interstate relations: state A's actions result in state B feeling threatened, which motivates state B to react in a way that, in turn, threatens state A. A classic case of a reinforcing cycle in international affairs was the outbreak of World War I in 1914, when the assassination of the Austrian crown prince provoked a series of mutu-

FIGURE 6.2 Balancing Loops in Power Relations

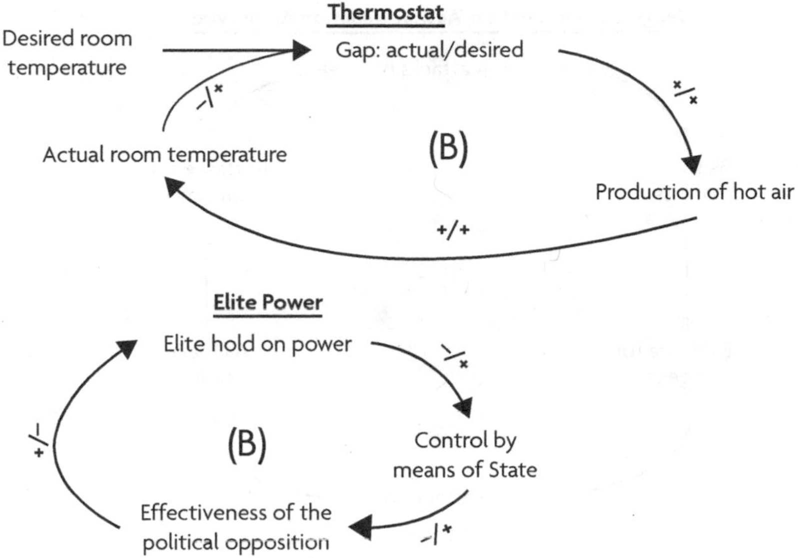

Source: Robert Ricigliano, *Making Peace Last: A Toolbox for Sustainable Peacebuilding* (Boulder, CO: Paradigm Publishers, 2012), 115. Reproduced with permission.

ally reinforcing retaliatory moves by Austria, Russia, Germany, France, and Great Britain, plunging Europe into a cataclysmic war (see figure 6.3).

Most complex social systems exist in a dynamic equilibrium that involves a combination of reinforcing loops, which provoke change within a system, and balancing loops, which help preserve stability. Under normal conditions, the balancing loops are robust enough to counteract the disruptive forces unleashed by the reinforcing loops. But when a tipping point is reached, and the reinforcing loops overwhelm the capacity of the balancing loops, a radical transformation of the system becomes possible.

The Fix That Backfires archetype (see figure 6.3) illustrates the combination of two competing loops—a balancing one and a reinforcing one—that may coexist in a country whose government is seeking to suppress a violent insurgency by an ethnic independence movement. In response to violent acts by the insurgents, the government seeks to restore stability by imposing extreme security measures. Although these measures are successful in the short run, the government crackdown also reinforces the ethnic grievances and tensions that provoked the insurgency in the first place, potentially reinforcing the cycle of violence. If the government security forces

FIGURE 6.3 Vengeance-Retaliation and the Fix That Backfires

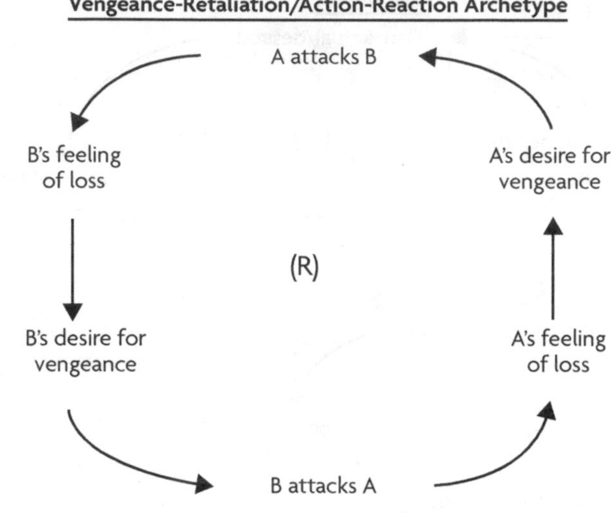

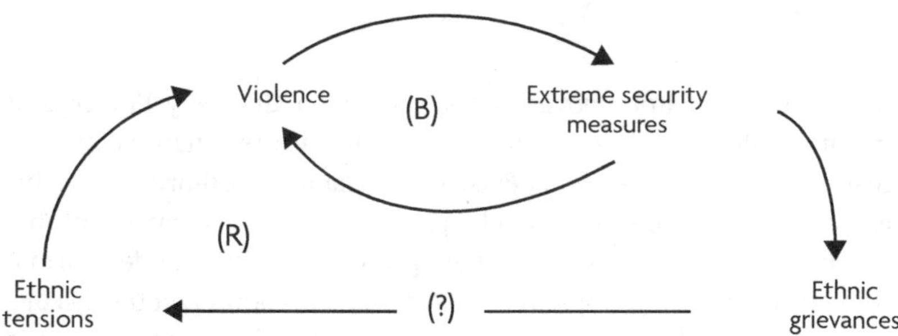

Source: Ricigliano, *Making Peace Last*, 129. Reproduced with permission.

have enough capacity to disrupt the insurgents' activities, the situation will remain stable. But if the reinforcing loop of ethnic tensions overwhelms the balancing loop of the security crackdown, the country may descend into civil war.

Systems maps can take a wide range of forms—from flow charts to simple loops to highly elaborate "spaghetti monsters" that may require hours to decipher.[5] David Kilcullen, an adviser to the U.S. Defense Department in Iraq and Afghanistan, has used systems maps to provide guidance for U.S. stabilization and counterinsurgency efforts in those countries. In 2007 and

2008, Kilcullen served as senior counterinsurgency adviser to David Petraeus, commanding general of the Multinational Force in Iraq, who implemented the successful surge strategy to mitigate insurgent and sectarian violence in Iraq. Kilcullen's systems maps for Iraq were generally simple and easy to read.

> Most complex social systems exist in a **dynamic equilibrium**, which involves a combination of reinforcing loops, which provoke change within a system, and balancing loops, which help preserve stability.

One of Kilcullen's maps summarized a strategy for breaking the cycle of violence between rival Shia and Sunni militias. The visual focal point of this map was a reinforcing loop drawn in red, showing escalating violence involving extremist Shia and Sunni groups. The map also indicated a series of tactical interventions that might help interrupt the cycle of escalation, which were depicted as green bars across the red arrows, for example, "Gated communities prevent Shia extremists from entering Sunni areas." Larger-scale initiatives carried out by U.S. and coalition forces were shown in blue, for example, "Joint Security Stations protect people in their homes," and "Market and district hardening programs . . . protect public places against terrorism." This diagram summarized, in an easily understandable form, both the logic by which sectarian violence had escalated in Iraq and several layers of interventions by the U.S. and Iraqi governments that could help restore peace among rival sectarian groups. Kilcullen's diagram provided U.S. military commanders with an intuitive road map for planning their efforts to mitigate sectarian violence.[6]

Systems mapping can also be used to stimulate discussion among participants in a peacebuilding process and to identify points of agreement and disagreement about the causes of a conflict (see box 6.1). Koenraad Van Brabant of Interpeace sometimes sketches out a systems map as a focal point for discussion in a collaborative conflict assessment workshop. This kind of "tentative visualization" of a conflict, says Van Brabant, "can become very stimulating of discussions" with diverse stakeholders. You can check the analysis by asking them whether the picture resonates well with how they see it. . . . And you can get interesting and insight-generating debate going about WHY the system persists as it

> The objective of a systems mapping exercise is not to achieve perfect accuracy, but rather to enable analysts and decision makers to "listen to the system" and understand the dynamic relationships among its various parts.

BOX 6.1 How to Use Systems Mapping

Systems mapping is particularly valuable when, in Rob Ricigliano's words, it provides a forum for a "process of dialogue and learning" about complex conflict dynamics. Unlike narrative analysis, which can be used even by people with no prior knowledge of a given conflict, systems mapping requires a thorough understanding of the interactions among key actors in a conflict zone. For this reason, it is most appropriate for use at the conclusion of a conflict assessment workshop, as a tool for synthesizing the findings of the assessment process, rather than as an introductory exercise.

Participants may wish to begin a systems mapping exercise by sketching out various *balancing loops* that preserve equilibrium within the system and *reinforcing loops* that may destabilize the system unless they are counteracted by balancing forces. After mapping these various loops and their interconnections, the participants may wish to examine how new factors introduced into the system—international development assistance programs, an influx of refugees, or the entry of an international peacekeeping force into a conflict zone, for example—are likely to influence the balance of forces within it. This deliberative process may help analysts and decision makers gain deeper insight into complex conflict dynamics. It may also help them anticipate the feedback loops and second-order effects that can cause an intervention or an investment in a conflict zone to have unexpected consequences—either positive or negative.

is, who mostly benefits from it, who would be open to and most opposed to change, etc."[7] Brabant was trained in a systems approach to conflict analysis by the Reflecting on Peace Practice Program at CDA Collaborative Learning Projects. CDA has concentrated on developing relatively simple systems tools for use by field practitioners. They have also generated a series of archtypes (similar to Ricigliano's) and use systems maps to identify points of leverage for inducing change in the conflict system.[8]

As with scenarios, one of the challenges of systems mapping is to provide enough detail to capture key conflict dynamics without overwhelming and confusing the audience with excessive information. In determining the appropriate level of detail to put into a given systems map, it is useful to keep in mind that the objective of a systems mapping exercise is not to achieve perfect accuracy. Rather, such an exercise should foster a conversation that enables a group of policymakers and program implementers to jointly "listen to the system" and understand the dynamic relationships within it. Ricigliano describes systems mapping as performance art:

> [It is] not about recreating reality, or even about the map itself, but is [instead] about the process of dialogue and learning that goes into producing a map.

Questions for Practitioners

- Which of the conflict mapping or systems mapping methods discussed here could be useful in your work? Would it be more valuable to use them casually, sketching out a rough diagram to provide a visual focal point for a conversation, or in a more formal setting such as a workshop or presentation?
- What are the keys to an effective conflict map or systems map? How does one draw a map that is intuitive and visually accessible—even to people who were not present in the workshop or dialogue in which the map was produced—and that conveys significant new information about conflict dynamics?

The group act of drawing a systems map requires participants to discuss their perceptions, assumptions, and beliefs about the social context they are studying. The discussion makes them set priorities (for example, what is important and why) and it requires participants to make their implicit assumptions about cause and effect explicit. It is a check on each person's unconscious filters and theories of change.[9]

Conclusion

Like a structured conflict assessment process, a systems mapping exercise can provide the basis for strategic conversations between conflict analysts and decision makers about the critical dynamics of an emerging conflict and about how feedback loops within the conflict system may cause policy decisions to have unintended effects. If carried out jointly by representatives of multiple groups operating in a conflict zone, systems mapping exercises can also assist in the development of a shared strategic narrative that can help diverse organizations coordinate their policies and programs more effectively.

Notes

1. Paul Rincon, "Violence Follows Common Patterns," BBC News, December 16, 2009, http://news.bbc.co.uk/2/hi/science/nature/8416951.stm (accessed May 6, 2012).
2. Aaron Mannes and V. S. Subrahmanian, "Calculated Terror: How a Computer Model Predicts the Future in Some of the World's Most Volatile Hotspots," Foreign Policy, December 15, 2009; www.foreignpolicy.com/articles/2009/12/15/calculated_terror (accessed May 6, 2012).
3. On social network analysis, see Charles Kadushin, *Understanding Social Networks: Theories, Concepts, and Findings* (New York: Oxford University Press,

2012); and "Social Network Analysis," Wikipedia.com, http://en.wikipedia.org/wiki/Social_network#Social_network_analysis (accessed May 6, 2012).

4. Robert Ricigliano, *Making Peace Last: A Toolbox for Sustainable Peacebuilding* (Boulder, CO: Paradigm Publishers, 2012), 115.
5. For an example of an overly complex systems map, see Dion Nissenbaum, "The Great Afghan Spaghetti Monster," *Checkpoint Kabul*, December 20, 2009, http://blogs.mcclatchydc.com/kabul/2009/12/the-great-afghan-spaghetti-monster.html (accessed May 6, 2012).
6. See David Kilcullen, "Breaking the Cycle of Sectarian Violence in Iraq," Powerbase.info, www.powerbase.info/index.php?title=Image:Kilcullen_RAND_Presentation.JPG (accessed May 6, 2012).
7. Koenraad Van Brabant, personal communication with the author, January 2012.
8. CDA Collaborative Learning Projects, Reflecting on Peace Practice Program, "Participants Training Manual," available at www.cdainc.com/cdawww/pdf/manual/rpp_training_participant_manual_rev_20090104_Pdf.pdf
9. Ricigliano, *Making Peace Last,* 108–09.

7 SCENARIO ANALYSIS

Key Points

- Scenario analysis is a valuable tool for strategic planning in uncertain and volatile conditions. It enables an organization to anticipate and rehearse its responses to disruptive changes.
- Effective scenarios are compelling stories about alternative futures, constructed on the basis of assumptions about predetermined trends and critical uncertainties in an organization's operating environment.
- Scenarios are "not a group of quasi-forecasts, one of which may be right." They describe "different worlds, not just different outcomes in the same world."
- Analysts can establish and track indicators to assess which scenarios are becoming more or less likely over time.
- When senior decision makers internalize the logic of the scenarios, they can provide a common lexicon and a shared road map for guiding program planning and implementation.

Scenario analysis is a technique frequently used in the corporate world, and increasingly in the fields of intelligence analysis and conflict management, to support medium- and long-term strategic planning efforts. It is especially valuable when an organization confronts critical uncertainties in the future business environment and when managers need to develop strategic plans that will allow their organization to succeed under diverse environmental conditions. Jay Ogilvy and Peter Schwartz of the Global Business Network write that "scenarios are narratives of alternative environments in which today's decisions may be played out. They are not predictions. Nor are they strategies. Instead they are more like hypotheses of different futures specifically designed to highlight the risks and opportunities involved in specific strategic issues."[1]

Ideally, according to Ogilvy and Schwartz, "scenarios should be written in the form of absorbing, convincing stories that describe a broad range of alternative futures relevant to an organization's success." Such stories have the virtue of serving as an effective bridge from analysis to policy planning and implementation: "Thoughtfully constructed, believable plots help managers to become deeply involved in the scenarios and perhaps gain new understanding of how their organization can manage change as a result of this experience.... Moreover, scenarios with engrossing plots can be swiftly communicated throughout the organization and will be more easily remembered by decision-makers at all levels of management."[2]

Yet scenario builders must be careful to avoid locking in on a particular scenario by confusing the exercise with reality.[3] The more compellingly scenarios are developed, the greater the risk of this outcome. Scenarios should be seen as tools for expanding one's understanding of the range of potential trajectories of a conflict situation, rather than narrowing one's focus to a single potential future (see box 7.1).

Scenario-Building Techniques

A wide range of techniques can be used for generating compelling and informative scenarios. Most of these techniques use the following three steps as a starting point:

- *Establish a decision focus.* "For scenarios to be truly useful learning and planning tools," Ogilvy and Schwartz observe, "they must teach lessons that are highly relevant" to an organization's decision makers. "In other words, they must speak to decisions or direct concerns."[4]
- *Brainstorm a list of key factors.* This brainstorming aims to identify "driving forces and key trends" that "are the most significant elements in the external environment," and that "drive the plots and determine their

outcome." The assessment team's discussion of the context, grievances, and mitigating factors in a conflict environment should provide the starting point for this brainstorming session. Ogilvy and Schwartz emphasize that the brainstorming should consider "five general categories of forces and trends: social, technological, economic, environmental, and political forces that interact with one another to create complex and interesting plots."[5]

- *Distinguish predetermined elements from uncertainties.* Certain key forces identified in the brainstorming session may be "inevitable or predetermined" trends "that are unlikely to vary significantly in any of the scenarios." Other forces may be identified as *critical uncertainties*: that is, forces that "are most likely to define or significantly change the nature of the scenarios."[6]

BOX 7.1 How to Use Scenario Analysis

Scenario analysis exercises can be a useful bridge between a collaborative conflict assessment workshop (see chapter 4) and an organization's planning process (see chapter 9). Unlike a conflict assessment, which aims to provide a snapshot of a conflict at the present time, a scenario analysis seeks to identify and explore the implications of a range of potential future trajectories of the conflict. Thus it can be a powerful tool for enhancing the organization's strategic foresight by enabling it to anticipate and rehearse its responses to evolving conditions in a potential conflict zone.

Scenario analysis is particularly valuable when an organization confronts fundamental uncertainties either in its external or in its internal operating environment: Will a civil war erupt in a neighboring country? Will global oil prices double in the next five years? Will our agency suffer draconian cuts in our federal budget allocation? Will our NGO receive an unexpected bequest from a major donor? An organization's leaders are often reluctant to develop contingency plans for disruptive events such as these, perhaps because they don't want to engage in idle speculation or because they don't want to appear either excessively fearful or unrealistically optimistic about the future. Consequently, when disruptive events occur, the organization is unprepared to respond in an agile and strategic manner.

One advantage of scenario analysis methodology is that it is explicitly not intended to be a predictive tool. Rather, it is intended to explore a range of alternative futures and to enable an organization's analysts and decision makers to discuss the implications of each of these futures, as well as how the organization can best respond to emerging challenges and opportunities. Participants in a scenario analysis exercise should beware of prematurely locking in on a particular scenario by viewing one potential future outcome as inevitable.

The initial steps of a scenario analysis are, first, to establish a decision focus for the exercise; second, to brainstorm a list of driving forces and key trends that will drive the plots of the scenarios; and, third, to distinguish predetermined forces and trends from those that are critical uncertainties.

Inductive and Deductive Approaches

Based on these initial steps, the team begins to identify a few *scenario logics*, or plot lines of the narratives. At this stage, the predetermined trends are factored into all of the scenarios, whereas the critical uncertainties play out in multiple directions. Analysts and planners typically take one of two methodological approaches to scenario development: either *inductive*, from specific observations to generalizations, or *deductive*, from general principles to specific conclusions.[7]

The inductive approach can take a variety of forms. One version involves building scenarios around one or more emblematic events. For example, how might Iran's acquisition of nuclear weapons influence political dynamics in the Middle East? Or, what impact might a one-meter rise in the sea level, resulting from global climate change, have on conflicts in the South China Sea?

Another version begins by identifying an *official future*, which is "the future that the decision makers really believe, either explicitly or implicitly, will occur." The official future is usually a "plausible and relatively non-threatening scenario, featuring no surprising changes to the current environment." The assessment team then examines the key drivers of the official future—the factors that would need to be present for it to occur. For example, if the official future in the energy industry involves stable petroleum prices through 2020, this scenario might require both the leveling off of growth in global energy demand and the discovery of major new oil reserves around the world. By altering one or more of the uncertainties surrounding this scenario, such as continuing rapid growth in global energy demand or lesser-than-expected discoveries of new oil reserves, one can

The **inductive approach** to scenario building may begin with a specific event or development (for example, the acquisition of nuclear weapons by Iran or a one-meter rise in the global sea level) and explore its implications and potential consequences.

construct alternative narratives with very different results.[8]

The **deductive approach** to scenario building develops multiple scenario logics by varying the outcomes of the critical uncertainties that drive the scenarios. This technique can be used to develop a grid of four scenarios, built around two critical uncertainties.

Other practitioners prefer the deductive approach to scenario building. The petroleum conglomerate Royal Dutch Shell pioneered this approach in a series of long-range strategic planning exercises that it initiated in the early 1970s. At that time, Shell had benefited from more than two decades of robust and steady growth in global oil demand and had steadily expanded its production and distribution capacity to match the growing market. But the company's senior managers were concerned by the results of a Year 2000 study they had commissioned that had concluded that the rate of expansion of the company's production capacity could not be sustained indefinitely. Some time before the year 2000, the study had predicted, global demand for oil would begin to exceed the potential supply, resulting in higher prices and volatility in the oil market.

In response to this prediction, Shell's management initiated a series of strategic planning exercises to gain insight into the potential evolution of the oil industry over the next fifteen years. The first round of these exercises, carried out in 1970, confirmed the judgment of the Year 2000 study that the then-current rate of expansion of oil production was unsustainable over the long run. In the second round of exercises, carried out the following year, Shell's strategic planning unit developed four scenarios about the development of the oil industry between 1971 and 1985. These scenarios were built around two critical uncertainties—the level of global oil supply and the level of global oil demand. Figure 7.1 presents a grid to compare the four scenarios.

Each of the four scenarios provided a coherent and plausible plot leading to the future depicted in that quadrant of the grid.

- *Keep on Gushing* (high supply, high demand). This was the official or surprise-free future, on the basis of which Shell had conducted its long-term planning efforts until that point.
- *Squeeze Play* (low supply, high demand). This scenario posited that the Organization of Petroleum Exporting Countries (OPEC) would triple the rates paid to oil producers in the upcoming renegotiation of the

FIGURE 7.1 Royal Dutch Shell Scenario Analysis, 1971

Supply	Low (Demand)	High (Demand)
High	**Atomic Age** Increased demand for coal and nuclear energy at the expense of oil	**Keep on Gushing** Steadily increasing supply and demand **("surprise-free" scenario)**
Low	**Hard Times** Constrained global economic growth resulting in low oil demand and prices	**Squeeze Play** Tripling of oil producing states' royalties in 1975, leading to global recession

Demand

Source: Author's compilation. Titles of the four scenarios added by author.

Tehran Agreement, which was scheduled to occur in 1975. This development would constrain supply and drive up oil prices, ultimately plunging the world's industrial economies into a severe recession.

- *Hard Times or Stagnation* (low supply, low demand). In this scenario, global economic growth would slow substantially, resulting in flat or declining demand for oil and limiting oil prices and oil producers' take.
- *Atomic Age* (high supply, low demand). The world's industrial economies would aggressively expand their use of alternative fuels, primarily nuclear power and coal. Oil demand and prices would remain flat or decline.

These scenarios provided valuable—and disturbing—information for Shell's senior managers. Although the surprise-free scenario was attractive, the other three scenarios all posed significant challenges to Shell's long-term profitability. This initial phase of scenario generation provided little information about the relative probability of each scenario. But, over the following year, Shell's strategic planning unit conducted further research on projected global oil reserves and on economic conditions in the various OPEC states. This research allowed them to predict that the second scenario, Squeeze Play, was by far the most likely. Shell's management was thus forewarned, a year before the OPEC oil embargo and global recession of 1973 and 1974, of the prospect of severe shocks to the global oil market. It used this information to shield the corporation from the worst effects of this crisis.[9]

Scenarios are "not a group of quasi-forecasts, one of which may be right." They describe "different worlds, not just different outcomes in the same world," providing decision makers with a way to "re-perceive reality."

Scenarios are most effective when they convey a vivid and compelling story. They should depict not only the potential futures that people within an organization consider most likely or most desirable, but illuminate a range of futures with both positive and negative features. In the words of Pierre Wack, who helped develop the Shell scenarios of the early 1970s, decision scenarios "are not a group of quasi-forecasts, one of which may be right. Decision scenarios describe different worlds, not just different outcomes in the same world." By providing decision makers with a way to re-perceive reality, scenario analysis can be an invaluable tool for helping organizations operate effectively in complex, ambiguous, and volatile environments.[10]

Scenario Analysis in Conflict Management

A wide range of governmental and nongovernmental institutions use scenario analysis to anticipate and prepare for potential international conflicts. Within the U.S. government, the CIA's Global Futures Project prepares reports such as *Global Trends 2025*; the U.S. National Intelligence Council produces publications such as *Global Governance 2025: At a Critical Juncture*; and the U.S. Joint Forces Command assesses emerging challenges for the U.S. military, discussed in documents such as *The Joint Operating Environment 2030*.

In 2008, the RAND Corporation conducted a scenario exercise to support the U.S. Marine Corps' military planning for Iraq's al-Anbar Province, which had been one of the most volatile regions of Iraq before the Anbar Awakening of 2006 and 2007. The exercise examined five scenarios for the province's political evolution between 2008 and 2011, ranging from a worst-case scenario involving a Sunni-Shia civil war to a best-case scenario of peaceful power sharing and intercommunal reconciliation:

- Sunni Fight for Survival, the worst case, in which "a renewed insurgency pits uniting Sunnis against the Shia-dominated central government in Baghdad"
- Every Clan for Itself, a violent scenario, based on "greater fragmentation within al-Anbar, with nascent cohesion breaking down along tribal, clan, and family lines"
- Iron Fist, in which "strong government control exerted from Baghdad keeps a lid on muted violence and holds restive Anbaris in check"
- Glueless in Baghdad, involving a weak central government in Baghdad that "motivates provincial leaders to take greater charge over local affairs, leading to improved security and delivery of services"
- Path to Stability, the best case, in which "the Anbari provincial government and the central government work out effective power-sharing, reconciliation, and reconstruction arrangements"

These scenarios were constructed on the basis of eight key drivers of events that the participants anticipated would play a role in al-Anbar Province over the next three years. The four most important drivers were

- whether an effective central government develops in Baghdad;
- adequacy of the financial flows, especially into the province;
- how Anbaris self-identify, for example, as Iraqis first, or more narrowly along ethnic-sectarian and tribal lines; and
- the relative effectiveness of the provincial government in al-Anbar.

One of the most important findings of the exercise was that the U.S. Marine Corps had only limited capacity to influence some of the most important drivers of events in al-Anbar. According to the study's authors, this finding highlighted the importance of "seeking leverage even where it will be hard to do so and maximizing leverage opportunities where they already exist."[11] By remaining "fully alert to how alternative al-Anbar trajectories may unfold as U.S. forces begin to draw down," Marine Corps leaders could

FIGURE 7.2 The Road to Democracy

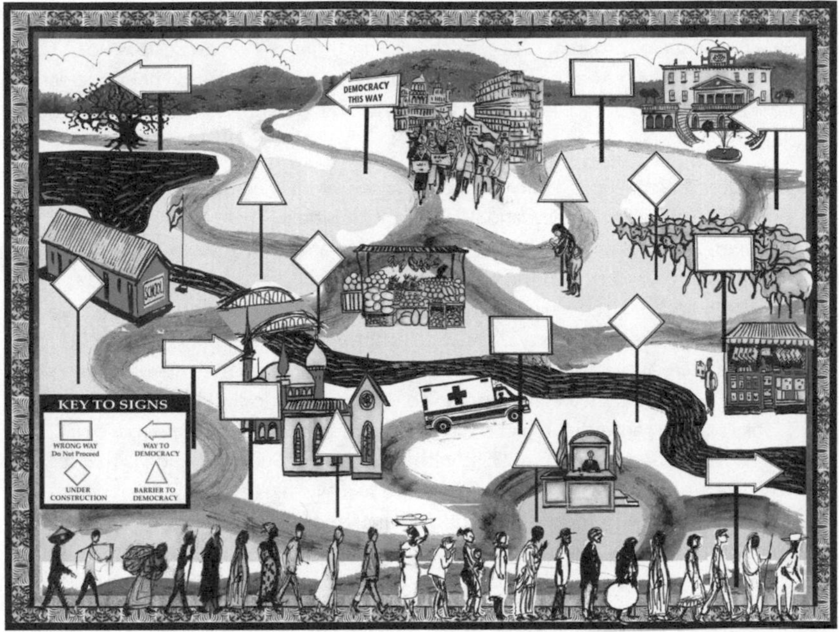

Source: Drawing by Micha Archer, artmicha.com, inspired by "The Road to Democracy," published in Street Law (SA), Centre for Socio-legal Studies, University of Natal, Durban SA and National Institute for Citizen Education in the Law in Washington DC, *Democracy for All: Education Towards a Democratic Culture* (Kenwyn, South Africa: Juta and Co., 1994), 14–15.

"focus on potential points of leverage against the drivers that will determine which of the alternate paths the province takes over the course of the next three years."[12]

Visualizing Scenarios

One way to maximize the vividness and impact of a scenario exercise is to draw a picture that can serve as a visual focal point for discussion. In the early 1970s, the Royal Dutch Shell strategic planning team was looking for a visual device to convey its predictions about the coming squeeze in global oil markets. The team members drew a picture of a placid river that would plunge into white-water rapids around the next bend. They used the phrase *the Rapids* to designate the constriction of global oil supply and energy

BOX 7.2 Mapping the Road to Democracy

Linda Bishai, senior program officer at the U.S. Institute of Peace, uses the Road to Democracy scenario exercise in training programs on democratization held in Sudan and in Washington, DC. In a 2012 interview, she described the value of the exercises:

> The democracy map is a very simple, cartoon-like drawing of people who are on the road to democracy, and it is filled with pitfalls. There are washed out bridges, and broken boulders across the road, and wrong turns, and other things that go wrong with the trip.
>
> The map has been very useful for us as an introduction to some of the things that make democracy difficult to achieve, so that people in transitional countries are aware of the difficulties and the many things they need to keep an eye on while they are in transition to democracy. It looks like a cartoon, it looks a child's game. But in fact it has been used successfully with people of all ages, with Americans here at USIP, with professors in Sudan. The ideas that it invokes are very complex ones. People have to really think carefully about what are the risks of a democratic transition, what are the obstacles, what are the indicators that they are actually approaching democracy. It helps them analyze their own situation and what democracy means to them. It also provides a reality check that democratization is not easy to achieve and that it's a long, long process that they will have to keep being engaged in over many years.
>
> I think the democracy map is a useful visual guide for imagining the different scenarios that a society might encounter on its road to stable democracy. One good thing about the journey metaphor is that you are taking it together as a group of people, as a society, as a nation. So there is an assumption of meeting everyone's needs built into that idea. It's not a journey the individual takes; democratic transitions happen when groups transition, not when individuals transition.

price inflation that they anticipated in the near future. This phrase became a shorthand expression among leaders of business units throughout the corporation in orienting their strategic planning efforts.

Trainers at the U.S. Institute of Peace sometimes use drawings as a focal point for scenario exercises in professional education programs both in the United States and overseas. One example is a map of the Road to Democracy scenario, which has proved to be a useful device for focusing discussion in courses on democratization and on the prevention of electoral violence (see figure 7.2 and box 7.2).[13] The map depicts a network of roads, with blank signs that point the "way to democracy," along with others indicating potential barriers to be overcome and wrong turns to be avoided. Participants in the workshops brainstorm collectively to produce text to write on each of the blank signs.

Selecting and Tracking Indicators

Whatever the method the analytical team uses for building its scenarios, a critical component of the exercise is to identify a set of indicators that will serve as signposts along the route. By tracking these indicators on a continuing basis, analysts and decision makers can assess which of the scenarios are becoming more or less likely, and adjust their planning accordingly.

For example, a central element of the scenario exercise for al-Anbar Province was the creation of a list of twenty-seven indications and warnings of the five scenarios, which were intended to serve as signposts for identifying future trajectories of al-Anbar Province. Most of these indicators could be tracked on the basis of unclassified open-source reporting, such as

- "2010 national elections consolidate power in the hands of a single party or bloc" (an indicator of Sunni Fight for Survival or Iron Fist);
- "Sunni integration into national politics continues," and "Expatriate Iraqi elites return" (indicators of Path to Stability); and
- "Ministry of Interior stops paying police" (an indicator of Sunni Fight for Survival or Every Clan for Itself).

Other indicators—"Arab Gulf funding for Sunni resistance groups," or "Growth of al-Qaeda in Iraq (AQI) underground and return of its influence in al-Anbar"—required access to classified intelligence reporting to track.[14] As Richards Heuer and Randy Pherson observe,

> A critical question that is not often asked is whether a given indicator would appear only in the scenario to which it is assigned or also in one or more alternative scenarios. Indicators that could appear in several scenarios are not considered diagnostic, suggesting that they are not particularly useful in determining whether a specific scenario is emerging. The ideal indicator is highly consistent for the world to which it is assigned and highly inconsistent for all other worlds."[15]

In the al-Anbar scenario exercise, the diagnostic value of each of the indicators was not a function of the classification level of the data on which it

> Analysts can establish and track indicators to assess which scenarios are becoming more or less likely over time. The ideal indicator "is highly consistent for the world to which it is assigned and highly inconsistent for all other worlds."

was based, but rather of the degree to which that indicator pointed specifically to a particular scenario. Certain indicators, such as "Expatriate Iraqi elites return" and "Arab Gulf funding for Sunni resistance groups," were each associated with only one of the five scenarios. Such indicators had more diagnostic value than others, such as "Sunnis lose political representation in 2010 national elections," which were associated with two or three of the five.

After the completion of this scenario exercise in December 2008, U.S. Marine Corps intelligence analysts in al-Anbar Province used the matrix of indications and warnings to track events in the province on a continuing basis. They developed a quantitative index that allowed them to determine the extent to which political conditions in the province were moving toward certain scenarios and away from others. Their tracking of the indicators was so sufficiently fine-grained that they were able to come up not only with aggregate scores for the province as a whole, but also for individual communities in the province such as Fallujah, Ramadi, Habbanyiah, and Haditha. They used these findings to advise U.S. military and civilian authorities about how best to deploy their resources in al-Anbar.

Linking Vision to Action

The central challenge facing scenario builders is to move beyond the realm of interesting stories to effective scenarios that capture the imagination and transform the decision-making calculus of an organization's leaders. Even more difficult is to create scenarios that can help create a common operating picture for representatives of diverse organizations working in the same conflict zone—from the U.S. Marines to the United Nations (UN) or World Bank to international humanitarian nongovernmental organizations (NGOs) to local civil society organizations.

> A scenario exercise can provide a common lexicon that helps diverse organizations working in a conflict zone develop a shared understanding of the conflict's dynamics and of potential conflict management opportunities.

According to Pierre Wack, Royal Dutch Shell's strategic planning team struggled with this challenge during the early 1970s. Even after having demonstrated the inevitability of future shocks to the global oil market in its 1972 scenario exercises, the planning team's briefings "sparked some intellectual interest but . . . failed to change behavior in much of the Shell organization." Wack explains this result:

> Reality was painful: most studies dealing with the future business environment, including these first scenarios, have a low "existential effectiveness." (We can define existential effectiveness as single-mindedness, but the Japanese express it much better: "When there is no break, not even the thickness of a hair, between a man's vision and his action.") A vacuum cleaner is mostly heat and noise; its actual effectiveness is only around 40 percent. Studies of the future, particularly when they point to an economic disruption, are less effective than a vacuum cleaner.[16]

Based on this insight, Shell's planners transformed the orientation of their work. Rather than simply aiming to provide accurate predictions, they sought to understand the core concerns of Shell's managers and to orient their analysis accordingly. Recognizing that managers base their decisions on a particular "mental model of the world," they attempted to "design scenarios so that managers would question their own model of reality and change it when necessary, so as to come up with strategic insights beyond their minds' previous reach."[17]

In business, the obstacles to achieving a common view of the world and adapting it to changing environmental conditions are less formidable than in international affairs. For a business enterprise, the definition of success is unambiguous: continuing growth and financial profitability. But in international affairs, success is harder to measure—or even define. Different organizations—or even different individuals within the same organization—may perceive their common objectives in contrasting ways. For example, various governments, international organizations, and NGOs operating in a single district in Afghanistan may define their goals multiple ways. One organization may focus on counterterrorism, another on counternarcotics. Yet others may be working to train security forces, promote effective local governance, prevent human rights abuses, enhance primary schooling, or empower female entrepreneurs. Measuring the success of any one of these initiatives is difficult. Evaluating whether all of them together effectively advance a shared international project in Afghanistan is harder still.

Randy Pherson is a former CIA analyst who served as the national intelligence officer for Latin America on the U.S. National Intelligence Council (NIC) from 1996 to 2000. His company, Pherson Associates, teaches advanced analytic techniques to analysts in intelligence agencies and the private sector. During his time at the NIC, Pherson organized scenario exercises on a range of Latin American countries. One such exercise helped inform the design of the U.S. State Department's Plan Colombia. Another, which focused on U.S.-Mexico relations, led the State Department to reorganize its Mexico desk to focus more attention on issues in the southwest borderlands, not just on government-to-government relations.

One of the most valuable results of a successful scenario exercise, according to Pherson, is "to give people a common lexicon."[18] Regarding the challenge of how to use scenarios to transform organizational decision making, he says it is essential that decision makers, along with analysts, participate in the exercise. Pherson always sought to involve several senior policymakers (such as a deputy assistant secretary in one of the State Department's regional bureaus or a director from the National Security Council) in his scenario exercises, both to provide "ground truth" concerning U.S. government perspectives on the issues and to subsequently communicate the key learning points of the exercise back to their home institutions. He observes, "I have rarely seen a policymaker internalize a scenario by reading a paper. They need to participate in the exercise." If the scenarios are sufficiently credible to decision makers that "a few people internalize their logic," then "the indicators become actionable" and provide a road map for guiding policy decisions.[19]

> To "internalize the logic" of the scenarios, it is important for senior decision makers to participate personally in the exercise. "I have rarely seen a policymaker internalize a scenario by reading a paper," says former national intelligence officer Randy Pherson.

A scenario exercise that Pherson organized on Haiti provided an example of how an indicator may be transformed into a road map. In this exercise, the best-case scenario, called Turning the Corner, posited that the Haitian government might successfully achieve political stability if medium-sized businesses in the country were to grow robustly enough to expand employment opportunities and tax revenues to the state. As a result of this exercise, U.S. State Department officials were able to envision a potential path toward a more prosperous and stable Haiti. According to Pherson, they began to say, "Let's implement Turning the Corner." The U.S. Department of Commerce was tasked with developing a strategy to support the growth of medium-sized businesses in Haiti. Leaders of NGOs active in Haiti were also briefed on the exercise, and consulted about how they could help work toward this objective. In other words, a joint conflict analysis helped provide a road map for coordinated action toward a shared objective.[20]

Some organizations have used scenarios as part of regular coordinating meetings of management teams. They sometimes begin meetings by updating and refining the scenarios based on new information, using this conversation as a starting point for assessing how to respond to emerging developments in the operating environment. For example, the UN Office for the Coordination of Humanitarian Assistance (OCHA) and some international humanitarian NGOs use scenarios to develop contingency plans for natural disasters such as floods or crop failures, as well as political emergencies such as armed conflicts or denial of humanitarian access to IDP camps. In volatile conflict situations, an organization's team leaders may meet on a weekly or even daily basis to evaluate whether the indicators point toward the improvement or the deterioration of conditions on the ground, and to revise their programmatic plans accordingly.

Conclusion

Scenario analysis exercises can provide the basis for strategic conversations between conflict analysts and decision makers about the critical uncertainties of an emerging conflict, and about how an organization's policies are likely to fare under changing environmental conditions. Pierre Wack writes that scenario analysis can help managers "break out of a one-eyed view" of the world and "rediscover the original entrepreneurial power of foresight in contexts of change, complexity, and uncertainty."[21]

In joint conflict analysis exercises, representatives of diverse organizations can come together to develop a shared perspective on the forces driving a particular conflict, and on the sources of social and institutional resilience that might help mitigate it. Such a common operating picture can be a starting point for more effective and integrated approaches to preventing and mitigating violent conflict. Scenario analysis can support this effort by providing a structured format for synthesizing insights from the exercise, as well as vivid and compelling stories that provide a shared vocabulary for discussing the conflict and capturing the imagination of decision makers from diverse organizations. The next two chapters address in more detail the challenges of incorporating conflict analysis into program planning and implementation.

Questions for Practitioners

- How does your organization anticipate and prepare for potential disruptive events? Do you have established procedures for risk assessment and contingency planning? Who in your organization is responsible for analyzing the operating environment and developing strategic plans? Do you discuss potential risks and opportunities, and how best to respond to them, on a regular basis with your colleagues in staff meetings or other settings?
- Could your organization benefit by using scenario planning? If so, would it be preferable to use it in a formal process (like the U.S. Marine Corps planning exercise on Iraq's al-Anbar Province) or more informally, for example, by brainstorming about potential future developments on a regular basis in staff meetings? How might you persuade your colleagues and supervisors of the potential value of this analytical method for your organization?

Notes

1. Jay Ogilvy and Peter Schwartz, "Plotting Your Scenarios" (Emeryville, CA: Global Business Network, 1998), 1, www.gbn.com/articles/pdfs/gbn_Plotting%20Scenarios%20new.pdf (accessed May 7, 2012).
2. Ibid.
3. The author thanks an anonymous peer reviewer of this manuscript for calling attention to the risk of locking in on a given scenario by viewing one potential future as necessary and inevitable.
4. Ogilvy and Schwartz, "Plotting Your Scenarios," 2.
5. Ibid., 3.
6. Ibid., 4.
7. Ibid., 4–7.
8. Ibid., 4–5.
9. Pierre Wack, "Scenarios: Uncharted Waters Ahead," *Harvard Business Review* 63, no 5 (Sept.–Oct. 1985): 73–89; "Shooting the Rapids," *Harvard Business Review* 63, no. 6 (Nov.–Dec. 1985): 139–50.
10. Wack, "Shooting the Rapids," 150.
11. James B. Bruce and Jeffrey Martini, "Whither Al-Anbar Province? Five Scenarios Through 2011" (occasional paper, RAND Corporation, Santa Monica, CA, 2010), ix–xi.
12. Ibid.
13. Linda Bishai, interview by the author, Washington, DC, March 2012.
14. Bruce and Martini, "Whither Al-Anbar Province?" 10–11.

15. Richards J. Heuer and Randolph H. Pherson, *Structured Analytic Techniques for Intelligence Analysis* (Washington, DC: CQ Press, 2010) 140–41.
16. Wack, "Shooting the Rapids," 107.
17. Ibid.
18. Randy Pherson, interview by the author, Washington, DC, November 2010.
19. Ibid.
20. Ibid.
21. Wack, "Shooting the Rapids," 134.

PART III

FROM ANALYSIS TO ACTION

8

NAVIGATING COGNITIVE MINEFIELDS

Key Points

- **Conflict analysis** is a social as well as an intellectual process. A conflict analysis, whatever its quality, provides no value to an organization unless its audiences absorb its findings and act accordingly.
- **Groupthink** is a process of collective self-censorship that occurs when the search for unanimity among the members of a group trumps "their motivation to realistically appraise alternative courses of action." Members of a group can reduce the likelihood of groupthink by encouraging expression of diverse views and valuing dissenting perspectives.
- **Black swans** are unpredictable disruptive events outside an organization's horizon of expectations. Analysts and decision makers can diminish the negative impact of black swans by broadening their risk modeling and by planning more effective responses to unwelcome contingencies.
- **Psychic numbing** is the distortion of thinking that results from efforts to suppress emotional responses to a problem. Analysts and decision makers can counter the effects of psychic numbing by acknowledging the essential role of emotion in human decision making and by creating a space for rational and emotional responses to a problem to complement each other in deliberative processes.

According to Greek myth, the Trojan maiden Cassandra was cursed by Apollo to foresee the future but to never be believed. Her warning that Greek soldiers were hiding in the wooden horse outside the city gates fell on deaf ears, and that night Troy was sacked and burned to the ground. Although Cassandra was perhaps the only conflict analyst to labor under a divine curse, she was far from the last to have her warnings ignored. Our lexicon is full of mocking expressions for those who bring unwelcome news—a Cassandra, a Chicken Little, a Boy Crying Wolf—or those who display excessive concern for the victims of suffering—a bleeding heart, for example. To be called such a name is to have one's credibility and seriousness impugned.

The previous chapters have discussed analytical methods for understanding and anticipating the trajectory of violent conflicts. Yet because conflict analysis is a practical rather than a purely academic pursuit, accuracy alone is not enough. The value of a conflict analysis is measured by the extent to which it enables an organization to counteract threats and seize opportunities in a volatile environment.

We now explore strategies for maximizing the impact of a conflict analysis within an organization. This chapter examines institutional and cognitive factors that can limit an organization's ability to absorb and act on new information. *Groupthink* stems from the tendency of an organization to exert explicit or implicit pressure to suppress dissenting views. *Black swans* are unanticipated and disruptive events beyond an organization's horizon of expectations. *Psychic numbing* is the distortion of thinking that results from efforts to suppress emotional responses to a problem. By staying alert to these cognitive minefields, you can anticipate potential challenges in communicating with your colleagues and reframe your message to reach your audiences more effectively.

Groupthink

Groupthink, a term coined by the psychologist Irving Janis, refers to a "mode of thinking that people engage in when they are deeply involved in a cohesive in-group, when the members' strivings for unanimity override their motivation to realistically appraise alternative courses of action." Groupthink is characterized by "a deterioration of mental efficiency, reality-testing, and moral judgment that results from in-group pressures."[1]

Groupthink occurs when the strivings for unanimity among the members of a group "override their motivation to realistically appraise alternative courses of action."

Janis's study compared a series of cases of disastrous group decisions by high-level U.S. officials, such as the Bay of Pigs invasion of 1961 and the escalation of the Vietnam War, with successful decision-making processes including the Cuban Missile Crisis and the framing of the Marshall Plan. He identified eight symptoms of groupthink that undermined the effectiveness of an organization's decision-making process:

- an illusion of invulnerability, which creates excessive optimism and encourages extreme risk taking;
- an unquestioned belief in the group's inherent morality, inclining the members to ignore the ethical or moral consequences of their decisions;
- collective discounting of warnings;
- stereotyped views of enemy leaders as either too evil to warrant genuine attempts to negotiate or too weak or stupid to counter the group's risky plan;
- self-censorship of deviations from apparent group consensus;
- a shared illusion of unanimity, partly resulting from self-censorship of deviations, augmented by the false assumption that silence means consent;
- direct pressure on any member who expresses dissent; and
- the emergence of self-appointed "mindguards" who protect the group from adverse information.[2]

In 1960, John F. Kennedy won the presidential election in part by depicting Vice President Richard Nixon as "soft on Cuba." This was a convenient charge, because Nixon had himself secretly proposed a plan to overthrow the Castro regime and thus, ironically, was unable to call publicly for Castro's ouster during the campaign. When Kennedy was inaugurated as president in January 1961, he inherited the Eisenhower administration's secret plan for Cuba, which had been prepared by the CIA.

Kennedy's top foreign policy advisers were a supremely intelligent and self-confident group and included Defense Secretary Robert McNamara

Symptoms of groupthink include the shared illusion of unanimity, stereotyped views of enemy leaders, collective discounting of warnings, and pressure on any member of the group who expresses dissent.

(former president of the Ford Motor Company), Secretary of State Dean Rusk (who had headed the Rockefeller Foundation and served in high-level positions at the State Department), and National Security Adviser McGeorge Bundy (former dean of arts and sciences at Harvard University). Harvard historian Arthur Schlesinger, another member of the president's inner circle, described the atmosphere during Kennedy's first months in office as one of "buoyant optimism." According to Schlesinger, "Everyone around [Kennedy] thought he had the Midas touch and could not lose. . . . *Euphoria reigned; we thought for a moment that the world was plastic and the future unlimited.*"[3]

But the CIA's plan, which involved dispatching a group of fourteen hundred Cuban exiles to overthrow the Castro regime, had glaring weaknesses that were overlooked by President Kennedy and his advisers. The Bay of Pigs invasion of April 1961 became a catastrophe that damaged the prestige and international standing of the new administration. Among the most egregious miscalculations were the following:

- Kennedy and his advisers assumed that the invasion plan and its connection to the CIA would remain secret—even after details of the plan had been widely reported by the American news media during the weeks leading up to the invasion.
- The advisory group assumed that the invasion would inspire a mass uprising in Cuba against the Castro regime—despite the CIA's lack of evidence to suggest that such a revolt was likely, and polling data indications that the overwhelming majority of Cubans supported Castro.
- The group assumed that, if the exile brigade met with resistance at the landing site, its members could retreat to the Escambray Mountains. None of Kennedy's top advisers bothered to consult a map of Cuba, which would have revealed that eighty miles of impenetrable swamps and rain forest separated the Bay of Pigs from the Escambray Mountains.

In analyzing accounts of the deliberations over the Bay of Pigs invasion plan by President Kennedy and his advisory group, Janis found evidence of each of the eight symptoms of groupthink. In contrast to the group's self-image as representing the best and the brightest, Kennedy's advisers regarded Castro as a "weak 'hysteric' leader whose army was ready to defect." Although several members of the advisory group harbored misgivings about the soundness of the plan, they refrained from expressing their concerns "out of a fear of being labeled 'soft' or undaring in the eyes of their colleagues," or to avoid gaining a reputation as a "nuisance." Those who did voice opposition to the plan were excluded from key meetings or censored by "mindguards," who sought to shield the president from dissent. Schlesinger reports that the president's brother, Attorney General Robert Kennedy, reproached him for his criticisms of the plan at a party shortly before the invasion: "You may be right or you may be wrong, but the President has made his mind up. Don't push it any further. Now is the time for everyone to help him all they can."[4]

Concerning the failures of the decision-making process leading up to the Bay of Pigs invasion, Janis concludes that

> the failure of Kennedy's inner circle to detect any of the false assumptions behind the Bay of Pigs invasion plan can be at least partially accounted for by the group's tendency to seek concurrence at the expense of seeking information, critical appraisal, and debate. . . . Most crucial were the symptoms that contributed to complacent overconfidence in the face of vague uncertainties and explicit warnings that should have alerted the members to the risks of the clandestine military operation—an operation so ill conceived that among literate people all over the world the name of the invasion site has become the very symbol of perfect failure.[5]

Eighteen months after the Bay of Pigs disaster, in October 1962, a new crisis erupted over Cuba that became the most dangerous moment of the Cold War. President Kennedy has not escaped criticism for his handling of the Cuban Missile Crisis. Some observers have argued that he was too quick to dismiss the possibility of a negotiated settlement with the Soviet leadership, opting instead for a game of nuclear chicken. Others have contended that Kennedy's previous aggressive actions against Cuba, most notably in the Bay of Pigs invasion, contributed to the deployment of Soviet missiles to Cuba.

> During the Cuban Missile Crisis of October 1962, President Kennedy's advisory group established a far more productive, deliberative process than in the Bay of Pigs disaster of the previous year—even though many of the principal participants remained the same—by avoiding some key pitfalls of groupthink.

But the deliberative process that Kennedy established within his advisory group (the Executive Committee of the National Security Council, or Ex Comm) during the thirteen days of the Cuban Missile Crisis differed dramatically from that of the Bay of Pigs deliberations—despite the fact that many of the principal participants were the same. Kennedy and his advisers were able to develop a probing and constructive consensus-building process that enabled the U.S. government to force the removal of the Soviet missiles from Cuba without escalating to war. Kennedy adopted several practices to avoid the pitfalls of groupthink:

- *Examine the opponent's perspective.* In the early days of the missile crisis, the members of Ex Comm, with the strong backing of the Joint Chiefs of Staff, were leaning toward authorizing a preemptive military strike against the missile sites in Cuba—a course of action that could have easily escalated into nuclear war. At a critical point in the deliberations, the president's brother Robert asked whether such a strike might be perceived as a Pearl Harbor in reverse. Former secretary of state Dean Acheson, whom the president had invited to the meeting, denounced this notion as "silly" and "unworthy" of consideration by the president.[6] But Robert Kennedy's comment provoked a searching discussion within Ex Comm about the morality of the proposed preemptive strike, contributing to the choice of a less risky blockade against Cuba. Rather than assuming that the U.S. government was inherently good and its enemies evil, the members of Ex Comm were willing to acknowledge the moral ambiguity of their position.

- *Create constructive conflict within the group.* During the deliberations leading up to the Bay of Pigs invasion, President Kennedy at one point invited Senator J. William Fulbright, a strong critic of the invasion plan, to make his case to the advisory group. But Kennedy undermined the effectiveness of this presentation by asking for an up-or-down vote on the plan immediately afterwards, but no substantive discussion of Fulbright's points. During the Cuban Missile Crisis, by contrast, Kennedy encouraged constructive conflict by forming two working groups, one charged with advocating a military strike on Cuba and the other making the case for the blockade option. He also established an environment within his advisory council that fostered open debate, such as the conversation over the morality of a Pearl Harbor in reverse. Over the course of the deliberations, many members of Ex Comm, including the president, changed their minds about issues of vital importance.

- *Break context to avoid context traps for participants.* A further benefit of forming multiple working groups is that it changes the physical setting and hierarchical relationships that shape the discussions. The working group setting, in which the president was not present, provided a lower-stakes environment in which the members of Ex Comm could deliberate more freely.
- *Limit the early influence of a senior leader.* At the beginning of the Cuban Missile Crisis, President Kennedy established the parameters of the decision to be made, insisting that the missiles be eliminated from Cuba, but he assigned Ex Comm to determine how best to achieve this goal. The president frequently removed himself from the room during Ex Comm meetings to create a less inhibited atmosphere for debate. Kennedy himself initially supported the air strike option, but he changed his mind as the discussions continued.
- *Ensure a heterogeneous group.* A diverse group is less likely to fall captive to the same blind spots and false assumptions, because people from different backgrounds tend to see the world through different eyes. President Kennedy enlisted several outside experts to participate in Ex Comm meetings, including Dean Acheson and Llewellyn Thompson, who had served as U.S. ambassador to the Soviet Union. Thompson's participation was especially valuable, because he had vacationed with Khrushchev at his dacha and was able to offer unique insights into the Soviet leader's psychology and motives.

An effective decision-making process does not ensure a positive outcome. Despite all of Ex Comm's care in its deliberations, the United States and the Soviet Union came to the brink of nuclear war in October 1962, and the confrontation could have easily ended catastrophically. But by systematically articulating and assessing diverse views, President Kennedy and his advisers were able to find a middle path through the crisis that had the greatest chance of success.[7]

> Groupthink is less likely when senior leaders actively encourage the expression of diverse views and validate dissenting perspectives. Techniques for fostering a constructive consensus-building process include establishing a heterogeneous group of decision makers, examining the opponent's perspective, creating constructive conflict within the group, and limiting the early influence of a senior leader.

Groupthink: Questions for Practitioners

- Do you recognize any signs of groupthink in your own organization? If so, what are the causes of this phenomenon, and how does it affect your organization's work?
- Can you take steps to counteract groupthink in your workplace? If you serve in a leadership role, can you establish a working environment that encourages the expression of diverse views, such as by ensuring a heterogeneous group, fostering constructive conflict, and limiting the early influence of a senior leader? If you serve in a subordinate role, can you help shift the group dynamics in a more positive direction, such as by expressing appreciation for dissenting views, or by "breaking context traps" through individual communications outside the group setting?
- What responsibility do you bear for a faulty decision driven by groupthink? Groupthink is often motivated by powerful institutional forces seeking to maintain consensus within an organization. In some situations, you may put your reputation and your career at risk by resisting groupthink. Under what circumstances is it appropriate to accept or abstain from a faulty decision-making process that you cannot change? Under what circumstances do you have an obligation to express dissent, even in the face of potential reprisals?

Black Swans

The financial analyst Nassim Nicholas Taleb defines a black swan as "a random event satisfying the following three properties: large impact, incomputable probabilities, and surprise effect." In principle, a black swan event may be either negative (the September 11 terrorist attacks) or positive (the rise of global social networking technologies). But because the event is unprecedented, it is difficult or impossible to predict.[8]

The notion of the black swan is related to a psychological phenomenon identified by Amos Tversky and Daniel Kahneman called the *availability heuristic*. They define this phenomenon as the tendency to "assess the frequency of a class or the probability of an event by the ease with which instances or occurrences can be brought to mind."[9] In other words, people tend to consider potential events more likely to occur if they are vivid and easy to imagine.

A **black swan** is a random event with large impact, incomputable probabilities, and surprise effect.

Contemporary American parenting practices provide an example of the effects of distorted risk assessment on public health. According to the Centers for Disease Control and Prevention, the five things most likely to cause injury to children up to age eighteen are car accidents, homicide (usually at the hands of someone they know), child abuse, suicide, or drowning. But the five things American parents worry most about, according to Mayo Clinic surveys, are kidnapping, school snipers, terrorists, dangerous strangers, and drugs. Because parents have a disproportionate fear that their children will be kidnapped by strangers if allowed to play alone outside, they engage in the statistically much riskier practice of driving their children to friends' houses or organized activities, at the same time encouraging sedentary habits that increase long-term health risks such as obesity and diabetes.[10]

Another type of black swan event is the *off-model risk*. For example, in the years leading up to the global financial crisis of 2008, the risk models used by many banks and other financial institutions failed to account for the possibility of a sustained decline in real estate prices. Likewise, Taleb cites the example of the largest casino in the world, which uses an elaborate risk model "geared towards reducing the losses resulting from cheaters." But he notes that "the four largest losses incurred or narrowly avoided by the casino fell completely outside their sophisticated model." These included the loss of about $100 million when an irreplaceable performer in the casino's main show was maimed by a tiger, a plot by a disgruntled contractor to blow up the building, and the near-loss of a gambling license because of employee fraud. According to Taleb, "A back-of-the-envelope calculation shows that the dollar value of these off-model risks swamp the on-model risks by a factor of close to 1000 to 1."[11]

As Taleb points out, the "vicious property of a Black Swan is its surprise effect." At any given time, nothing in the environment points to the likelihood of the event. Indeed, it is "the surprise element that either causes the Black Swan or at least exacerbates its consequences. If there were anything convincing about the need for protection, then agents would have taken preventive or protective actions." Taleb cites the September 11 terrorist attacks on the World Trade Center as an example of this phenomenon: "If such a possibility were deemed worthy of attention, fighter planes would have circled the city above the twin towers, airplanes would have had locked bulletproof doors, and the attack would not have taken place, period."[12]

> People generally overestimate the likelihood of vivid and compelling scenarios that they can easily call to mind. Conversely, they may underestimate the probability and impact of less vivid or more complex scenarios.

Even though black swans cannot be predicted, the concept may be useful in sensitizing practitioners to the potential impact of off-model risks—such as the steep decline in housing prices that triggered the global financial crisis of 2008, or the tsunami of 2011 in northern Japan that simultaneously knocked out multiple backup safety systems at a nuclear power generation complex. Organizations can increase the comprehensiveness and rigor of their risk analysis in various ways. For example, the scenario analysis techniques discussed in chapter 7 can be useful in anticipating and rehearsing an organization's responses to a wide range of alternative futures. Likewise, stress tests—such as those conducted on U.S. banks after the financial crisis of 2008 and 2009—can shed light on how a system or organization is likely to perform under catastrophic conditions.

Managing a Black Swan: The FAA on 9/11

The responses of Federal Aviation Administration (FAA) personnel to the 9/11 attacks offer both positive and negative examples of institutional adaptation to black swan events. This discussion—based on *The 9/11 Commission Report* and on published interviews and testimony compiled by the commission staff—examines the FAA's handling of two urgent issues that morning: first, its success in arriving at the unprecedented decision to order the immediate landing of every airplane then flying over U.S. territory; and, second, the failure of FAA headquarters to request that fighter jets be scrambled to intercept the hijacked planes.

The 9/11 attacks unfolded over the space of less than two hours on a Tuesday morning. At 8:14 a.m. Eastern time, American Airlines Flight 11 was hijacked en route from Boston to Los Angeles. At 8:46 a.m., Flight 11 struck the North Tower of the World Trade Center in New York City; at 9:03 a.m., United Airlines Flight 175 collided with the South Tower of the World Trade Center; and at 9:37 a.m., American Airlines Flight 77 crashed into the Pentagon. At 10:03 a.m., the passengers of United Airlines Flight 93 forced the plane to crash in eastern Pennsylvania, preventing the potential destruction of the White House or the U.S. Capitol.

The use of a commercial airliner as a guided missile was not unprecedented: in 1994, an Algerian terrorist group had plotted unsuccessfully to fly a hijacked Air France plane into the Eiffel Tower. But FAA protocols assumed that the goal of an airline hijacking would be extortion rather than the destruction of targets on the ground. Moreover, multiple simultaneous hijackings had never been carried out in the United States. The September 11 hijackers also hid their intentions, for example, by shutting off the transponders of their airplanes to make them harder to track by radar.[13]

Decision to Ground All Aircraft in the United States

On the morning of September 11, 2001, air traffic controller Ben Sliney reported for his first day of work as a national operations manager at the FAA's national Air Traffic Control System Command Center in Herndon, Virginia, which oversees daily air traffic flow throughout the United States. At 9:42 a.m.—just fifty-six minutes after the first plane struck the World Trade Center—Sliney made the unprecedented decision to order all of the nearly forty-five hundred civilian aircraft then flying in U.S. airspace to land at the nearest airport. Remarkably, Sliney made this decision without consulting either the office of FAA administrator Jane Garvey or that of Secretary of Transportation Norman Mineta. The sequence of events leading up to Sliney's decision—which may have prevented one or more additional hijackings that day—is worth examining in detail, because it illustrates the importance of agility in recognizing and responding to unpredictable events.

To some extent, personal characteristics of Sliney and the Command Center's other senior officials helped facilitate this decision. Although new to this job, Sliney had spent more than twenty years as a military and civilian air traffic controller and supervisor before beginning a second career as a securities lawyer. The Command Center's facility manager Linda Schuessler, whose background was in administration rather than operations, deferred to Sliney's expertise—huddling with him and the other national operations manager every three minutes to review the evolving situation. But two other factors were also essential: first, Sliney's *alertness to new information* and his willingness to question his own preconceptions on the basis of this information; and second, the *clarity of the operational mission* of the national Air Traffic Control System Command Center.[14]

In an interview with the staff of the 9/11 Commission, Sliney said that, in his experience, "hijacks followed a usual course of events that included negotiations and an eventual resolution to the event." Within minutes of learning of the hijacking of American Airlines Flight 11, however, he received several pieces of information that did not match this profile: the plane was not responding to radio calls, it was flying erratically, it had switched off its transponder, and the Boston Air Traffic Control Center reported hearing a transmission from the cockpit that "we have more planes."

Because Sliney had a clearly defined picture of a typical hijacking event, he was alert to the anomalies in the seizing of Flight 11 and immediately directed his air traffic controllers to identify any other aircraft displaying certain suspicious signs. The controllers began tracking about a dozen such aircraft, writing notes on a white board that Sliney set up in the middle of the room. But only at 9:02 a.m., when the second aircraft struck the World Trade Center, did Sliney realize that the hijackers were piloting the planes. As he recalled in a 2006 interview, "I could not believe that an American or any carrier pilot would fly a plane into a building. I don't care what the hijacker was doing. Even if he had several guns to his head. He would have ducked it in the Hudson. He would have done something to avoid the loss of life on the ground. That's their code."[15]

Sliney told the 9/11 Commission that "the biggest deficit was the lack of notice that such an event was possible, and that if he had such information he would have ordered all aircraft to land regardless of destination at the first report of a hijacking."[16]

As for clarity of mission, according to the records of Sliney's interview with the 9/11 Commission, he decided that he had the authority to order the grounding of all aircraft flying over U.S. territory "under his responsibility for the safe air use of the National Air Space"—despite the fact that there was no historical precedent for such an action. He issued this order as soon as he learned that a third hijacked airplane had crashed into the Pentagon.[17]

Air traffic controllers, by virtue of the nature of their job, need to be prepared to take quick and decisive action. Their paramount responsibility is to protect the safety of the flying public, and so they may be inclined to focus less on the letter of administrative regulations than on doing whatever is necessary to protect human lives.

Failure to Request Military Support

In 2001, FAA protocols for responding to hijackings were cumbersome: they required air traffic controllers to notify their supervisors, who would in turn pass this information up through several further layers of management to FAA headquarters. At headquarters, a designated hijack coordinator had the authority to ask the Pentagon's National Military Command

Center (NMCC) to scramble military aircraft to escort the flight. Only the president and secretary of defense had the authority to order the military to shoot down a civilian airplane.

When officials at the national Air Traffic System Command Center informed FAA headquarters about the hijacking of American Airlines Flight 11, they were initially told that the FAA's hijack coordinator was unavailable and that only he was authorized to request military assistance. Over the next ninety minutes, controllers both at the national Command Center and at several regional centers made direct, ad hoc contact with various military bases—disregarding the FAA protocols—to request that the military scramble fighter jets to pursue the hijacked planes.

At 8:46 a.m., in response to a call from the Boston Air Route Traffic Control Center, the U.S. Air Force's Northeast Air Defense Sector (NEADS) scrambled two fighter planes from Otis Air Force Base in Falmouth, Massachusetts. At 9:23 a.m., NEADS scrambled two additional fighters from Langley Air Force Base in Hampton, Virginia—but these planes initially flew eastward over the Atlantic Ocean, rather than toward Washington, DC, and the pilots were never briefed about why they had been scrambled. Only at 10:07 a.m.—after United Flight 93 had already crashed in Pennsylvania—did NEADS first learn of the hijacking of Flight 93. The lead pilot of the Langley planes told the 9/11 Commission, "I reverted to the Russian threat. . . . I'm thinking cruise missile threat from the sea. You know you look down and see the Pentagon burning and I thought the bastards [had] snuck one by us. . . . [Y]ou couldn't see any airplanes, and no one told us anything."[18]

From the time of the first hijacking at 8:14 a.m. to the crash of Flight 93 at 10:03 a.m., personnel at FAA headquarters made no request to the U.S. Air Force that it scramble fighter jets to pursue any of the hijacked planes. At 9:49 a.m., twelve minutes after the Pentagon had been struck, controllers at the national Air Traffic Control System Command Center estimated that the fourth hijacked airplane, Flight 93, was twenty-six minutes away from Washington. Even at this point, FAA headquarters staff rebuffed a request from the Command Center to call for assistance from the Air Force—or even to notify military commanders at the NMCC about the inbound plane.

> FAA Headquarters: They're pulling Jeff [Griffith, deputy director of air traffic] away to go talk about United 93.
>
> Command Center: Uh, do we want to think, uh, about scrambling aircraft?
>
> FAA Headquarters: Oh, God, I don't know.

Responding to a Black Swan: Questions for Practitioners

- Have you sought to identify and evaluate off-model risks? Although some events are truly unpredictable, an organization can expand its horizon of expectations through scenario analysis exercises and study of history. For example, the risk models used by many global financial institutions in 2008 excluded the possibility of a sustained decline in housing prices—which led them to overlook the systemic risks posed by mortgage-backed securities. Likewise, although the attack on Pearl Harbor in December 1941 came as a shock to Americans, the Japanese navy had used a similar stratagem in 1904, when it had launched a surprise attack on the Russian Pacific fleet in Port Arthur at the outset of the Russo-Japanese War.
- Do you test your assumptions against new information? It is useful to explicitly identify the assumptions that inform your analysis, and to reevaluate them as new information becomes available. For example, during the first few weeks of the Rwandan genocide in 1994, most international diplomatic and media reports depicted this crisis primarily as a civil war between rival military factions, rather than as a mass killing of unarmed civilians. Many international observers of Rwandan politics found it difficult to imagine that genocide was occurring—in part because Rwanda possessed none of the industrialized apparatus of mass murder (trains, concentration camps, gas chambers) that Nazi Germany had used to perpetrate the Holocaust. If analysts had explicitly tested their civil war hypothesis against a genocide hypothesis (see related discussion in chapter 3), they might have recognized the one-sided nature of the violence more quickly.
- Does your organization have a coherent and unambiguous mission, or does it face double binds that may inhibit its ability to respond to crises? In the chaotic conditions that can follow a black swan event, an organization may be paralyzed if its staff does not have a clear understanding of its fundamental objectives and priorities. On the morning of September 11, 2001, the staff of the FAA's national and regional air traffic control centers understood that their overriding objective was to protect public safety. This shared understanding facilitated a coherent and agile response to the crisis. Their response included the decision to ground all aircraft in U.S. airspace and various ad hoc efforts to obtain military support, which violated established FAA procedures. At FAA headquarters, by contrast, officials confronted the double bind between protecting public safety and promoting air commerce. The FAA's inflexible and hierarchical decision-making protocols also limited the organization's adaptability and may have discouraged individual initiative on the part of headquarters staff.

> Command Center: Uh, that's a decision somebody's going to have to make probably in the next 10 minutes.
>
> FAA Headquarters: Uh, ya know everybody just left the room.[19]

In part, the contrasting behavior of the air traffic controllers and the officials at FAA headquarters reflected differences between an operational culture, which rewards decisive action, and an administrative culture, which frequently penalizes it. But the headquarters staff may also have fallen prey to a dilemma known as a double bind—a situation in which individuals are forced to reconcile two mutually incompatible messages or values. A senior FAA official illustrated the nature of this double bind in his 2004 testimony to the 9/11 Commission:

> The FAA Act of 1958 is clear: next to safety, the job of the FAA is to support the military and promote air commerce. Air commerce in the United States is a $900 billion a year industry. It is the engine of our economy. That is why many of the decision makers regarding aviation on 9/11 were planning how to start up the National Airspace System the instant we shut it down.[20]

In other words, the FAA's mission emphasized two paramount objectives: to keep air traffic safe and to keep air traffic flowing smoothly. On the morning of September 11, these objectives were directly at odds with one another. Unlike the air traffic controllers, who were charged solely with preserving air safety, the staff at FAA headquarters faced the additional challenge of attempting to reconcile—and weighing the relative importance of—these two opposing goals. It is not surprising that this added burden had a negative impact on the decision-making ability of senior FAA officials.

Psychic Numbing

One of the primary functions of any bureaucratic institution is to systematize information management and decision making. To be legitimate, a decision must conform to certain established procedures rather than be based on emotional appeals.

But social psychologists have shown that emotion is a key aspect of virtually all human decision making. Medical studies have found that individuals whose bodies are deprived of the hormone testosterone descend into listlessness and that they lack any motivation to work or socialize. In decision-making processes, emotions play an analogous role: they help motivate, orient, and focus the will to act. As psychologist Paul Slovic observes, "Information must convey feeling to be meaningful and to be used in judgments and decisions."[21]

> Emotions play a critical role in human decision making. Emotions complement rational analysis by motivating, orienting, and focusing one's will to act.

Studies by Slovic and other psychologists have shown that when people are asked to give money to help malnourished children in Africa, they donate more than twice as

The **collapse of compassion** in response to statistics documenting large-scale suffering can lead to inaction in the face of mass murder or genocide.

much when they are shown a picture of an individual victim than when they are confronted with statistics of mass suffering. Slovic calls this phenomenon the collapse of compassion. As he observes, "Our capacity to feel (good or bad) is limited." Even when the number of victims is as small as two, our level of empathy begins to decline. When confronted with vast numbers of suffering people, emotional responses to the suffering essentially shut down. Slovic argues that this lack of feeling can lead to "inaction as large losses of life occur in mass murder or genocide."[22]

The phenomenon of psychic numbing is related to a syndrome known as compassion fatigue, which is common among humanitarian aid workers. The nonprofit Compassion Fatigue Awareness Project describes it as follows:

> Day in, day out, workers struggle to function in care giving environments that constantly present heart wrenching, emotional challenges. Affecting positive change in society, a mission so vital to those passionate about caring for others, is perceived as elusive, if not impossible. This painful reality, coupled with first-hand knowledge of society's flagrant disregard for the safety and well being of the feeble and frail, takes its toll on everyone from full time employees to part time volunteers. Eventually, negative attitudes prevail.[23]

The absence of an emotional response to a given issue can impede rational decision making, but an excessively strong emotional response can be equally problematic. A decision maker who becomes obsessed with an issue, or who identifies too intensely with a victim group, may be spurred to take rigid and even counterproductive actions. A key challenge for conflict analysts is to recognize and account for the centrality of emotion in decision making without resorting to maudlin or manipulative appeals—which, in any event, will likely backfire when one's readers are seasoned foreign policy professionals. Paul Slovic describes the ideal decision-making process as involving a "dance of emotion and reason," in which our feelings complement but do not overwhelm our rational faculties.[24]

Conclusion

Irving Janis identifies seven typical defects of decision-making processes in organizations afflicted by groupthink:

Psychic Numbing: Questions for Practitioners

- Is there room for emotional intelligence in your organization? What kinds of emotions are perceived as acceptable in your workplace? Are your colleagues and supervisors attuned to their emotions? Is it viewed as legitimate to discuss your emotional response to a given issue, or does your organization pride itself on the hard-headed rationality of its institutional culture? Remember that psychic numbing is not the same as pure rationality; rather, it is the distortion of one's thinking and decision making that results from efforts to suppress emotional responses to a problem. There is nothing soft-headed or weak about openly introducing emotional or moral concerns into a deliberative process.
- Can you reframe emotional and moral issues in rational terms? Emotional responses to a problem should complement but not overwhelm our rational faculties. Can you reframe an emotional or moral issue so as to stress its relevance to your organization's interests—for example, by emphasizing the destabilizing effects of a famine in Somalia, rather than the catastrophic suffering that the famine is causing?

- incomplete survey of alternatives,
- incomplete survey of objectives,
- failure to examine risks of preferred choice,
- failure to reappraise initially rejected alternatives,
- poor information search,
- selective bias in processing information at hand, and
- failure to work out contingency plans.[25]

The other two cognitive pitfalls discussed in this chapter, black swans and psychic numbing, can also contribute to some or all of these decision-making defects. Black swans result partly from the human tendency to exaggerate the probability of easily imaginable events, and to discount the possibility of disruptive events outside one's horizon of expectations. This tendency can result in faulty risk analysis, biased and incomplete information processing, and the failure to examine alternative courses of action and contingency plans. Psychic numbing can lead analysts and decision makers to discount the significance of events and future risks that do not trigger a strong emotional response. Conversely, when analysts and decision makers experience intense emotional responses to a given event or risk, they may exaggerate its significance and respond in rigid or counterproductive ways.

A healthy organization takes active steps to counteract each of these negative tendencies. Its leaders and operational staff emphasize the importance of carefully defining the organization's strategic objectives and assessing the relative merits of alternative courses of action. They examine the risks as well as the rewards of the chosen strategy, and they seek out information that will enable them to reassess their decisions on an ongoing basis. Finally, they seek to anticipate and plan for contingencies that may transform the organization's operating environment in positive or negative ways.[26]

Although most of these responsibilities are primarily the domain of an organization's decision makers and program implementers rather than its analysts, each of them has a strong analytical component as well. The next, and final, chapter examines in more detail the role conflict analysts can play in supporting effective organizational planning and program implementation processes.

Notes

1. Irving L. Janis, *Groupthink: Psychological Studies of Policy Decisions and Fiascoes*, 2nd ed. (Boston, MA: Houghton Mifflin, 1983), 9.
2. Ibid., 174–75.
3. Ibid., 214 (italics in original).
4. Ibid., 19–30, 35–36, 39–40.
5. Ibid., 47.
6. Evan Thomas, *Robert Kennedy: His Life* (New York: Simon & Schuster, 2000), 216.
7. Janis, *Groupthink*, 132–58.
8. Nassim Nicholas Taleb, "The Black Swan: Why Don't We Learn That We Don't Learn?" (January 2004), 6, http://russwbeck.files.wordpress.com/2009/04/44_2004.pdf (accessed May 10, 2012); *The Black Swan: The Impact of the Highly Improbable*, 2nd ed. (New York: Random House, 2010).
9. Amos Tversky and Daniel Kahneman, "Availability: A Heuristic for Judging Frequency and Probability," *Cognitive Psychology* 5, no. 2 (1973): 207–32.
10. Lisa Belkin, "To Keep a Child Safe, Just. . .," *New York Times*, September 19, 2010, WK 4.
11. Taleb, *The Black Swan*, 129–30.
12. Ibid., xxiii.
13. National Commission on Terrorist Attacks Upon the United States, *The 9/11 Commission Report* (Washington, DC: Government Printing Office), 1–34, 344–45.

14. Ibid., 35–46.
15. "United 93: An Interview with National Operations Manager Ben Sliney," Blackfilm.com, April 21, 2006, www.blackfilm.com/20060421/features/bensliney.shtml (accessed May 10, 2012).
16. 9/11 Commission Staff, "Interview with Benedict Sliney," May 21, 2004, www.scribd.com/doc/17053258/T8-B2-FAA-Command-Center-Ben-Sliney-Fdr-52104-MFR-717 (accessed May 10, 2012).
17. Ibid.
18. Ibid., 45.
19. Ibid., 29.
20. Jeff Griffith, "Written Testimony to the National Commission on Terrorist Attacks Upon the United States," June 9, 2004, http://govinfo.library.unt.edu/911/hearings/hearing12/griffith_statement.pdf (accessed May 10, 2012).
21. Paul Slovic, personal communication with the author, March 2008.
22. Deborah A. Small, George Loewenstein, and Paul Slovic, "Sympathy and Callousness: The Impact of Deliberative Thought on Donations to Identifiable and Statistical Victims," *Organizational Behavior and Human Decision Processes* 102 (2007): 143–53; Paul Slovic, "If I Look at the Mass I Will Never Act: Psychic Numbing and Genocide," *Judgment and Decision Making* 2 (2007): 1–17.
23. Compassion Fatigue Awareness Project, "What is Compassion Fatigue?" www.compassionfatigue.org/pages/compassionfatigue.html (accessed May 10, 2012).
24. Paul Slovic, personal communication with the author, September 2008. On the role of emotion in decision making, see also David Rock, *Your Brain at Work: Strategies for Overcoming Distraction, Regaining Focus, and Working Smarter All Day Long* (New York: HarperCollins, 2009), 101–18.
25. Janis, *Groupthink*, 175.
26. Research on the neuroscience of decision making demonstrates the importance of self-reflective deliberative processes. See for example Rock, *Your Brain at Work*, especially 87–97; and Frank Partnoy, *Wait: The Art and Science of Delay* (New York: Public Affairs, 2012).

9

CONFLICT ANALYSIS IN THE PLANNING PROCESS

Key Points

- **Framing the strategic narrative.** The first step of the planning process is to define and contextualize the problem using a strategic narrative about the conflict, within which actors orient their decisions.
- **Defining your objectives.** It is essential to articulate clear, specific, and measurable objectives that address not only the concerns of one's organization, but also those of local and international partners.
- **Conducting a situation or SWOT analysis.** The situation analysis examines an organization's internal strengths (S) and weaknesses (W), along with opportunities (O) and threats (T) in the external environment, which helps illuminate how an organization can match its strengths to the operating environment.
- **Designing a plan of action.** Based on a capacity assessment that inventories the resources of institutions operating with similar objectives in the same space, as well as key gaps in existing programs, an organization can identify the most productive activities.
- **Measuring progress and adapting to change.** The metrics employed in an evaluation process need to be tailored to measure specific effects of the program under assessment. A carefully designed evaluation process will enable decision makers to document both successes and failures and to adapt programs to maximize their effectiveness.

In the absence of a common worldview among an organization's managers, writes strategic planning expert Pierre Wack, "decentralized strategic decisions will result in management anarchy."[1] The section on groupthink in the previous chapter showed how institutions can create and enforce a shared worldview among their employees, even when this perspective has only a tenuous connection to reality. This chapter discusses more constructive consensus-building strategies that analysts and decision makers can use both within their organizations and with partner institutions.

Although coordination with institutional partners is principally a leadership function and not an analytical one, conflict analysts can play a valuable role in the process by helping synchronize the *situational awareness* of representatives of diverse organizations working in the same space. Effective coordination of conflict management efforts must begin with a shared understanding of the operating environment and the functions that various indigenous and third-party groups can perform within it. Such a *common operating picture* needs to be grounded in an accurate and thorough conflict analysis. It also needs to be sustained and broadened through ongoing conversations with partner institutions and continually adapted in response to changing conditions on the ground.

Framing the Problem

Framing an issue means placing it within a broader interpretive context. The frame provides information about both the logic of the problem and the course of action to address it.[2] A frame provides the basis for a strategic narrative about the nature and stakes of a conflict, within which the various actors orient their decisions.

Twentieth-century German history provides a vivid example of the importance of framing in international affairs. At the beginning of the century, German leaders used the concept of encirclement to frame discussions of the country's relationships with other European powers, Russia to the east and France and Great Britain to the west. They warned that Germany would be overwhelmed by its rivals unless it aggressively defended its territory and interests. This competitive strategic narrative contributed to the escalation of international tensions in Europe and the outbreak of World

> A **strategic narrative** defines the interpretive context within which actors orient their decisions, identifying the nature and stakes of a conflict.

War I. But after World War II, the concept of integration became dominant: most Germans now view their nation's well-being as dependent on high levels of cooperation with other European states. This frame has become so deeply ingrained that many observers now consider a war between Germany and France to be inconceivable.

> The lack of a consistent frame for understanding a given conflict can cripple efforts to forge an effective and coordinated conflict management strategy.

The absence of a coherent frame for a problem can be equally consequential. The international efforts to rebuild Afghanistan since 2001 show how a mission can be undermined by the lack of a shared and consistent strategic vision. The U.S. government and its international partners have framed their strategic objectives in Afghanistan in a wide range of ways. At various times, and in various contexts, they have emphasized the goals of democratization, promoting human rights, counterterrorism, counterinsurgency, counternarcotics, humanitarian assistance, economic development, and governance reform, among others. Just as the overall objectives of the mission have sometimes been unclear, there has been inconsistency in identifying the foes against whom U.S. and international military forces have been fighting. Is the opponent al-Qaeda, the Taliban, hardline elements of the Taliban, or simply anti-Coalition forces? Although it may be appropriate for such a large-scale mission to have multiple goals and multiple foes, an effective strategic narrative requires a clear explanation of how the objectives of the campaign connect with each other and which of them have the highest priority.

According to Ali Ahmad Jalali, who served as Afghan interior minister from 2003 to 2005, the lack of a coherent frame has been a critical weakness of international efforts to stabilize Afghanistan:

> The absence of a shared vision for Afghanistan has blurred the distinction between means and ends. Too often, means have defined goals, tactics have driven strategy, supply has determined demands, and short-term necessities have taken precedence over long-term priorities. This failed vision has led many to question whether the U.S.-led operation is aimed at securing Afghanistan, reshaping the whole of South Asia, or simply setting the conditions for a responsible exit plan.[3]

Defining the strategic objectives of a mission is typically the responsibility of an organization's senior leaders, not of working-level conflict analysts or operational staff. Nonetheless, a practitioner may encounter situations in which strategic guidance is lacking or unclear, or in which one is receiving inconsistent or conflicting guidance from different quarters. In such situations, it is essential to listen carefully to the organization's decision makers to try to understand their deepest concerns—the issues that keep them awake at night. The narrative analysis techniques outlined in chapter 5 may be useful for this purpose. Orienting analysis around the key problems the organization is grappling with may help senior leaders navigate apparently intractable terrain.

Fictional Case Study: Governance Reform in Afghanistan

Take the fictional example of a large international NGO called Helping Hands Global (HHG), which provides development assistance in Afghanistan's volatile Kandahar and Helmand provinces. Although HHG is based in the United States, most of its local staff members are Afghan nationals; the remaining few are Americans and Europeans. HHG has operated in Afghanistan for more than twenty years, setting up its Kabul office shortly after the Soviet withdrawal from the country in 1989. Most of HHG's budget comes from private charitable donations, but the organization also accepts funding from the USAID and European development agencies.

Due to its long presence in Afghanistan and its carefully cultivated relationships with local community leaders, HHG has operated successfully, during the Taliban regime and since, focusing primarily on infrastructure projects such as schools, health clinics, and water projects. Over the past several years, HHG's programs have increasingly focused on poverty reduction and promoting livelihoods, in part by using a cash-for-work approach to building infrastructure projects in rural Afghanistan. Unfortunately, the operating environment for international NGOs in southern and eastern Afghanistan has continued to deteriorate, leading a number of humanitarian organizations to suspend operations there. Although HHG has so far avoided attacks on its staff members, several representatives of other NGOs in Helmand Province have been kidnapped or murdered in recent months, and a number of new schools and health clinics have been burned or taken over by the Taliban.

Recently, the head of HHG's Kabul office was approached by the USAID mission director in Afghanistan. The mission director invited HHG to submit a proposal to "enhance local governance in Helmand Province by strengthening civil society institutions," to be supported by USAID's democracy and governance program funds for Afghanistan. This project would be a new field of work for HHG. The HHG country team leader is interested in this idea, because the instability of the region is increasingly threatening HHG's core projects, and a more peaceful and stable political environment will be critical to the organization's long-term success in southern Afghanistan.

In consultation with HHG's senior leaders at its home office in Wichita, Kansas, the Afghanistan country team leader decides to form a strategic planning group in Kabul, charged with three assignments:

- assessing the feasibility and desirability of initiating USAID-funded governance programs in Helmand Province;
- identifying the ideal focus, objectives, and structure of any pilot programs HHG might develop to promote democracy and good governance; and
- designing an evaluation mechanism to assess the results of the pilot programs and inform HHG's decisions as to whether and how to proceed.

In framing the problem for the strategic planning group, HHG's leaders focus on a specific issue of central relevance for the organization's ongoing programs, rather than on the broader concerns of the U.S. government and other international actors. The problem statement might be summarized as follows: "Political instability is threatening the viability of HHG's development projects in Helmand Province." The core question the strategic planning group must consider is whether new USAID-funded governance programs in Helmand could help mitigate this threat.

Defining Objectives

In some cases, senior leaders will provide a clear and unambiguous statement of an organization's strategic objectives, for example, "Relieve humanitarian suffering resulting from flooding in Pakistan," or "Prevent Iran from acquiring nuclear weapons." In other cases, the strategic guidance may be inconsistent or unclear.

In the absence of precise guidance from above, the planning team may need to frame its statement of the organization's strategic objectives. In doing so, it is useful to keep in mind three principles:

- The objectives should be clear, specific, and measurable. For example, during World War II, President Franklin Roosevelt provided precise benchmarks for the success of the U.S. war effort: "the unconditional surrender of Germany and Japan." In World War I, by contrast, President Woodrow Wilson had articulated American war aims in less tangible and more grandiose terms: "to make the world safe for democracy." Not surprisingly, many Americans were disheartened and disillusioned after the conclusion of World War I, which resulted in the defeat of Germany and Austria, but not the global triumph of democracy. In more recent times, campaigns such as the war on drugs and the war on terrorism have also lacked specific metrics for success, which has made it problematic to assess whether they are accomplishing their objectives.
- As discussed, the objectives should reflect senior leaders' key concerns. The assessment team may need to consult with decision makers within the organization if these are not immediately evident.
- The objectives should be compatible with those of partner organizations. To enlist the support of other organizations for a mission, strategic objectives must be framed in terms consistent with the missions of those groups. For example, in Afghanistan, humanitarian NGOs generally do not want to be perceived as participating in a counterterrorism or counterinsurgency campaign. Likewise, the phrase war on terrorism (or war on al-Qaeda) creates particular sensitivities in Germany, whose post–World War II constitution restricts the German army to a defensive role. For this reason, German political leaders have been reluctant to describe their country's military deployment to Afghanistan as a contribution to a war effort.

By effectively framing its strategic objectives, an organization may be able to enhance its influence and strengthen its alliances. Sometimes, even the most radically opposed organizations may find common ground. For example, in Afghanistan, the head of an NGO promoting women's literacy was able to obtain the protection of local Taliban leaders for her organization's work by persuading them that increased literacy was vital to the promotion of women's health, a fundamental value of Islam espoused in the Quran.

> It is essential to articulate **clear, specific, and measurable** strategic objectives that reflect the key concerns of your organization's senior leaders.

In the case of our fictional HHG planning team, the organization's

> An organization can often strengthen its alliances and enhance its influence in a conflict zone by framing its strategic objectives in terms that resonate with the concerns of local and international partners.

mission statement provides a starting point: "Helping communities help themselves by laying a foundation for sustainable development." Until now, HHG has defined sustainable development primarily in terms of livelihoods and public infrastructure. But the organization's leaders have concluded that these economic improvements will not be sustainable in the absence of a more stable political environment. Thus they believe that supporting governance programs is a natural extension of the organization's core mission—provided that HHG has the capacity to effectively design and deliver such programs. Another point of reference is USAID's website, which describes the goal of the agency's democracy and governance programs as to help "develop a stable, legitimate, and democratic state in which the voices of Afghan people are heard."[4]

But both statements are too vague to provide specific metrics for success. Moreover, many of HHG's local partners in Kandahar and Helmand provinces question the sincerity and credibility of the U.S. government's motives. They argue that U.S. leaders care only about protecting America from terrorism and exploiting Afghanistan's natural resources, not about helping the Afghan people. President Obama himself has defined America's objectives in Afghanistan as to "disrupt, dismantle, and defeat al Qaeda in Afghanistan and Pakistan, and to prevent its capacity to threaten America and our allies in the future."[5] HHG's Afghan partners also claim that American support for local leaders in the region, which is part of a tribal engagement strategy to defeat the Taliban, has reinforced the power of some of the most corrupt and ruthless individuals in these communities. Taliban leaders have capitalized on this distrust, denouncing as "enemies of the Islamic Emirate" the "infidels" and "puppets" who collaborate with the "imperialist invaders."

Based on these considerations, the HHG planning team arrives at the following recommendations concerning the proposal to establish USAID-funded democracy and governance programs in Helmand Province.

- First, any such programs should do no harm, either by increasing the physical risks to HHG staff and local partners or by undermining the effectiveness of existing HHG programs in Helmand Province.
- Although HHG should conform to its established policy of financial transparency, openly acknowledging USAID as the program funder, it

should take care to frame its governance programs as locally based and locally owned. To the greatest extent possible, the programs should be operated by Afghan nationals rather than international staff. HHG should also emphasize that its local governance programs are intended to respond to the needs of rural Afghan communities, rather than serving the agenda of American military forces or the central Afghan state, which is widely perceived as corrupt.

- HHG's governance programs could potentially serve one or more of three valuable objectives: reinvigorate local traditional governing institutions that have been undermined by Taliban assassinations of tribal elders, the rise of local warlords and drug lords, and other developments since 2001; empower disenfranchised groups (such as those based on ethnicity, economic status, or gender) by enabling them to make their voices heard in local governing processes; combat corruption by increasing the transparency of public spending in rural communities.

These three objectives have the virtues of being clear, specific, and measurable. Whether they are realistic and feasible, especially in light of the do-no-harm principle, must be addressed in subsequent stages of the planning process.

Although the strategic planning group's assignment focuses on establishing USAID-funded governance programs, its members recognize that broader and more fundamental questions concerning HHG's future in Afghanistan are at stake. Can the organization continue to operate safely in the increasingly volatile security environment? Can it continue to concentrate primarily on humanitarian and development assistance, or does it need to focus more explicitly on issues of conflict resolution and effective governance as well? Can it maintain its reputation for impartiality and integrity if it uses U.S. government funds to become directly engaged in local politics as well as economic assistance? Can the organization successfully manage potential tensions regarding its programming between USAID and other major stakeholders, especially the Afghan central government and the U.S. departments of Defense and of State? To address these questions, the HHG strategic planning group decides to conduct a comprehensive situation analysis.

Situation Analysis

Whereas a conflict assessment seeks to illuminate the motives and perspectives of the parties to a conflict, a situation analysis examines the conflict

Framing the Problem and Defining the Objectives: Questions for Practitioners

- Has the organization articulated a strategic narrative about the problem it seeks to solve? Have leaders defined operational objectives in *clear, specific,* and *measurable* terms? Are these objectives mutually compatible, or are there tensions or contradictions among competing objectives? Is there consensus within the organization about its goals, or are there significant areas of disagreement or confusion within the staff concerning this issue?
- Can you play a role in helping reframe your organization's strategic narrative? In many large organizations, working-level staff have limited access to internal deliberations over the institution's strategic objectives and priorities. If this is the case, how can you work to shape your activities and programs so as to maximize their clarity of purpose and their impact?

from the practitioner's institutional perspective. A situation analysis attempts to identify the capabilities and resources that an organization and other third-party interveners can use to influence the conflict's outcome and to assess how well these capabilities match up against the opportunities and threats in the conflict environment. Some practitioners use the term *SWOT analysis* as a synonym for situation analysis.

As illustrated in figure 9.1, a SWOT analysis can be organized into a two-by-two grid, in which the top two cells depict factors internal to the organization and the bottom two cells depict factors in the external environment.

The situation analysis begins by assessing the organization's strengths and weaknesses with regard to its strategic objectives. What resources and tools does it control that may help solve the problem? Are there particular

FIGURE 9.1 SWOT Analysis

	POSITIVE	NEGATIVE
INTERNAL	**STRENGTHS**	**WEAKNESSES**
EXTERNAL	**OPPORTUNITIES**	**THREATS**

comparative advantages that distinguish the organization from other groups operating in the same space? Does the organization have any critical gaps in its resources and expertise, or vulnerabilities that others may exploit?

Next, the analysis examines key opportunities and threats in the external environment, utilizing the analytical techniques discussed earlier in this guide, as well as the principles discussed below concerning the escalation and de-escalation of violent conflict.

Such a situation analysis can provide guidance as to how best to deploy an organization's resources to capitalize on opportunities and neutralize threats. It can also serve as a starting point for coordinating more effectively with other groups whose missions overlap by helping identify the resources and comparative advantages that diverse institutions bring to the task at hand.

Assessing Strengths and Weaknesses

To continue with the example, HHG has a number of institutional strengths in its Afghanistan programs:

- established relationships with community leaders in Helmand Province, based on HHG's two decades of work in Afghanistan;
- local expertise and a talented staff of Afghan nationals, a number of whom are ethnic Pashtuns from Helmand;
- substantial funding from USAID;
- support from U.S. diplomatic and military authorities in Afghanistan; and
- a generally positive reputation within Pashtun communities in Helmand Province.

But HHG also has several weaknesses that could hamper its ability to implement governance programming:

> Assessing an organization's distinctive **strengths** is an essential step toward identifying its comparative advantages over other groups operating in the same space and with similar objectives.

- Afghan suspicion of U.S. government motives, which extends to USAID-funded contractors;
- lack of institutional experience and knowledge concerning democracy and governance programming;
- lack of representation of certain ethnic groups, such as Balochis and Kuchis, among HHG's Afghan staff members; and
- uncertainty concerning long-term U.S. government commitment to sustain USAID-funded programs in Afghanistan.

Based on this analysis, the strategic planning team would look for ways to maximize the benefits from HHG's institutional strengths and compensate for its weaknesses. The organization's key comparative advantage is that it has both strong local knowledge and connections to international actors, which enable it to secure substantial resources for its programs. HHG's institutional weaknesses fall into three categories:

- *Easy fixes*. Certain problems, such as the lack of experience in democracy and governance programming and lack of Afghan staff from particular minority groups, could be remedied by hiring additional staff and contractors to fill these gaps.
- *Necessary inconveniences*. The uncertainty concerning USAID's long-term commitment to funding governance programs in Helmand Province means that HHG will need to focus initially on short-term programs or find alternative sources of funding to sustain its commitments.
- *Potential red flags*. The potential perception among community leaders in Helmand Province that HHG's governance programs are part of an imperialist agenda to subjugate the region could undermine the effectiveness of the organization's other programs and endanger its staff and local partners. The issue would warrant careful consideration before HHG decided to proceed in this direction.

In assessing an organization's **weaknesses** with respect to its strategic objectives, it is useful to differentiate among challenges to program implementation that are **easy fixes, necessary inconveniences,** and **red flags.** Issues that represent potential red flags must be considered and accounted for in the planning process.

Recognizing Opportunities and Threats

The various analytical tools discussed in this guide—conflict assessment frameworks, narrative analysis, conflict mapping, systems mapping, and scenario analysis—can be used to anticipate potential changes in a conflict environment. Ideally, these tools will be used as part of an ongoing collaborative process to establish and refine an operating picture shared by organizations involved in managing the conflict.

In assessing the likelihood of improvement or deterioration of conditions in a conflict zone, it is useful to keep in mind several principles concerning the escalation and de-escalation of violent conflict (discussed in chapter 2).

- *Conditions for escalation*: high perceived divergence of interest between the rival parties and low stability. Escalation of violence can be sparked by a trigger event that heightens the parties' perceived divergence of interests or increases instability, such as a contested election or census, a terrorist attack, a natural disaster, or an economic crisis.
- *Conditions for de-escalation*: a more gradual and halting process. Conditions for de-escalation include the parties' grudging acceptance of each other as interdependent partners and the existence of perceived common ground between the parties.

In both escalation and de-escalation, the perceptions of the situation by the rival parties are extremely important. When the parties believe that their interests are mutually exclusive, conflict can easily escalate. Conversely, when they come to perceive themselves as mutually interdependent and as having common ground on important issues, conflict is likely to de-escalate.

In the polarized political climate of Helmand Province, it will be critical for HHG to avoid fanning the flames of the conflict by creating perceptions that it is supporting an imperialist agenda to subjugate the people of the province. Although this view may appear far-fetched from a Western perspective, such perceptions have created difficulties for the Provincial Reconstruction Team (PRT) in Helmand. After the United Kingdom took over leadership of the Helmand PRT in early 2006, the security situation in the province deteriorated, partly as a result of aggressive British counternarcotics efforts that alienated those who benefited from the opium trade. A common explanation among people of the province for the worsening security situation in 2006 was that "the British were consciously sabotaging

Helmand" to "avenge the Battle of Maiwand" of 1880, in which Afghan insurgents had decimated a British military force in Helmand.[6] As we saw in chapter 5, such mythic histories can play a powerful role in shaping political perceptions and motivating insurgent movements.

In light of these considerations, HHG's strategic planning team identifies several opportunities and threats in the operating environment of Helmand Province that need to be considered before establishing governance programs. The opportunities stem from various factors that unite the interests of important constituencies in Helmand, such as

- the desire of traditional elites to restore their eroded authority;
- continuing respect for these elites among many members of their communities;
- popular disaffection with the abusive practices of the Taliban and local warlords;
- widespread outrage over corruption, including embezzlement of public funds and development assistance money; and
- near-universal war fatigue and a desire for peace.

The threats involve factors that magnify perceptions of division, both among the various groups within the province and between the provincial populace and external forces, including not only foreign military and civilian personnel, but also agents of the Afghan central state. Such threats include

- increasing volatility both in Helmand and in neighboring areas of Pakistan;
- efforts by the Taliban to further destabilize the province by propaganda, terrorist attacks, and the kidnapping and murder of foreign military and civilian personnel as well as those perceived as collaborators with the occupying forces;
- popular perceptions of the Afghan central state and provincial government as illegitimate and corrupt;

Opportunities are conditions in the external environment that may enhance an organization's ability to implement its programs and to help de-escalate conflict.

- efforts by local warlords and drug lords to maintain their power and profits by fomenting chaos in the region; and
- uncertainty regarding the long-term presence and objectives of U.S. and other international forces in Helmand, along with the risk of future military actions that may antagonize communities by killing civilians.

Threats are conditions in the external environment that have the potential to escalate conflict and that may jeopardize an organization's ability to implement its programs successfully.

Designing a Plan of Action

The next step of the analysis is to synthesize the key findings to make recommendations to HHG's leadership. In carrying out this task, it is important to assess how other groups operating in the same space understand their missions and how their resources and programs may have the potential to support or undermine an organization's work.

At this stage of the process, the HHG strategic planning team broadens its analytical lens to focus on those other organizations: for example, the U.S. military, USAID, NATO, the Afghan central state, the Helmand provincial government, Pakistan, the UN, the World Bank, international and local NGOs, and traditional local governing councils. One objective here is to conduct a capacity assessment as well as to identify key gaps in existing programs.

Another objective of this analysis is to point out potential synergies and frictions between the organization's programs and those of other organizations. For example, the U.S. military has invested considerable resources in a tribal engagement strategy that has enlisted traditional local leaders in Helmand and Kandahar provinces to support U.S. counterinsurgency efforts against the Taliban. In some cases, these investments may have helped strengthen traditional local governing institutions, but in other cases, they may have undermined such institutions by increasing the power of local warlords.

A **capacity assessment** identifies the programs and resources of various institutions operating with similar objectives in the same space, as well as key *gaps* in existing programs.

After assessing the capacity and programmatic objectives of other local, national, and international actors in Helmand Province, the HHG strategic planning team revisits the three programming options it identified at the outset of its planning process.

Option 1. Reinvigorate local governing institutions
The content and structure of such programs would need to reflect the result of a thorough needs assessment involving various constituencies in the target communities. Potential avenues for supporting traditional governing institutions might include providing travel funds for *shuras* involving the leaders of multiple communities in a given district, supporting dialogues between traditional leaders and representatives of the provincial or district governments concerning the optimal division of responsibilities or giving cell phones to tribal elders to enhance their ability to administer local affairs.

The HHG planning group concludes that this option would entail relatively little risk either to local participants in the project or to HHG's other programs, provided that the organization is capable of delivering services that are responsive to locally articulated needs. By seeking to reinvigorate existing governing institutions, HHG would be working with the grain of local culture rather than against it. Such projects might encounter resistance from the Taliban but would be unlikely to result in strong opposition from the communities at large.

Option 2. Empower marginalized groups
This option has the advantage of coinciding closely with the objectives of USAID's grant program, which seeks to promote "the development and growth of a politically active civil society in Afghanistan with an emphasis on women-focused organizations . . . by providing technical assistance, capacity building training, and grant support to civil society organizations."[7] But such programs could potentially work at cross purposes with option 1 programs by fomenting suspicions that HHG's goal is to overturn traditional social hierarchies and rebuild Afghan culture according to an American model.

HHG's planners conclude that staff will need to carefully balance the goal of supporting the establishment of more transparent, accountable, and responsive governing institutions against the need to cultivate and maintain support for their programs from existing local elites.

Option 3. Increase transparency of public spending

On its face, this option is appealing because disgust over corruption in Helmand is widespread and visceral, and corrupt practices undermine the legitimacy and effectiveness of Afghan governing institutions. HHG's planning team notes that certain organizations have developed low-cost methods to counter corrupt practices in rural Afghanistan. For example, the American NGO Mercy Corps has begun to track the funds disbursed in its cash-for-work programs by using GPS-enabled digital cameras to verify the completion of projects in Afghan villages.[8]

Unfortunately, corruption also has powerful constituencies that might be antagonized by an aggressive anticorruption campaign. In 2007, for example, several Afghan staff members employed by a USAID contractor were murdered while working on bridge construction projects on the Helmand River. It was later learned that one of the bridges they were building "would have made the poppy fields of a local drug baron accessible to monitoring and eradication forces." The chief engineer on this project was assassinated shortly after the NGO refused a request by a delegation of elders to halt construction on the bridge. Some elements of the Taliban also benefit from corruption, reportedly extorting up to 30 percent of the budget of assistance projects in parts of Helmand Province.[9]

The HHG planning team concludes that option 3 may not pass the do-no-harm test. The team members are concerned that a robust anticorruption program could provoke retribution against HHG staff members or local partners. They therefore recommend that HHG adopt Mercy Corps' procedures for tracking expenditures on cash-for-work projects but that it refrain from initiating any more ambitious anticorruption effort until it has higher confidence in the likelihood of success and the safety of the operating environment.

In framing its recommendations, the HHG strategic planning group may wish to explicitly state the premises that undergird its analysis, because the soundness of its policy proposals depend on the validity of the assumptions on which they are based. The planning group's central assumption aligns with a saying of Tip O'Neill, the longtime speaker of the U.S. House of Representatives: "All politics is local." In other words, the planning team believes that the appeal of the Taliban in Helmand Province stems less from the power of global jihadist ideology than from localized factors such as unemployment (which provides economic incentives to join the insurgents), the marginalization of disenfranchised groups (who see joining the Taliban as a path to empowerment), and the desire for revenge (on the part of Helmandis who have lost members of their families or tribes to attacks by international or Afghan national forces).[10] The members of the HHG strategic planning team believe it is too simplistic to view the Taliban and its sympathizers as implacably opposed to any and all international engagement in Helmand Province. The planners are guardedly optimistic that, if implemented in a sensitive manner, local governance programs may be welcomed by the residents of some communities in the region.

The HHG planning team could use a *participatory rural appraisal* (PRA) to test the soundness of its operating assumptions and refine the details of its programmatic proposals. A PRA is a process used by many NGOs and other development organizations to incorporate the knowledge and views of rural people in designing conflict-sensitive development projects in their communities. According to the development scholar Robert Chambers, "decentralization and empowerment" are the key principles that undergird participatory appraisals: "Decentralization means that resources and discretion are devolved, turning back the inward and upward flows of resources and people. Empowerment means that people, especially poorer people, are enabled to take more control over their lives and secure a better livelihood with ownership and control of productive assets as one key element."[11]

The PRA can take various forms, depending on the nature and objectives of the proposed program. One international aid organization operating in Pakistan uses a five-step analytical process to enhance the effectiveness and conflict sensitivity of its local development projects:

- *Household surveys.* The organization's local staff members randomly select households in a given community, interviewing the inhabitants about the potential impact of a proposed project on conditions of life in the community and seeking to identify possible negative impacts.

- *Focus group discussions.* Based on the initial household surveys and other research, program planners identify eight to twelve key influentials representing various elements of the community, who are capable of providing expert knowledge about social and economic relationships within the community. The goal of the focus group discussion is to generate consensus about how to maximize the benefits of the project to the community while avoiding negative side effects such as intensifying conflict by inadvertently creating advantages for one social group over another.

- *Participatory mapping.* Residents of a community are asked to construct, on the ground or on paper, maps using materials such as sticks, stones, leaves, chalk, or pens. The person who holds the stick or pen talks about what is most important to him or her. As maps take shape, more people typically become involved and want to contribute and make sequential changes. Participatory mapping techniques may be used to identify social relationships within a village, wealth rankings, public services, resources such as farms, forests, aquifers, disease patterns, and so forth.
- *Transect walk.* The researchers walk along a path through the community to verify and visualize the findings from the household surveys, focus group discussions, and participatory mapping exercises.
- *Venn diagrams.* This tool is used to visualize patterns of influence and conflicts within a community. For example, the influence of religious leader A may be depicted as a small circle overlapping with one part of a community, and the influence of religious leader B may be shown as a larger circle with a more substantial area of influence.[12]

By using these various tools for structuring interviews and discussion groups, as well as visualizing their findings, the designers and implementers of development programs can minimize the possibility that their projects will unleash unanticipated and counterproductive effects.

Measuring Progress and Adapting to Change

A careful situation analysis can be helpful in identifying emerging factors in a conflict environment that may support or impede an organization's ability to accomplish its mission. But, for this information to be useful, the organization must have the capacity to learn from its successes and failures, and to adapt to changing conditions on the ground. Its analysts and decision makers must also be able to exchange relevant information with institutional partners on a regular basis, so that collaborative efforts continue to mutually reinforce efforts to mitigate the conflict. Thus it is essential to devote institutional resources to systematic monitoring and evaluation efforts, especially for new or evolving projects.

The specific procedures used for monitoring and evaluation vary across organizations. Many governmental and nongovernmental development agencies use a *logical framework matrix,* or *logframe,* to define the objectives of a given project and the procedures to be used for assessing its success (see appendix 8). Whatever the details of the instrument, a monitoring and evaluation plan should involve several components:

- *Timeline for evaluation.* In the case of the fictional HHG pilot program, an interim evaluation might be completed six months after the program's initiation and a comprehensive evaluation after one year. The organization's leadership might also establish certain indicators that would trigger an immediate reassessment of the program, for example, Taliban threats or attacks against HHG staff, local partners, or facilities in Helmand.
- *Metrics for success or failure.* For an evaluation to be reliable, it must measure effects that are relevant and specific to the program under assessment. For example, HHG might wish to compare the overall level of security in a given village before and after the implementation of one of its pilot governance programs by measuring the number of attacks on civilians, the extent of Taliban activity in the village, and so forth. But, given that HHG's governance program would be just one of many factors influencing security in the village, this data would not provide persuasive evidence of a causal relationship between the two. It would be more useful to identify metrics more closely related to the program activities, such as the
  - number and outcomes of disputes adjudicated by traditional governing institutions,
  - number and outcomes of disputes adjudicated by Taliban authorities,
  - survey data on villagers' attitudes toward tribal elders and Taliban insurgents, or
  - level of threats or violent acts against tribal elders by insurgents.
- Various conflict metrics are discussed in chapter 3. Two examples of such metrics instruments are Measuring Progress in Conflict Environments (MPICE) and the Tactical Conflict Assessment and Planning Framework (TCAPF).

> The metrics employed in an evaluation process should be designed to measure specific effects of the program under assessment, rather than more general trends in a conflict zone.

- *Baseline data collection.* To assess the impact of a project, it is essential to collect baseline data on the chosen metrics at its outset. In some cases, it may be possible for the assessment team to obtain relevant baseline data from other organizations. For example, Gallup WorldView conducts detailed public opinion surveys on a wide range of issues in countries around the world. For sub-Saharan Africa, Afrobarometer publishes regular national-level surveys on various issues related to economic well-being and political stability, and the Fund for Peace's UnLock project publishes district-level data on violent conflict for several countries in West and Central Africa.[13]
- *Follow-up data collection and analysis.* On the basis of follow-up surveys at the conclusion of the evaluation period, the team can complete a quantitative and qualitative assessment of the project's impact. This assessment will inform HHG's decisions as to whether to refine, expand, or terminate its democracy and governance programs in Helmand Province. If the results are positive, it will also serve the important function of documenting the project's accomplishments and justifying the continuation of funding from USAID.

> By comparing the results of baseline and follow-up data collection, analysts and planners can document the successes and failures of programs and recommend appropriate changes to program design and implementation.

In addition to examining the environment of the village level, it will be important for HHG's assessment team to track developments in the environment of Helmand Province and Afghanistan on a continuing basis. By scanning the horizon for emerging opportunities and threats, and by remaining alert to potential synergies with other groups operating in the same space, the organization's staff can engage in a continuing strategic conversation about how best to use its resources to promote the cause of peace.

Conclusion

To work effectively in conflict zones, practitioners need to adopt habits of *reflective practice*, which has been defined as "the capacity to reflect on action so as to engage in a process of continuous learning."[14] Gary Rolfe summarizes the process of reflective practice as follows: *action* (the "what") is followed by *learning* (the "so what"), which is followed by *adaptation* (the "what next"), which in turn shapes future actions in an ongoing cycle.[15]

The five-step process described in this chapter for integrating conflict analysis into program planning and implementation draws on these principles of reflective practice. In planning, as in conflict analysis, self-assessment is an essential starting point. The initial two steps of this cycle, *framing the problem* and *defining objectives,* require practitioners to reflect on their perceptions of a conflict environment and the role of their organizations within that environment. Likewise, the *situation analysis* begins with an assessment of the strengths and weaknesses of an organization, and how they influence its capacity to achieve its strategic objectives in the conflict zone. The planning team then moves to an assessment of opportunities and threats in the external environment, as well as the organization's *comparative advantages* with respect to other groups working in the same space. Having defined and implemented a plan of action based on this analysis, the organization's analysts, planners, and program implementers move on to the stage of measuring progress and adapting to change. This model of continuous learning and adaptation, by both individuals and their organizations, seamlessly integrates conflict analysis into the practice of international conflict management.

Situation Analysis, Planning, and Measuring Progress:
Questions for Practitioners

- Does your organization assess its strengths and weaknesses as part of its planning process? How does your organization capitalize on its particular comparative advantages over other institutions operating in the same space? How does it compensate for its weaknesses—does it, for example, establish strategic partnerships to address gaps in institutional resources or expertise? What role can you play in helping your organization develop a more mindful approach to planning its operations in conflict environments?
- How effective and useful are your organization's procedures for monitoring and evaluating the impact of its programs in conflict zones? Does your organization actively seek to learn from past successes and failures, or is the principal goal of monitoring and evaluation processes to document the success of your programs in order to justify continued funding? How can you help encourage habits of reflective practice in your workplace?

Notes

1. Pierre Wack, "Scenarios: Uncharted Waters Ahead," *Harvard Business Review* 63, no. 5 (Sept.-Oct. 1985): 89.
2. On the concept of framing, see Erving Goffman, *Frame Analysis: An Essay on the Organization of Experience* (London: Harper and Row, 1974); David A. Snow and Robert D. Benford, "Ideology, Frame Resonance, and Participant Mobilization," *International Social Movement Research* 1 (1988): 197–217.
3. Ali Ahmad Jalali, "Afghanistan: Long-term Solutions and Perilous Shortcuts," *Prism* 1, no. 4 (September 2010): 58.
4. U.S. Agency for International Development, "About USAID/Afghanistan," http://afghanistan.usaid.gov/en/about/about_usaid_afghanistan (accessed May 7, 2012).
5. Barack Obama, "Remarks by the President in Address to the Nation on the Way Forward in Afghanistan and Pakistan" (press release, Office of the Press Secretary, The White House, December 1, 2009), www.whitehouse.gov/the-press-office/remarks-president-address-nation-way-forward-afghanistan-and-pakistan (accessed September 14, 2012).
6. Jean MacKenzie, "The Battle for Afghanistan: Militancy and Conflict in Helmand," Counterterrorism Strategy Initiative Policy Paper (Washington, DC: New America Foundation, 2010), 5–6; http://counterterrorism.newamerica.net/sites/newamerica.net/files/policydocs/helmand2.pdf (accessed May 7, 2012).
7. U.S. Agency for International Development, "Initiative to Promote Afghan Civil Society," Fact Sheet, June 2010, http://afghanistan.usaid.gov/documents/document/document/974 (accessed May 7, 2012).
8. Wired.com, "Using Google Earth and GPS to Track Afghanistan Cash," February 25, 2010, www.wired.com/dangerroom/2010/02/using-laptops-cameras-and-gps-to-track-afghanistan-cash (accessed May 7, 2012).
9. MacKenzie, "The Battle for Afghanistan," 13–14.
10. Ibid., 8–13.
11. Robert Chambers, "Challenging the Professions: Frontiers for Rural Development" (London: ITDG, 1993).
12. These methods for participatory rural appraisals are discussed in Neela Mukherjee, *Rural Appraisal: Methodology and Applications* (New Delhi: Concept Publishing, 1993).
13. Gallup WorldView, https://worldview.gallup.com/signin/login.aspx?ReturnUrl=%2f; Afrobarometer, www.afrobarometer.org; The Fund for Peace UNLocK Program, www.fundforpeace.org/global/?q=unlock-library (accessed October 2, 2012).
14. Donald Schön, The Reflective Practitioner: How Professionals Think in Action (New York: Basic Books, 1983), 18.
15. Gary Rolfe, *Knowledge and Practice* (London: South Bank University Distance Learning Centre, 2001).

CONCLUSION: THE VALUE OF COLLABORATIVE CONFLICT ANALYSIS

Since the end of the Cold War, the nature of international conflict has become more complex. In the absence of two sharply defined geopolitical blocs, political alignments among states have become more amorphous in much of the world. Nonstate actors such as militant movements and international criminal networks have become increasingly important in fueling and perpetuating conflict. At the same time, other nonstate actors, such as NGOs and international corporations, as well as transnational organizations, such as the United Nations and the African Union, have increasingly emphasized preventing and managing violent conflict. The global security environment is likely to become even more complicated over the next generation, as a result of ongoing developments such as environmental degradation, resource shortages, technological advances, and weapons proliferation.

Conflict analysis is an essential skill for practitioners whose work is affected by these complex security challenges. The various analytical tools discussed in this guide can help illuminate emerging trends in complex, volatile, and ambiguous environments. They can enable practitioners to better anticipate threats and opportunities and to respond to unforeseen events with greater agility and insight.

This guide portrays conflict analysis not only as an intellectual enterprise, but also as a social one. For conflict analysis to be useful, it must do more than help various stakeholders better understand a conflict. It must also provide decision makers and program implementers with actionable insights as to how to respond to evolving conditions in the conflict environment. To accomplish this goal, the analysis needs to penetrate the core of decision makers' minds, where possible futures are rehearsed and judgment exercised. Collaborative conflict analysis can lay a foundation for effective program planning by helping forge a common operating picture among diverse organizations engaged in conflict management activities, and by identifying programming gaps and areas of comparative advantage.

The first part of this book examines various analytical perspectives that shed light on the strategic, political, socioeconomic, psychological, and cultural dimensions of violent conflict. It also discusses quantitative tools for conflict risk assessment and early warning, such as the Failed States Index and the Peace and Conflict Instability Ledger. Such tools can provide a valuable first cut at the data, helping identify regions at greatest risk of conflict. But quantitative approaches are generally of limited utility in identifying specific conflict drivers and potential options for conflict mitigation strategies. For this reason, the bulk of the guide focuses on qualitative analytical tools such as conflict assessment frameworks, narrative analysis, systems mapping, scenario exercises, and situation analysis. These analytical approaches can help provide more nuanced insights into the dynamics of a given conflict, the risks of escalation, and potential strategies for conflict prevention or management.

Although each of these qualitative methods can be used by an individual analyst, each is also potentially more productive when used in a group exercise involving both analysts and decision makers.

In an exercise using a *conflict assessment framework*, the framework will typically specify a methodology for organizing the deliberations, which may combine breakout groups for certain sessions and plenary meetings for synthesizing the findings of the assessment. Some assessment processes, such as those using the UN Strategic Assessment tool, the UN Post Conflict Needs Assessment (PCNA), or U.S. Interagency Conflict Assessment Framework (ICAF), are structured so as to incorporate a range of individual and institutional perspectives at various steps of the process.

For example, a comprehensive ICAF process can take several months. It may begin with individual consultations with Washington-based policymakers, intelligence analysts, and independent experts, followed by a daylong workshop bringing together various governmental and nongovernmental experts. After this preliminary phase, the facilitators of the process travel to the country in question, conducting field surveys and interviews of U.S. embassy staff. The ICAF exercise may culminate with a multiday exercise at the U.S. embassy involving both American diplomats and locally employed staff, and sometimes representatives of other institutions as well. This painstaking process can highlight as well as help bridge differences of opinion among various stakeholders, such as Washington-based desk officers and embassy staff, enabling the various country specialists to develop a more informed shared perspective on key trends affecting stability in the country.

In a *narrative analysis exercise*, several small working groups may be established, each one analyzing the perspective on a conflict situation articulated by one of the rival groups. In a joint debriefing session, the groups can compare notes and identify key differences and areas of common ground among the various conflict narratives.

Conflict mapping or *systems mapping* may also be used as part of a collaborative exercise to synthesize and distill the key findings of a conflict analysis process. Robert Ricigliano, a leading authority on systems mapping, notes that a mapping exercise is "not about recreating reality, or even the map itself, but is about the process of dialogue and learning that goes into producing a map."[1] In the course of this dialogue, participants are forced to "set priorities" as to which factors are most important and why, as well as to "make their implicit assumptions about cause and effect explicit." The mapping exercise structures the dialogue in a manner that helps participants identify and reevaluate their assumptions about the drivers of a conflict and potential conflict management opportunities.

A *scenario analysis exercise* may begin with a plenary session in which the participants brainstorm to identify key factors and critical uncertainties relevant to the decision focus. Based on this discussion, the participants can proceed to identify several scenario logics they deem worthy of further exploration in smaller working groups. In the concluding plenary session, each working group can tell the story it has created based on its assigned scenario logic. The juxtaposition of several vivid and compelling alternative futures can yield unexpected insights about the potential trajectories of a conflict.

A *situation analysis* seeks to shed light on emerging opportunities and threats in a volatile environment and to assess how well the organization is prepared to navigate the challenges ahead. For the first two steps of a situation analysis, framing the strategic objectives and identifying comparative advantages, it is essential for the assessment team to consult with experts both within and outside their organization. Productive cooperation with institutional partners is possible only if the strategic objectives of the various organizations are mutually compatible, so partner organizations need to carefully consult with one another about how best to articulate their goals. Likewise, partner organizations need to understand not only their own capabilities and resource gaps, but also those of groups working in the same space if they wish to avoid duplications or omissions in their programming.

Although this guide emphasizes the importance of integrating conflict analysis into institutional processes for program planning and implementation, practitioners must be sensitive to the operational culture of their organization. In some institutions, for example, small humanitarian NGOs, there may be no distinction between the roles of analyst, decision maker, and program implementer. Each staff member working in a conflict zone may perform all of these roles at various times. At the opposite end of the spectrum, large Western intelligence agencies frequently draw a bright line between the functions of analyst and policymaker. In such institutions, analysts may be formally or informally barred from making policy recommendations so that their impartiality is not undermined.

In whatever manner these various responsibilities are allocated within an organization, certain general principles may be articulated concerning the function and responsibilities of the conflict analyst. The role of the analyst is not to be a policymaker or an advocate for a particular course of action. Nor is it the analyst's responsibility to resolve the problem for the organization's decision makers.

Rather, the analyst's objective should be to help decision makers better think through the problem and evaluate potential options for addressing it. Analysts can help frame the context for decisions by an organization's leaders and staff. Moreover, by fostering conversation both within and across organizational boundaries, analysts can help forge a shared vocabulary and common operating picture that can enhance collaboration among organizations working in a conflict zone. In sum, conflict analysts should not seek to become decision makers, but rather to help decision makers become better conflict analysts themselves.

Note

1. Robert Ricigliano, *Making Peace Last: A Toolbox for Sustainable Peacebuilding* (Boulder, CO: Paradigm Publishers, 2012), 115.

APPENDIX 1

Estimating Mortality from Violent Conflict

Researchers typically use one of two methods for estimating conflict mortality: direct counting of deaths, based on news reports and other sources of information deemed to be reliable, or indirect estimates extrapolated from retrospective household surveys in conflict zones. The most authoritative global databases on conflict mortality are compiled jointly by the Uppsala Conflict Data Program (UCDP) and the Peace Research Institute, Oslo (PRIO), which rely on a direct counting methodology. UCDP and PRIO define an *armed conflict* as a "contested incompatibility that concerns government and/or territory where the use of armed force between two parties, of which at least one is the government of a state, results in at least 25 battle-related deaths in one calendar year."[1] The UCDP/PRIO Armed Conflict Dataset includes only "battle-related deaths," defined as "all deaths, military as well as civilian, incurred in battle." UCDP and PRIO produce other datasets on conflict-related mortality as well, for example, a One-Sided Violence Dataset that focuses on mass atrocities against civilians. But because these numbers reflect only independently verified attacks on civilians by military actors,[2] they may understate the extent of the violence—in part because independent observers are frequently not present in the most violent areas of a conflict zone. Furthermore, the UCDP/PRIO definition of "armed conflicts" excludes "non-state conflicts," defined as "the use of armed force between two organized armed groups, neither of which is the government of a state, which results in at least 25 battle-related deaths in a year." Between 1990 and 2009, UCDP/PRIO counted 287 nonstate armed conflict dyads in Africa alone, some of which resulted in thousands of deaths.[3]

Estimating conflict mortality from household survey data is a more labor-intensive process, which has typically been done at the national rather than the global level. For example, the International Rescue Committee (IRC) has conducted a series of surveys in the Democratic Republic of the Congo (DRC) that sought to determine the level of "excess mortality" among civilians caused by the Congolese Civil War between 1998 and 2007, based on tens of thousands of interviews in communities around the country.[4] Likewise, a 2008 study published in *The British Medical Journal* used data on sibling deaths from war injuries, which was obtained from the World Health Organization's 2002–2003 World Health Survey, to produce retrospective estimates on mortality from war in thirteen countries.[5] Like the direct counting methodology, the household survey technique has limitations. Because it extrapolates data from the local to the national level, it is essential that the sampled communities be representative of the nation as a whole. Estimates of excess mortality also depend on the availability of reliable baseline data on mortality during peacetime, which is often lacking.

The shortcomings of each of these approaches can result in vast discrepancies in the results. For example, the UCDP/PRIO Armed Conflict Dataset estimates that 24,416 battle-related deaths and 59,688 deaths from "one-sided violence" against civilians occurred in the Democratic Republic of the Congo between 1998 and 2007.[6] By contrast, the IRC has estimated that 5.4 million "excess deaths," primarily from disease or malnutrition, occurred in the DRC during those years—sixty-four times the UCDP/PRIO number.[7] But critics have argued that the IRC study overestimated conflict-related mortality in the Congolese war by surveying unrepresentative districts in the DRC and making flawed assumptions about baseline peacetime mortality rates in the DRC. The statistician Patrick Ball asserts that distortions in the baseline mortality figures inflate the death toll in the IRC reports by a factor of three or four—so that a more accurate estimate of conflict-related deaths in the DRC would be 1.5 to 2 million.[8]

Likewise, UCDP/PRIO estimates that 1,055 battle-related deaths occurred in Rwanda during the 1994 genocide[9]—because the vast majority of the half a million to one million victims were unarmed civilians, and hence were not included in this figure. For Sudan between 2003 and 2005, UCDP/PRIO estimates about five thousand battle-related deaths and about seven thousand deaths from one-sided violence[10]—whereas many experts have estimated the mortality from the genocidal violence in Sudan's Darfur region during that period at two hundred thousand or higher.[11]

Even at the global level, methodological differences can result in diametrically opposed conclusions about trends in mortality from conflict. The 2009–2010 Human Security Report, which uses UCDP/PRIO data, argues that overall national mortality rates have actually declined 90 percent of the time during periods of civil war since 1970—in part because wars tend to be so localized that conflict-related deaths are outweighed by long-term positive trends in the country as a whole.[12] By contrast, the study in *The British Medical Journal* based on retrospective household surveys produced mortality estimates three times as high as the UCDP/PRIO Armed Conflict Dataset, and concluded that "there is no evidence to support a recent decline in war deaths."[13]

The enormous variations in these mortality statistics suggest that a degree of humility is warranted in making assertions about the death toll from conflict in the contemporary world.[14] Andrew Mack observes, "The reality is that, despite better conflict datasets and a huge expansion of humanitarian activity since the end of the Cold War, we still know extraordinarily little about the true extent of the human costs of war."[15] The Human Security Report Project has called for the UN to conduct national demographic and health surveys at the outset of any peacekeeping operation to help remedy these deficiencies.

Notes

1. Uppsala Conflict Data Program, "Definitions," www.pcr.uu.se/research/ucdp/definitions (accessed July 30, 2012).
2. Uppsala Conflict Data Program, "How are UCDP data collected?" www.pcr.uu.se/research/ucdp/faq/#How_are_UCDP_data_collected (accessed July 30, 2012).
3. Paul Williams, *War and Conflict in Africa* (Malden, MA: Polity Press, 2011), 22–23.
4. International Rescue Committee, "Measuring Mortality in the Democratic Republic of the Congo," www.rescue.org/sites/default/files/resource-file/IRC_DRC MortalityFacts.pdf (accessed July 30, 2012).
5. Ziad Obermeyer, Christopher J.L. Murray, and Emmanuela Gakidou, "Fifty Years of Violent War Deaths from Vietnam to Bosnia: Analysis of Data from the World Health Survey Programme," *British Medical Journal* 336, no. 7659 (June 28, 2008): 1482–86.
6. The UCDP/PRIO figure for battle-related deaths in the Democratic Republic of Congo is calculated from "UCDP Battle-Related Deaths Dataset v.5-2011, 1989–2010," www.pcr.uu.se/research/ucdp/datasets/ucdp_battle-related_deaths_data set%20 (accessed July 30, 2012). The number cited is the sum of column K, "Battle Deaths Best Estimate," lines 186–94, 612–13, 752, and 843–44. The figure for deaths from one-sided violence is calculated from "UCDP One-sided Violence Dataset v 1.3-2011, 1989–2010," www.pcr.uu.se/research/ucdp/datasets/ucdp_one-sided_violence_dataset (accessed July 30, 2012). The number cited is the sum of column D, "Fatalities Best Estimate," lines 84–92, 428–38, 505–13, 559–63, 582–88, 659, 665–67, and 675–81.
7. International Rescue Committee, "Measuring Mortality in the DRC."
8. Tina Rosenberg, "The Body Counter: Meet Patrick Ball, a statistician who's spent his life lifting the fog of war," *Foreign Policy*, March/April 2012, www.foreignpolicy.com/articles/2012/02/27/the_body_counter (accessed July 30, 2012).
9. The UCDP/PRIO figure for battle-related deaths in Rwanda in 1994 is taken from the UCDP battle-related deaths dataset, column K, "Battle Deaths Best Estimate," line 608.

10. The UCDP/PRIO figure for battle-related deaths in Sudan from 2003 to 2005 is calculated from the UCDP battle-related deaths dataset, column K, lines 313–15. The figure for deaths from one-sided violence is calculated from the UCDP one-sided violence dataset, column D, lines 151–53, 456–58, and 573–75.

11. For a review of studies on conflict mortality in Darfur between 2003 and 2005, see Olivier Degomme and Debarati Guha-Sapir, "Patterns of Mortality Rates in Darfur Conflict," *The Lancet* 375 (January 23, 2010): 294–300. See also GAO, "Darfur Crisis: Death Estimates Demonstrate Severity of Crisis, but Their Accuracy and Credibility Could Be Enhanced" (Washington, DC: Government Accountability Office, 2006), www.gao.gov/new.items/d0724.pdf (accessed July 30, 2012).

12. Human Security Report Project, Human Security Report 2009-2010, www.hsrgroup.org/human-security-reports/20092010/text.aspx (accessed July 30, 2012).

13. Obermeyer, Murray, and Gakidou, "Fifty Years of Violent War Deaths."

14. On this point, see Anita Gohdes, Megan Price, and Patrick Ball, "The Mismeasure of War," Human Rights Data Analysis Group (accessed July 30, 2012).

15. Andrew Mack, "Global Political Violence: Explaining the Post-Cold War Decline," Coping with Crisis Working Paper Series (New York: International Peace Academy, March 2007), 13.

APPENDIX 2

Early Warning Watchlists and Reports

AlertNet—*Humanitarian Aid and Disaster News*. Humanitarian news network with more than three hundred contributing organizations. www.alertnet.org

Center for American Progress—*Enough Project*. An advocacy project that seeks to promote more effective action to prevent and respond to genocide and crimes against humanity. Focuses mainly on Central and East Africa. www.enoughproject.org

Center for Global Policy, George Mason University—*Political Instability Task Force Reports*. Statistical forecasting of political instability events around the globe. http://globalpolicy.gmu.edu/pitf

Center for International Development and Conflict Management, University of Maryland—*Peace and Conflict Instability Ledger*. Biennial report tracking global trends in conflict, democratization, and instability. www.cidcm.umd.edu/pc

Center for Systemic Peace—*State Fragility Index and Matrix*. Assessment of state fragility for 163 countries based on effectiveness and legitimacy indicators for security, governance, economic, and social dimensions of state performance. www.systemicpeace.org/SFImatrix2009c.pdf

Fund for Peace—*Failed States Index*. Ranks 177 states in order of their vulnerability to violent internal conflict and societal deterioration. www.foreignpolicy.com/story/cms.php?story_id=4350

Genocide Prevention Advisory Network—*Assessing Country Risks of Genocide and Politicide*. An informal, international network of experts on the causes, consequences, and prevention of genocide and other mass atrocities. www.gpanet.org/content/barbara-harffs-risk-assessments.

Genocide Watch. Seeks to raise awareness and influence public policy to prevent and stop genocide. www.genocidewatch.org

Human Security Centre, University of British Columbia—*Human Security News Service*. Daily compilation of human security–related news and research from fifty online media sources, wire services, and more than one hundred think tanks and university research centers. www.humansecuritygateway.com

Intergovernmental Authority on Development (IGAD)—*Conflict Early Warning and Response Mechanism* (CEWARN). Provides early warning information on cross-border pastoral conflicts in the Horn of Africa. www.cewarn.org

International Crisis Group—*CrisisWatch*. Monthly updates on conflicts around the globe. Data available since September 2003. www.crisis group.org

ISN Security Watch—*International Relations and Security Network*. Offers security-related news stories, reference and background information, and analyses every weekday. www.isn.ethz.ch

Minorities at Risk Project, University of Maryland—*Minorities at Risk*. Quantitative and qualitative data on 283 ethnic minority groups, indicating whether the group is at risk of rebellion, protest, or state repression. www.cidcm.umd.edu/mar

Minority Rights Group International—*Peoples Under Threat*. Campaigns worldwide with more than one hundred partners in more than sixty countries to ensure that disadvantaged minorities and indigenous peoples can make their voices heard. www.minorityrights.org/9885/peoples-under-threat/peoples-under-threat-2010.html

SwissPeace—*FAST International*. Provided monthly updates on conflicts in twenty-five countries. Operational from 1998 to 2008. www.swisspeace.ch/typo3/en/peace-conflict-research/early-warning

UN Interagency Standing Committee—*Humanitarian Early Warning Service* (HEWSweb). Compilation of humanitarian early warnings and forecasts for natural hazards and socio-political developments. www.hewsweb.org

UN Office for the Coordination of Humanitarian Affairs (OCHA)—*ReliefWeb*. Global hub for time-critical humanitarian information on complex emergencies and natural disasters. www.reliefweb.int/rw/dbc.nsf/doc100?OpenForm

U.S. Agency for International Development (USAID)—*Famine Early Warning System*. Early warning and food security information to prevent famine and ameliorate food insecurity. www.fews.net/Pages/default.aspx

West Africa Network for Peacebuilding (WANEP)—*West Africa Early Warning Network* (WARN). Offers early warning studies about countries in the region. www.wanep.org/aboutwanep.htm

APPENDIX 3
Conflict Metrics

Brookings Institution—*Index of State Weakness in the Developing World.* Ranked list of 141 developing countries based on twenty indicators of economic, political, security, and social welfare. www.brookings.edu/reports/2008/02_weak_states_index.aspx

Carleton University—*Country Indicators for Foreign Policy*. Statistical information conveying key features of the political, economic, social and cultural environments of countries around the world. www.carleton.ca/cifp

Center for International Development and Conflict Management, University of Maryland—*Center for Systemic Peace, Global Conflict Trends.* Global information regarding seven interrelated aspects of contemporary, complex, international interventions and external influences. www.systemicpeace.org/conflict.htm

Institute for Economics and Peace—*Global Peace Index*. Ranks 158 countries by their peacefulness and identifies some of the drivers of peace. www.visionofhumanity.org/gpi/results/rankings.php

International Peace Research Institute, Oslo (PRIO)—*Armed Conflict Location and Event Data* (ACLED). This dataset codes the location of all reported conflict events in fifty countries in the developing world since 1997. www.acleddata.com

Massachusetts Institute of Technology—*Cascon System for Analysing International Conflict*. Computerized history-based conflict analysis system, with information on eighty-five post–World War II conflicts. http://web.mit.edu/cascon

Pennsylvania State University. *Correlates of War*. Quantitative datasets on interstate, extrastate, and intrastate wars. www.correlatesofwar.org

Stockholm International Peace Research Institute (SIPRI). Collection of databases, including chronology of global conflicts, and facts on armed conflicts and peacekeeping, arms production and trade, armed forces, conventional and nuclear weapons. www.sipri.org/contents/webmaster/databases.

Uppsala University—*Uppsala Conflict Data Program*. Databases on armed conflicts, trends, and peace agreements. www.pcr.uu.se/research/UCDP

UK Department for International Development (DFID)—*Proxy List of Fragile States*. Ranks developing countries based on economic and social data such as primary school enrollment, malnutrition, percentage of births attended by skilled health personnel, and percentage of one-year-olds immunized against measles. www.dfid.gov.uk/Pubs/files/fragile states-paper.pdf

U.S. Department of Defense and United States Institute of Peace—*Measuring Progress in Conflict Environments* (MPICE). Diagnostic tool for tracking progress of postconflict stabilization and reconstruction missions.

World Bank—*Country Policy and Institutional Assessment* (CPIA). Quantitative country rankings based on sixteen criteria related to economic management and institutional performance.

World Bank—*Governance datasets*. Compilation of datasets measuring the governance performance of countries, localities, and institutions. http://web.worldbank.org/WBSITE/EXTERNAL/WBI/EXTWBIGOVANTCOR/0,,contentMDK:20746316~pagePK:64168445~piPK:64168309~theSitePK:1740530,00.html

APPENDIX 4

Private Strategic Forecasters

Business Environment Risk Analysis—*Quick response country reports.* Country risk assessments of business environment. www.beri.com/hrrp.asp

Control Risks Group. Risk consultancy on complex or hostile business environments. www.control-risks.com

Economist Intelligence Unit. Analysis of political and economic trends in two hundred countries as well as an annual forecasting guide. www.eiu.com

Eurasia Group—*Global risk watch and reaction.* Political-risk analysis and industry research for sixty-five countries around the world, based on in-country sources and in-house analysts. www.eurasiagroup.net

Global Insight. Assesses and forecasts political, economic, regulatory, and business conditions in 186 countries. www.globalinsight.com

International Risk—*Fact sheets on political and business risk.* Reports on macro-level and micro-level factors relevant to political and business environments. www.intl-risk.com/fact-sheets/pbras.htm

Jane's Sentinel Security Assessments. Examines underlying reasons for instability and conflict for every state and territory in the world. http://sentinel.janes.com/public/sentinel

Medley Global Advisers. Policy intelligence—monetary, fiscal, and economic policy as well geopolitics—for policymakers, investment bankers, asset managers, and others. www.medleyadvisors.com

Oxford Analytica. Risk analysis and political/economic forecasts, daily briefings about global and regional geopolitical, economic, and social developments. www.oxan.com

PFC Energy—*Petroleum Risk Manager.* Online analytical tool for assessing political, economic, and petroleum sector risk in fifty oil-producing countries. www.pfcenergy.com

Political Risk Services Group—*International Country Risk Guide.* Index based on twenty-two variables concerning political, financial, and economic risks. www.prsgroup.com/ICRG_Methodology.aspx

STRATFOR—*weekly updates.* Private intelligence provider, offering geopolitical analysis of international political, economic, and security issues throughout the world. www.stratfor.com

Virtual Research Associates—*VRA GeoMonitor.* Web-based software tool providing political, economic, and social analysis and early warning in the form of graphs, tables, and maps. www.vranet.com

APPENDIX 5

Conflict Assessment Frameworks

3P Security Initiative (Lisa Schirch)—*Conflict Assessment for Peacebuilding Planning* (CAPP). Seeks to make the connection between conflict assessment and peacebuilding planning more explicit by prioritizing key factors driving conflict or supporting peace.

Collaborative for Development Action (Mary B. Anderson)—*Do-No-Harm (DNH) Analytical Framework.* Aims to help development practitioners avoid counterproductive assistance programming and identify opportunities for conflict mitigation. www.cdainc.com/dnh/docs/DoNoHarm Handbook.pdf

Conflict Prevention and Post-Conflict Reconstruction Network—*Peace and Conflict Impact Assessment* (PCIA). Development; emphasizes peacebuilding resources as well as conflict drivers. http://cern.ch/cpr/library/Tools/PCIA_HandbookEn_v2.2.pdf

Country Indicators for Foreign Policy (Carleton University)—*Country Fragility Analysis.* www.carleton.ca/cifp

UK Department for International Development (DFID)—*Conducting Conflict Assessments.* Methodology assessing conflict-related risks associated with development or humanitarian aid, and developing options for more conflict sensitive policies and programs.

Gesellschaft für Technische Zusammenarbeit (GTZ), Germany—*Conflict Analysis for Project Planning and Management.* www.gtz.de/en/themen/uebergreifende-themen/krisenpraevention/4091.htm

International Alert—*Conflict-Sensitive Approaches to Development.* www.conflictsensitivity.org/resource_pack.html

Netherlands Institute of International Relations—*Stability Assessment Framework.* Tool for integrating security, governance, and development programs. www.clingendael.nl/publications/2005/20050200_cru_paper_stability.pdf

OECD-DAC—*Handbook on Security System Reform.* A compliation of OECD-DAC guidance and good practice on conflict, peacebuilding, and security system reform programming. www.oecd.org/dac/conflictand-fragility/conflictpreventionpeacebuildingandsecuritysystemreforms srcd-rom.htm

Swedish International Development Cooperation Agency (SIDA)—*Manual for Conflict Analysis.*

UN Department of Political Affairs—*UN Strategic Assessment.* Mechanism for joint analysis and strategic discussions of conflict situations by senior decision makers in key UN departments.

UN Development Group, European Commission, and World Bank—*Post Conflict Needs Assessment* (PCNA). Used by national and international actors as an entry point for conceptualizing, negotiating, and financing a common shared strategy for recovery and development in fragile, post-conflict settings. www.undg.org/index.cfm?P=144

UN Development Program—*Conflict-Related Development Analysis.* Supports conflict-sensitive design. www.undp.org/cpr/whats_new/CDA_combined.pdf

USAID—*Conflict Assessment Framework* (CAF 2.0). Designed to help gain a deeper understanding of the causes of conflict and how to use development assistance more strategically in order to address them. http://pdf.usaid.gov/pdf_docs/PNADY740.pdf

USAID—*District Stability Framework* (DSF). Used by U.S. government civilian and military personnel to identify local causes of instability in conflict zones, devise programs to diminish the root causes of instability and conflict, and measure the effectiveness of programming. www.usaid.gov/our_work/global_partnerships/ma/dsf.html

USAID—*Tactical Conflict Assessment and Planning Framework* (TCAPF). Superseded by the District Stability Framework, which incorporates the four TCAPF questions into the first stage of its template for assessment and planning. www.carlisle.army.mil/ietcop/2007_workshop/TCAF%20Counterinsurgency.ppt

U.S. government (State, USAID, Defense)—*Interagency Conflict Assessment Framework.* Strategic-level assessment for conflict prevention and post-conflict reconstruction. www.crs.state.gov/index.cfm?fuseaction=public.display&shortcut=CJ22#whatisICAF

World Bank—*Conflict Assessment Framework.* A tool to assess the causes and consequences of conflict and resilience in order to develop conflict sensitive approaches to programming. http://siteresources.worldbank.org/INTCPR/214574-1112883508044/20657757/CAFApril2005.pdf

APPENDIX 6

U.S. Institute of Peace Narrative Analysis Framework

NARRATIVE ANALYSIS FRAMEWORK Subject: ____________ Date: ____________

	PRIMARY ACTORS	SECONDARY ACTORS	SO WHAT?
FIRST IMPRESSIONS • Pre-conditions for conflict • Why did this conflict happen now?			
WHO? • Primary actors (leaders & constituents) • Spoilers • Secondary actors (other states, multilateral organizations, businesses, diasporas, etc.) • Peacebuilding resources			
WHAT? **Positions** • What do the actors say the conflict is about? • What do they say they want?			
WHY? **Interests** • Unstated motives o Greed o Grievance o Gods **Needs** • Food, water, home, livelihood, dignity			

APPENDIX 6 *(continued)*

NARRATIVE ANALYSIS FRAMEWORK **Subject:** ______ **Date:** ______

	PRIMARY ACTORS	SECONDARY ACTORS	SO WHAT?
WHEN? • What "mythic histories" do the various parties tell? • When do they say the conflict broke out, and what events do they focus on? • When and how do they believe the conflict will end?			
WHERE? • Do the factions disagree about the identity of the contested territory? • How do such disagreements influence the conflict?			
HOW? • What is each side's "game plan"? • How does it hope to prevail in the conflict? • What weapons, organization & methods (both violent and nonviolent) does it use?			
CONCLUSIONS? • Missed opportunities for conflict prevention or resolution over the past 10 years. • Potential trajectory of the conflict over the next 1–2 years. • Current opportunities for productive engagement by third parties.			

APPENDIX 7

Conflict Mapping Tools

Atlas.ti—*Atlas.ti v6*. Consolidates large quantities of text, images, audio, video, and geo data. Provides analytical and visualization tools for interpretation. www.atlasti.com

CDA Collaborative Learning Projects. www.cdainc.com/cdawww/default

Centrifuge Systems—*Business Intelligence 2.0*. Tool for integrating and analyzing diverse data to identify threats and opportunities. www.centrifugesystems.com/technology/applications/bi.php

FrontlineSMS. Enables collaborative text messaging among large groups of people for collecting and sharing data. www.frontlinesms.com

Gesellschaft für Technische Zusammenarbeit (GTZ)—Conflict analysis for project planning and management. Methodology for mapping connections among diverse parties to a conflict. www.gtz.de/en/themen/uebergreifende-themen/krisenpraevention/4091.htm

i2 Group—*Analyst's Notebook*. Provides visualization and analytical tools to identify connections, patterns, and trends in complex datasets. www.i2group.com/template1.asp?id=5

International Network for Social Network Analysis—*Computer Programs for Social Network Analysis*. An annotated list of software packages for automated social network analysis. www.insna.org/software/software_old.html

Laboratory for Computational Cultural Dynamics, University of Maryland—*Stochastic Opponent Modeling Agents* (SOMA). A probabilistic logic program for finding the most probable action that extremist groups might take in a given situation. www.umiacs.umd.edu/research/LCCD/projects/soma.jsp

OpenStreetMap. A free editable map of the world that allows users to view, edit, and use geographical data collaboratively from anywhere. www.openstreetmap.org

Palantir—*Palantir government*. A platform for information analysis, designed to integrate fragments of data from a vast set of starting material. www.palantirtech.com

Pen-Link—*Lincoln and Pen-Link software*. Software for automated monitoring and analysis of telephone records and digital wireless communications for law enforcement and intelligence agencies. www.penlink.com

Ushahidi—Ushahidi (*testimony* in Swahili). Collaborative platform for "crowdsourcing" crisis information via text messaging, e-mail, or web form. www.ushahidi.com

APPENDIX 8

Template for a Logical Framework Matrix (Logframe)

Activity Description	Indicators	Verification	Assumptions
Goal or impact—the long-term development impact (policy goal) that the activity contributes at a national or sectoral level	How the achievement will be measured—including appropriate targets (quantity, quality, and time)	Sources of information on the goal indicator(s)—including who will collect it and how often	—
Purpose or outcome—the medium-term result(s) that the activity aims to achieve—in terms of benefits to target groups	How the achievement of the purpose will be measured—including appropriate targets (quantity, quality, and time)	Sources of information on the purpose indicator(s)—including who will collect it and how often	Assumptions concerning the purpose to goal linkage
Component objectives or intermediate results—this level in the objectives or results hierarchy can be used to provide a clear link between outputs and outcomes (particularly for larger multi-component activities)	How the achievement of the component objectives will be measured—including appropriate targets (quantity, quality, and time)	Sources of information on the component objectives indicator(s)—including who will collect it and how often	Assumptions concerning the component objective to output linkage
Outputs—the tangible products or services that the activity will deliver	How the achievement of the outputs will be measured—including appropriate targets (quantity, quality, and time)	Sources of information on the output indicator(s)—including who will collect it and how often	Assumptions concerning the output to component objective linkage

Source: Australian Agency for International Development (AusAID), *AusGuideline 3.3: The Logical Framework Approach*, October 2005. www.ausaid.gov.au/ausguide/Documents/ausguideline3.3.pdf (accessed September 16, 2012).

GLOSSARY

Asymmetry: A relationship in which one person or party has more power or leverage than another.

Avoiding: A strategy that seeks to evade conflict, either through inaction or withdrawing.

Balancing cycle: A destabilizing event counteracted by an opposing force that restores equilibrium in the system (also called a balancing feedback loop).

Black swan: A random event with a large impact, incomputable probabilities, and surprise effect.

Civil war: A large-scale armed conflict within a country fought either for control of all or part of a state, for a greater share of political or economic power, or for the right to secede. Analysts differ on how to define *large-scale,* but several sources say a conflict must cause at least one thousand war-related deaths a year to be labeled a civil war.

Collapsed state: A country in which national structures have essentially dissolved, leaving a near vacuum of authority.

Compromising: A strategy in which parties agree to accept a middle ground between their positions.

Confidence-building measures (CBMs): A range of methods to help overcome mutual distrust among nations and expand perceived common ground. Intended to reduce fear and suspicion by increasing the predictability of rival states' behavior. Also known as confidence and security building measures (CSBMs).

Conflict: Any situation in which two or more individuals or groups perceive their interests as mutually incompatible, and act on the basis of this perception.

Conflict analysis: A structured inquiry into the causes and potential trajectory of a conflict that seeks to identify opportunities for managing or resolving disputes.

Conflict assessment framework: A qualitative analytical tool to help forge a shared set of questions about the nature and potential trajectory of a conflict, a shared vocabulary with which to discuss opportunities for preventive actions.

Conflict curve: A conceptual tool that helps illustrate how conflicts tend to evolve over time, how different phases of conflict relate to one another, and how to identify different kinds of third-party interventions.

Conflict entrepreneur: Any group or individual whose profits depend on conditions that promote conflict. Most often used to describe those who engage in or directly benefit from illegal economic activity that promotes violence.

Conflict management: Efforts to prevent, limit, contain, or resolve conflicts—especially violent ones—while building the capacities of all parties involved in peacebuilding. *See also* Peacemaking, which tends to focus on halting ongoing conflicts and reaching partial agreements or broader negotiated settlements.

Conflict prevention: Measures taken to keep low-level or long-festering disputes from escalating into violence. Also efforts to limit the spread of violence if it does occur, or to avoid the recurrence of violence.

Conflict sensitivity: An approach to development assistance that involves designing and implementing programs so that they do no harm, and ideally help alleviate conflicts in the target communities.

Conflict spiral: A cycle of escalating hostile actions by rival parties. In a *threat spiral,* two parties escalate their threatening actions toward the other, as in an arms race. In a *retaliation spiral,* Party A's aggressive behavior causes Party B to blame A for harming its interests, which leads B to retaliate, and so forth.

Connector: A potential source of cohesion within or between groups. When leaders mobilize their constituents around a given connector, it may be transformed into a driver of peace.

Contending: A strategy in which one party attempts to impose its preferred solution on another.

Crimes against humanity: Mass killings and targeted attacks against civilians, including systematic rape. Described fully in the Rome Statute of the International Criminal Court, Article 7. To be found guilty, an individual must have developed or carried out a policy of widespread or systematic violations. Specific genocidal intent is not required.

Cross-cutting bonds: Cultural, social, or economic links among groups in a community, as when two ethnic groups are linked through civic organizations.

Divider: A potential source of polarization within or between groups. When leaders mobilize their constituents around a given divider, it may be transformed into a driver of conflict.

Do no harm: A maxim acknowledging that any intervention carries with it the risk of doing harm. Practitioners should proceed with programs only after careful consideration and widespread consultation, including with other institutions in the field so as not to duplicate or undermine their efforts. *See also* Conflict sensitivity.

Driver of conflict: A reinforcing cycle in which leaders mobilize their constituents around a divider, and the constituents in turn push their leaders toward escalating their divisive actions. *See also* Driver of peace.

Driver of peace: A reinforcing cycle in which leaders mobilize their constituents around a connector, and the constituents in turn push their leaders toward further conciliatory actions. *See also* Driver of conflict.

Early warning: An assessment of high-risk situations so as to provide timely notice of escalating violence.

Ethnic cleansing: Deliberate, organized, and usually violent expulsion of people from an area on the basis of their perceived ethnic, communal, sectarian, or religious identity.

Evaluation: Systematic collection and analysis of data on a program, both as to the process and outputs (materials and activities) and the impact or outcome (immediate and longer term effects). *See also* Metrics.

Failed state: A state lacking the authority, capacity, and legitimacy to govern its territory. Characterized by loss of physical control of its territory, or of the monopoly on the legitimate use of physical force therein; an inability to provide public services; and erosion of legitimate authority to make collective decisions. *See also* Collapsed state *and* Fragility.

Fragility: Can refer to humans, states, or the environment. A fragile state or weak state typically suffers from weak authority, capacity, and legitimacy.

Framing: Placing an issue within a broader interpretive context. Provides information about the logic of the problem and about the course of action that may be required to address it. *See also* Reframing, Strategic narrative.

Genocide: Defined by the UN Convention on the Prevention and Punishment of the Crime of Genocide (1948) as any of five types of acts committed "with intent to destroy, in whole or in part, a national, ethnical, racial or religious group, as such." These acts are "(1) killing members of the group; (2) causing serious bodily or mental harm to members of the group; (3) deliberately inflicting on the group conditions of life, calculated to bring about its physical destruction in whole or in part; (4) imposing measures intended to prevent births within the group; [and] (5) forcibly transferring children of the group to another group."

Groupthink: A process of collective self-censorship that occurs when the strivings for unanimity among the members of a group override their motivation to realistically appraise alternative courses of action.

Horizontal inequalities: Social or economic inequalities among different ethnic, geographic, religious, or cultural groups living in the same society.

Indicator: A diagnostic sign of a given condition, such as state failure or famine; also a metric, such as of a program's success. Can be either predictive, as an early warning sign of future events, or descriptive, as a diagnostic sign of a process already under way.

Interest-based negotiation: An approach in which the parties seek to reframe the conflict by focusing on their underlying interests and needs rather than on their stated positions.

Metrics: Measurable indicators of progress. The most useful gauge impact or outcomes such as fewer weapons-related deaths or increased literacy, rather than outputs, such as number of schools built or wells drilled.

Mutually hurting stalemate: A situation in which neither party thinks it can win a given conflict without incurring excessive loss, and in which both are suffering from the continuation of fighting.

Narrative analysis: A method for illuminating rival parties' subjective perspectives on a conflict by examining the stories the parties tell about their grievances and their desires.

Peacekeeping: Traditionally, action undertaken to preserve peace when fighting has been halted and to assist in implementing agreements. Typically authorized by the UN Security Council, operations usually include lightly armed military personnel and have the consent of the parties. Scope of activities has gradually broadened since the end of the Cold War to include a variety of civilian and humanitarian activities. *See also* Conflict management.

Perceived common ground: Perceived likelihood of finding an alternative that satisfies both parties' aspirations.

Problem solving: A strategy in which parties collaborate to create a mutually beneficial solution to a problem.

Psychic numbing: A distortion of thinking that results from efforts to suppress emotional responses to a problem.

Reframing: To redefine a problem, or to look at it from a new perspective, to find ways to reduce tensions, break a deadlock, or facilitate collaboration among diverse organizations.

Reinforcing cycle (or action-reaction cycle): A relatively minor event escalates into something of much greater magnitude. Also called a reinforcing feedback loop.

Ripeness: Period in a conflict when parties are most likely to be open to a negotiated settlement, usually due to conditions of a mutually hurting stalemate.

Scenario analysis: A method for developing vivid and compelling stories of potential alternative futures. Can be an invaluable planning tool for organizations operating in volatile and uncertain environments.

Security dilemma: Maxim in international relations theory that actions taken by one state to enhance its security will necessarily decrease the security of other states. By acting to defend itself, a state may inadvertently provoke aggressive reactions from its rivals.

Security reciprocity: Benefits that can accrue to both dominant and subordinate states by accepting binding international rules and institutions.

Situation analysis (SWOT analysis): A method that focuses on identifying an organization's internal strengths (S) and weaknesses (W), along with opportunities (O) and threats (T) in the external environment. This analysis helps illuminate how an organization can match its own capabilities to the demands of the operating environment.

Spoiler: An individual or group seeking to block or sabotage a peace process or the implementation of an agreement, usually because it threatens that party's power and interests. *See also* Conflict entrepreneur.

Strategic narrative: A shared story describing the nature and stakes of a conflict, around which actors orient their decisions. *See also* Framing.

Systems map: An analytical tool for visualizing and synthesizing information about patterns of interdependence among actors and institutions in complex social systems.

Trend analysis: An analytical method that looks at historical patterns along with current factors to project trends.

Trigger: An event that initiates or accelerates the outbreak of a conflict, such as the assassination of a leader, election fraud, or a political scandal.

War crimes: Crimes committed during armed conflict in violation of the laws of war or international humanitarian law, described fully in the Rome Statute of the International Criminal Court, Article 8. Most perpetrated against noncombatant and civilian populations; and include murder, torture, deportation, rape, hostage-taking, and forced labor.

Watchlist: A list of countries at risk for specific concerns, maintained by government agencies or nongovernmental organizations as early-warning mechanisms.

Window of opportunity: A period during which the chances for success in an endeavor are greatly increased.

Window of vulnerability: A moment at which the escalation of conflict becomes more likely, whether because of a trigger event, such as an assassination or a contested election, or because of more gradual developments such as food shortages or rising unemployment.

Yielding: A strategy involving the lowering of aspirations and conceding to another party.

RESOURCES

General Surveys

Beswick, Danielle, and Paul Jackson. 2011. *Conflict, Security and Development: An Introduction*. New York: Routledge.

Boulding, Kenneth E. 1962. *Conflict and Defense: A General Theory*. New York: Harper.

Burton, J. W. 1987. *Resolving Deep-Rooted Conflicts: A Handbook*. Lanham, MD: University Press of America.

——. 1990. *Conflict: Human Needs Theory*. London: Macmillan.

Carnegie Commission on Preventing Deadly Conflict. *Preventing Deadly Conflict: Final Report*. New York: Carnegie Corporation of New York. www.wilsoncenter.org/subsites/ccpdc/pubs/rept97/finfr.htm.

Carter, Candice C., ed. 2010. *Conflict Resolution and Peace Education*. New York: Macmillan. Central Intelligence Agency. 2009. "Guide to the Analysis of Insurgency." Document C05332177. Langley, VA: Central Intelligence Agency. www.fas.org/irp/cia/product/insurgency.pdf.

CDA Collaborative Learning Projects. 2012. Reflecting on Peace Practice: Participant Training Manual. Cambridge, MA: CDA Collaborative Learning Projects.

——. 2012. Reflecting on Peace Practice: Advanced Training of Consultants and Advisers Resource Manual. Cambridge, MA. CDA Collaborative Learning Projects.

Cheldelin, Sandra, Daniel Druckman, and Larissa Fast, eds. 2003. *Conflict*. New York: Continuum.

Covey, Jock, Michael J. Dziedzic, and Leonard R. Hawley. 2005. *The Quest for Viable Peace: International Intervention and Strategies for Conflict Transformation*. Washington, DC: United States Institute of Peace Press.

Crocker, Chester A., Fen Osler Hampson, and Pamela Aall, eds. 1999. *Herding Cats: Multiparty Mediation in a Complex World*. Washington, DC: United States Institute of Peace Press.

——. 2001. *Turbulent Peace: The Challenges of Managing International Conflict*. Washington, DC: United States Institute of Peace Press.

——. 2004. *Taming Intractable Conflicts: Mediation in the Hardest Cases*. Washington, DC: United States Institute of Peace Press.

——, eds. 2007. *Leashing the Dogs of War: Conflict Management in a Divided World*. Washington, DC: United States Institute of Peace Press.

——, eds. 2011. *Rewiring Regional Security in a Fragmented World*. Washington, DC: United States Institute of Peace Press.

Deutsch, Morton. 1973. *The Resolution of Conflict*. New Haven, CT: Yale University Press.

Deutsch, Morton, and Peter T. Coleman, eds. 2006. *The Handbook of Conflict Resolution: Theory and Practice*, 2nd ed. San Francisco: Jossey-Bass.

Fischer, Martina, Hans J. Gießmann, and Beatrix Schmelzle, eds. 2009. *Berghof Handbook for Conflict Transformation*. Berlin: Berghof Research Center for Constructive Conflict Management. www.berghof-handbook.net.

Fisher, Roger. 1969. *International Conflict for Beginners*. New York: Harper.

Fisher, Roger, and William Ury, with Bruce Patton. 1991. *Getting to Yes: Negotiating Agreement Without Giving In*, 2nd ed. New York: Penguin.

Fisher, Simon, Dekha Ibrahim Abdi, Jawed Ludin, Richard Smith, Steve Williams, and Sue Williams. 2005. *Working with Conflict: Skills and Strategies for Action*. London: Zed Books.

Folger, Joseph P., Marshall Scott Poole, and Randall K. Stutman. 2004. *Working Through Conflict: Strategies for Relationships, Groups, and Organizations*, 5th ed. New York: Addison Wesley Longman.

Galtung, Johan. 1996. *Peace by Peaceful Means: Peace and Conflict, Development and Civilization*. Oslo: International Peace Research Institute.

Hocker, Joyce, and William Wilmot. *Interpersonal Conflict*, 2nd ed. Dubuque, IA: William C. Brown.

Keen, David. 2008. *Complex Emergencies*. Cambridge: Polity.

Kriesberg, Louis. 2003. *Constructive Conflicts: From Escalation to* Resolution, 2nd ed. Lanham, MD: Rowman & Littlefield.

Lederach, John Paul. 1995. *Preparing for Peace: Conflict Transformation Across Cultures*. Syracuse, NY: Syracuse University Press.

——. 1997. *Building Peace: Sustainable Reconciliation in Divided Societies*. Washington, DC: United States Institute of Peace Press.

——. 2002. *A Handbook of International Peacebuilding: Into the Eye of the Storm*. San Francisco: Jossey-Bass.

——. 2003. *The Little Book of Conflict Transformation*. Intercourse, PA: Good Books.

Lund, Michael S. 1996. *Preventing Deadly Conflicts: A Strategy for Preventive Diplomacy*. Washington, DC: United States Institute of Peace Press.

Mitchell, Christopher, and Michael Banks. 1996. *Handbook of Conflict Resolution: The Analytical Problem-Solving Approach*. London: Pinter.

Pruitt, Dean, and Sung Hee Kim. 2004. *Social Conflict: Escalation, Stalemate, and Settlement*, 3rd ed. New York: McGraw Hill.

Ramsbotham, Oliver, Tom Woodhouse, and Hugh Miall. 2011. *Contemporary Conflict Resolution: The Prevention, Management, and Transformation of Deadly Conflicts*, 3rd ed. Cambridge: Polity.

Reychler, Luc, and Thania Paffenholz, eds. 2000. *Peacebuilding: A Field Guide*. Boulder, CO: Lynne Rienner Publishers.

Ricigliano, Robert. 2011. *Making Peace Last*. Boulder, CO: Paradigm Publishers.

Sandole, Dennis J. D., Sean Byrne, Ingrid Sandole-Staroste, and Jessica Senehi, eds. 2009. *Handbook of Conflict Analysis and Resolution*. London: Routledge.

Schirch, Lisa. 2004. *The Little Book of Strategic Peacebuilding: A Vision and Framework for Peace with Justice*. Intercourse, PA: Good Books.

——. 2013. *Conflict Assessment and Peacebuilding Planning: A Strategic, Participatory, Systems-Based Handbook on Human Security*. Bloomfield, CT: Kumarian Press.

Van Brabant, Koenraad. 2010. *Peacebuilding How? Good Practices in Conflict Analysis*. Interpeace Peacebuilding and Policy Resources. www.interpeace.org/index.php/publications/cat_view/8-publications/23-peacebuilding-and-policy-resources.

Wallensteen, Peter. 2007. *Understanding Conflict Resolution: War, Peace, and the Global System*, 2nd ed. Thousand Oaks, CA: Sage Publications.

——. 2011. *Peace Research: Theory and Practice*. New York: Routledge.

Williams, Paul D., ed. 2013. *Security Studies: An Introduction*. London: Routledge.

Wolff, Stefan, and Christalla Yakinthou, eds. 2011. *Conflict Management in Divided Societies: Theories and Practice*. New York: Routledge.

Zartman, I. William, ed. 2007. *Peacemaking in International Conflict: Methods and Techniques*, rev. ed. Washington, DC: United States Institute of Peace Press.

Conflict Early Warning and Risk Assessment

Adelman, Howard, and Astri Suhrke. 1996. "Early Warning and Conflict Management." In Joint Evaluation of Emergency Assistance to Rwanda.

The International Response to Conflict and Genocide: Lessons from the Rwanda Experience. Copenhagen: DANIDA.

Austin, Alex. 2004. "Early Warning and the Field: A Cargo Cult Science?" In *Berghof Handbook for Conflict Transformation*, eds. Martina Fischer, Hans J. Gießmann, and Beatrix Schmelzle. Berlin: Berghof Research Center for Constructive Conflict Management. www.berghof-handbook.net/std_page.php?LANG=e&id=34&parent=4.

Barton, Frederick, and Karin von Hippel, with Sabina Sequeira and Mark Irvine. 2008. "Early Warning? A Review of Conflict Prediction Models and Systems." PCR Project Special Briefing. Washington, DC: Center for Strategic and International Studies.

George, Alexander L., and Jane E. Holl. 1997. *The Warning-Response Problem and Missed Opportunities in Preventive Diplomacy*. New York: Carnegie Corporation of New York.

Goldstone, Jack A. 2008. "Using Quantitative and Qualitative Models to Forecast Instability." USIP Special Report 204. Washington, DC: United States Institute of Peace Press.

Marshall, Monty G., and Benjamin R. Cole. 2011. *Global Report 2011: Conflict, Governance, and State Fragility*. Vienna, VA: Center for Systemic Peace.

Taleb, Nassim Nicholas. 2007. *The Black Swan: The Impact of the Highly Improbable*. New York: Random House.

Woocher, Lawrence. 2008. "The Effects of Cognitive Biases on Early Warning." Paper presented at the International Studies Association Annual Convention. San Francisco (March 29, 2008).

Culture, Ethnicity, and Nationalism

Anderson, Benedict. 1983. *Imagined Communities: Reflections on the Origin and Spread of Nationalism*. London: Verso.

Augsberger, David W. 1992. *Conflict Mediation Across Cultures: Pathways and Patterns*. Louisville, KY: Westminster/John Knox Press.

Avruch, Kevin. 1998. *Culture and Conflict Resolution*. Washington, DC.: United States Institute of Peace Press.

Brown, Michael, ed. 2001. *Nationalism and Ethnic Conflict*. Revised ed. Cambridge: Massachusetts Institute of Technology Press.

Byman, Daniel L. 2002. *Keeping the Peace: Lasting Solutions to Ethnic Conflicts*. Baltimore, MD: The Johns Hopkins University Press.

Coser, Lewis A. 1956. *The Functions of Social Conflict*. New York: Free Press.

Esman, Milton J. 2004. *An Introduction to Ethnic Conflict*. Cambridge: Polity.

Grimshaw, A. D., ed. 1990. *Conflict Talk: Sociolinguistic Investigations of Arguments in Conversation*. Cambridge: Cambridge University Press.

Levinger, Matthew, and Paula Franklin Lytle. 2001. "Myth and Mobilization: The Triadic Structure of Nationalist Rhetoric." *Nations and Nationalism* 7, no. 2: 175–94.

Meyer, Karl E. and Shareen Blair. *Pax Ethnica: Where and How Diversity Succeeds*. New York: Public Affairs, 2012.

Mueller, John. 2004. *The Remnants of War*. Cornell Studies in Security Affairs. Ithaca, NY: Cornell University Press.

Varshney, Ashutosh. 2002. *Ethnic Conflict and Civic Life: Hindus and Muslims in India*. New Haven, CT: Yale University Press.

Development and Conflict

Anderson, Mary. 1999. *Do No Harm: How Aid Can Support Peace—or War*. Boulder, CO: Lynne Rienner.

Austin, Alex, Martina Fischer, and Oliver Wils, eds. 2003. *Peace and Conflict Impact Assessment. Critical Views on Theory and Practice*. Berlin: Berghof Research Center for Constructive Conflict Management.

Carment, David, Stewart Prest, and Yiagadeesen Samy. 2011. *Security, Development and the Fragile State: Bridging the Gap Between Theory and Policy*. New York: Routledge.

Chambers, Robert. 1993. *Challenging the Professions: Frontiers for Rural Development*. London: ITDG Publishing.

Clunan, Anne L., and Harold A. Trinkunas. 2010. *Ungoverned Spaces: Alternatives to State Authority in an Era of Softened Sovereignty*. Palo Alto, CA: Stanford University Press.

Organisation for Economic Co-operation and Development. 2006. *Whole of Government Approaches to Fragile States*. Paris: OECD Publishing.

——. 2011. *Investing in Security: A Global Assessment of Armed Violence Reduction Initiatives*. Paris: OECD Publishing.

Schmelze, Beatrix. 2005. *New Trends in Peace and Conflict Impact Assessment (PCIA)*. Berlink: Berghof Research Center for Constructive Conflict Management. www.berghof-handbook.net/documents/publications/dialogue4_pcianew_complete.pdf.

Spear, Joanna, and Paul D. Williams, eds. 2012. *Security and Development in Global Politics: A Critical Comparison*. Washington, DC: Georgetown University Press.

Stewart, Frances. 2004. "Development and Security." CRISE Working Paper 3. Oxford: Centre for Research on Inequality, Human Security, and Ethnicity. www.crise.ox.ac.uk/pubs/workingpaper3.pdf.

Uvin, Peter. 1998. *Aiding Violence: The Development Enterprise in Rwanda*. West Hartford, CT: Kumarian Press.

Van Brabant, Koenraad. 2010. *What Is Peacebuilding? Do No Harm, Conflict Sensitivity, and Peacebuilding*. Geneva: Interpeace Peacebuilding and Policy Resources. www.interpeace.org/index.php/publications/cat_view/8-publications/23-peacebuilding-and-policy-resources.

World Bank. 2011. *World Development Report 2011: Conflict, Security, and Development*. Washington, DC: World Bank.

Zartman, I. William, ed. 1995. *Collapsed States: The Disintegration and Restoration of Legitimate Authority*. Boulder, CO: Lynne Rienner.

Economics and Conflict

Arnson, Cynthia, and I. William Zartman, eds. 2005. *Rethinking the Economics of War: The Intersection of Need, Creed, and Greed*. Baltimore, MD: The Johns Hopkins University Press.

Ballentine, Karen, and Heiko Nitzschke, eds. 2005. *Profiting from Peace: Managing the Resource Dimensions of Civil War*. Boulder, CO: Lynne Rienner.

Ballentine, Karen, and Jake Sherman. 2003. *The Political Economy of Armed Conflict: Beyond Greed and Grievance*. Boulder, CO: Lynne Rienner.

Brauer, Jurgen, and J. Paul Dunne. 2012. *Peace Economics: A Macroeconomic Primer for Violence-Afflicted States*. Washington, DC: United States Institute of Peace Press.

Collier, Paul. 2000. *Economic Causes of Civil Conflict and Their Implications for Policy*. Washington, DC: World Bank.

——. 2007. *The Bottom Billion: Why the Poorest Countries Are Failing and What Can Be Done About It*. New York: Oxford University Press.

Collier, Paul, V. L. Elliott, Havard Hegre, Anke Hoeffler, Marta Reynal-Querol, and Nicholas Sambanis. 2003. *Breaking the Conflict Trap: Civil War and Development Policy*. Washington, DC: World Bank.

Klare, Michael T. 2002. *Resource Wars: The New Landscape of Global Conflict*. New York: Metropolitan Books/Henry Holt.

Miguel, Edward, Shanker Satyanath, and Ernest Sergenti. 2004. "Economic Shocks and Conflict: An Instrumental Variable Approach." *Journal of Political Economy* 112, no. 4: 725–53.

Ostby, Gudrun. 2008. "Horizontal Inequalities, Political Environment and Civil Conflict: Evidence from 55 Developing Countries." In *Horizontal Inequalities and Conflict: Understanding Group Violence in Multiethnic Societies*, ed. Frances Stewart. Basingstoke: Palgrave Macmillan.

Stewart, Frances. 2002. "Root Causes of Violent Conflict in Developing Countries." *British Medical Journal* 324 (February): 342. www.bmj.com/content/324/7333/342.full (accessed May 7, 2012).

——, ed. 2008. *Horizontal Inequalities and Conflict: Understanding Group Violence in Multiethnic Societies.* Basingstoke: Palgrave Macmillan.

Environment and Conflict

Bloomfield, David, Yash Ghai, and Ben Reilly. 1998. "Analysing Deep-Rooted Conflict." In *Democracy and Deep-Rooted Conflict: Options for Negotiators*, eds. Peter Harris and Ben Reilly. Stockholm: International Institute for Democracy and Electoral Assistance. www.idea.int/publications/democracy_and_deep_rooted_conflict/index.cfm.

Brown, Lester R. 2003. *Plan B: Rescuing a Planet under Stress and a Civilization in Trouble.* Washington, DC: Earth Policy Institute.

——. 2008. *Plan B 3.0: Mobilizing to Save Civilization.* Washington, DC: Earth Policy Institute.

Evans, Alex. 2010. "Resource Scarcity, Climate Change and the Risk of Violent Conflict." World Development Report 2011 Background Paper. Washington, DC: World Bank.

Homer-Dixon, Thomas. 1994. *Environmental Scarcities and Violent Conflict: Evidence from Cases.* Toronto: University of Toronto Press.

Parenti, Christian. 2011. *Tropic of Chaos: Climate Change and the New Geography of Violence.* New York: Nation Books.

Gender and Peacebuilding

Anderlini, S. N. 2006. "Mainstreaming Gender in Conflict Analysis: Issues and Recommendations." Social Development Papers no. 33. Washington, DC: World Bank.

——. 2007. *Women Building Peace: What They Do, Why It Matters.* Boulder, CO: Lynne Rienner Publishers.

——. 2010. *What Women Say: Participation and UNSCR 1325*. Cambridge, MA: International Civil Society Action Network.

Caprioli, Mary. 2003. *Gender Equality and Civil Wars*. Washington, DC: World Bank.

Cheldelin, Sandra I., and Maneshka Eliatamby, eds. 2011. *Women Waging War and Peace: International Perspectives of Women's Roles in Conflict and Post-Conflict Reconstruction*. New York: Continuum.

Greenberg, Marcia E., and Elaine Zuckerman. 2009. "The Gender Dimensions of Post-Conflict Reconstruction: The Challenges in Development Aid." In *Making Peace Work: The Challenges of Social and Economic Reconstruction*, ed. Tony Addison and Tilman Brück. Basingstoke: Palgrave Macmillan, UNU-WIDER.

Kuehnast, Kathleen, Chantal de Jonge Oudraat, and Helga Hernes, eds. 2011. *Women and War: Power and Protection in the 21st Century*. Washington, DC: United States Institute of Peace Press.

Neimains, Astrida. 2002. *Gender Mainstreaming in Practice: A Handbook*. New York: United Nations Development Program.

Genocide and Mass Atrocities

Bellamy, Alex J. "The Responsibility to Protect and the Problem of Military Intervention." *International Affairs* 84, no. 4: 615–39.

Downes, Alexander B. 2008. *Targeting Civilians in War*. Ithaca, NY: Cornell University Press.

Genocide Prevention Task Force. 2008. *Preventing Genocide: A Blueprint for U.S. Policymakers*. Washington, DC: U.S. Holocaust Memorial Museum, United States Institute of Peace, and the American Academy of Diplomacy.

Harff, Barbara. 2003. "No Lessons Learned from the Holocaust? Assessing Risks of Genocide and Political Mass Murder since 1955." *American Political Science Review* 97, no. 1: 57–73.

Kiernan, Ben. 2007. *Blood and Soil: A World History of Genocide and Extermination from Sparta to Darfur*. New Haven, CT: Yale University Press.

Ould-Abdallah, Ahmedou. 2000. *Burundi on the Brink 1993–1995: A UN Special Envoy Reflects on Preventive Diplomacy*. Washington, DC: United States Institute of Peace Press.

Power, Samantha. 2002. *"A Problem from Hell": America and the Age of Genocide*. New York: Basic Books.

Sewall, Sarah, Dwight Raymond, and Sally Chin. 2010. *Mass Atrocity Response Options (MARO): A Military Planning Handbook*. Cambridge, MA: Harvard University.

Slovic, Paul. 2007. "'If I Look at the Mass I Will Never Act': Psychic Numbing and Genocide." *Judgment and Decision Making* 2, no. 2: 1–17. http://journal.sjdm.org/vol2.2.htm (accessed September 17, 2012).

Straus, Scott. 2007. "Second-Generation Comparative Research on Genocide." *World Politics* 59(3): 476–501.

——. "Identifying Genocide and Related Forms of Mass Atrocity." Working Paper. Washington, DC: United States Holocaust Memorial Museum. www.ushmm.org/genocide/pdf/indentifying-genocide.pdf (accessed September 17, 2012).

——. 2012. "Wars Do End! Changing Patterns of Political Violence in Sub-Saharan Africa." *African Affairs* 111, no. 443: 179–201. http://afraf.oxfordjournals.org/content/111/443/179.full.pdf (accessed September 17, 2012).

U.S. Army Peacekeeping and Stability Operations Institute (PKSOI). 2012. *Mass Atrocity Prevention and Response Options (MAPRO): A Policy Planning Handbook*. Carlisle, PA: PKSOI.

Valentino, Benjamin. *Final Solutions: Mass Killing and Genocide in the 20th Century*. Ithaca, NY: Cornell University Press.

International Relations Perspectives

Guo, Rongxing. 2011. *Territorial Disputes and Conflict Management: The Art of Avoiding War*. New York: Routledge.

Gurr, Ted. 1970. *Why Men Rebel*. Princeton, NJ: Princeton University Press.

Hoffmann, Stanley, Robert O. Keohane, and John J. Mearsheimer. 1990. "Back to the Future, Part II: International Relations Theory and Post-Cold War Europe." *International Security* 15, no. 2: 191–99.

Ikenberry, G. John. 2001. *After Victory: Institutions, Strategic Restraint, and the Rebuilding of Order After Major Wars*. Princeton, NJ: Princeton University Press.

Iklé, Fred Charles. 1991. *Every War Must End*, rev. ed. New York: Columbia University Press.

Kennan, George. 1954. *Realities of American Foreign Policy*. Princeton, NJ: Princeton University Press.

Keohane, Robert O. 1988. "International Institutions: Two Approaches." *International Studies Quarterly* 32, no. 4: 79–96.

Mearsheimer, John. 2001. *The Tragedy of Great Power Politics.* New York: W. W. Norton.

Morgenthau, Hans. 1948. *Politics among Nations: The Struggle for Power and Peace.* New York: Alfred A. Knopf.

Nye, Joseph, with Robert Keohane. 2004. *Power in the Global Information Age: From Realism to Globalization.*

Putnam, Robert D. 1988. "Diplomacy and Domestic Politics: The Logic of Two-Level Games." *International Organization* 42, no. 3: 427–60.

Schelling, T. C. 1960. *The Strategy of Conflict.* Cambridge, MA: Harvard University Press.

Walt, Stephen M. 1987. *Origins of Alliances.* Ithaca, NY: Cornell University Press.

Waltz, Kenneth Neal. 1979. *Theory of International Politics.* Reading, MA: Addison-Wesley.

Monitoring and Evaluation

Blum, Andrew. 2011. "Improving Peacebuilding Evaluation: A Whole-of-Field Approach." Special Report 280. Washington, DC: United States Institute of Peace Press.

Agoglia, John, Michael Dziedzic, and Barbara Sotirin, eds. 2010. *Measuring Progress in Conflict Environments (MPICE): A Metrics Framework.* Washington, DC: United States Institute of Peace Press.

Hewitt, Joseph, Jonathan Wilkenfeld, and Ted Robert Gurr. 2007. *Peace and Conflict 2008.* Boulder, CO: Paradigm Publishers.

Human Security Report Project. 2008. *Human Security Brief 2007.* Vancouver, BC: Human Security Research Group.

Kennedy-Chouane, Megan Grace. 2010. "Improving Conflict Prevention and Peacebuilding Assistance Through Evaluation." *OECD Papers* 8, no. 1: 99–107. www.oecd-ilibrary.org/economics/improvingconflict-prevention-and-peacebuilding-assistance-through-evaluation_gen_papers-2010–5kgc6cl2vlvd.

National Research Council. 2007. *Tools and Methods for Estimating Populations at Risk from Natural Disasters and Complex Humanitarian Crises.* Washington, DC: National Academies Press.

Schön, Donald. 1983. *The Reflective Practitioner: How Professionals Think in Action.* New York: Basic Books.

Psychology of Conflict

Bies, Robert J., Thomas M. Tripp, and Roderick M. Kramer. 1997. "At the Breaking Point: Cognitive and Social Dynamics of Revenge in Organizations." In *Antisocial Behavior in Organizations*, eds. Robert A. Giacolone and Jerald Greenberg. Thousand Oaks, CA: Sage Publications.

Christie, Daniel J., Richard V. Wagner, and Deborah DuNann Winter. 2001. *Peace, Conflict, and Violence: Peace Psychology for the 21st Century*. Upper Saddle River, NJ: Prentice Hall.

Cobb, Sara. 1994. "A Narrative Perspective on Mediation." In *New Directions in Mediation*, eds. Joseph P. Folger and Tricia S. Jones. Thousand Oaks, CA: Sage Publications.

Janis, Irving. 1982. *Groupthink: Psychological Studies of Policy Decisions and Fiascoes*. 2nd ed. New York: Houghton Mifflin.

Levinger, George, and Jeffrey Z. Rubin. 1994. "Bridges and Barriers to a More General Theory of Conflict." *Negotiation Journal* 10, no. 3: 201–15.

Macintosh, James. 1996. *Confidence Building in the Arms Control Process: A Transformation View*. Ottawa: Department of Foreign Affairs and International Trade.

McNair, Rachel M. 2012. *The Psychology of Peace: An Introduction*, 2nd ed. Santa Barbara, CA: Praeger.

Pruitt, Dean G. 2007. "Readiness Theory and the Northern Ireland Peace Process." *American Behavioral Scientist* 50, no. 11: 1520–41.

——. 2012. "Social Conflict and Negotiation." In *Handbook of the History of Social Psychology*, eds. Arie W. Kruglanski and Wolfgang Stroebe. New York: Psychology Press.

Slovic, Paul. 2007. " 'If I Look at the Mass I Will Never Act': Psychic Numbing and Genocide." *Judgment and Decision Making* 2, no. 2: 1–17.

Small, Deborah A., George Loewenstein, and Paul Slovic. 2007. "Sympathy and Callousness: The Impact of Deliberative Thought on Donations to Identifiable and Statistical Victims." *Organizational Behavior and Human Decision Processes* 102, no. 2: 143–53.

Staub, Ervin. 2003. *The Psychology of Good and Evil: Why Children, Adults, and Groups Help and Harm Others*. New York: Cambridge University Press.

Taleb, Nassim Nicholas. 2010. *The Black Swan: The Impact of the Highly Improbable*, 2nd ed. New York: Random House.

Tversky, Amos, and Daniel Kahneman. 1973. "Availability: A Heuristic for Judging Frequency and Probability." *Cognitive Psychology* 5, no. 2: 207–32.

Volkan, Vamik D. 1997. *Bloodlines: From Ethnic Pride to Ethnic Terrorism*. New York: Farrar, Straus & Giroux.

——. 2004. *Blind Trust: Large Groups and Their Leaders in Times of Crisis and Terror*. Charlottesville, VA: Pitchstone Publishing.

Winslade, John, and Gerald Monk. 2000. *Narrative Mediation*. San Francisco: Jossey-Bass.

Strategic Forecasting and Scenario Planning

Bracken, Paul, Ian Bremmer, and David Gordon, eds. 2008. *Managing Strategic Surprise: Lessons from Risk Management and Risk Assessment*. New York: Cambridge University Press.

Brown, Michael E., ed. 2003. *Grave New World: Security Challenges in the 21st Century*. Washington, DC: Georgetown University Press.

Bruce, James B., and Jeffrey Martini. 2010. "Whither Al-Anbar Province? Five Scenarios through 2011." Occasional Paper 278-MCIA. Santa Monica, CA: RAND Corporation.

Campbell, Ashley. 2002. "The Private Sector and Conflict Prevention Mainstreaming: Risk Analysis and Conflict Impact Assessment Tools for Multinational Corporations." Country Indicators for Foreign Policy. London: Donor Committee for Enterprise Development. www.enterprise-development.org/page/conflict-assessments (accessed September 17, 2012).

Friedman, George. 2008. *The Next 100 Years: A Forecast for the 21st Century*. New York: Doubleday.

Heuer, Richards J., and Randolph H. Pherson. 2010. *Structured Analytic Techniques for Intelligence Analysis*. Washington, DC: CQ Press.

Quiggin, Thomas. 2007. *Seeing the Invisible: National Security Intelligence in an Uncertain Age*. Hackensack, NJ: World Scientific Publishing.

Schwartz, Peter. 1991. *The Art of the Long View: Planning for the Future in an Uncertain World*. New York: Currency Doubleday.

——. 2003. *Inevitable Surprises: Thinking Ahead in a Time of Turbulence*. New York: Gotham Books.

Schwartz, Peter, and Jay Ogilvy. 1998. *Plotting Your Scenarios*. Emeryville, CA: Global Business Network. www.gbn.com/consulting/article_details. php?id=24.

Senge, Peter M. 2006. *The Fifth Discipline: The Art and Practice of the Learning Organization*. New York: Doubleday.

U.S. Joint Forces Command. 2008. *The Joint Operating Environment 2030: Challenges and Implications for the Future Joint Force.* Suffolk, VA: United States Joint Forces Command Center for Joint Futures.

U.S. National Intelligence Council (NIC). 2008. *Global Trends 2025: A Transformed World.* Washington, DC: Government Printing Office. www.dni.gov/nic/NIC_2025_project.html.

Wack, Pierre. 1985. "Scenarios: Uncharted Waters Ahead." *Harvard Business Review* 63(5)(September-October): 73–89.

——. "Scenarios: Shooting the Rapids." *Harvard Business* Review 63, no. 6 (November-December): 139–50.

Systems Analysis

Kilcullen, David. 2006. "Counter-Insurgency Redux." *Survival* 48(4): 111–30.

Miller, John H., and Scott E. Page. 2007. *Complex Adaptive Systems: An Introduction to Computational Models of Social Life*. Princeton, NJ: Princeton University Press.

Ricigliano, Robert. 2011. *Making Peace Last.* Boulder, CO: Paradigm Publishers.

Van Brabant, Koenraad. 2010. *Peacebuilding How? Systems Analysis of Conflict Dynamics.* Geneva: Interpeace Peacebuilding and Policy Resources. www.interpeace.org/index.php/publications/cat_view/8-publications/23-peacebuilding-and-policy-resources.

Electronic Resources

Armed Conflict Location & Event Dataset (ACLED). www.acleddata.com

Berghof Conflict Research. *Berghof Handbook for Conflict Transformation.* www.berghof-handbook.net

Beyond Intractability. www.beyondintractability.org

CDA Collaborative Learning Projects. www.cdainc.com/cdawww/default

Center for Systemic Peace. 2009. *Global Trends in Armed Conflict 1946–2007.* www.systemicpeace.org/conflict.htm

Center for International Development and Conflict Management, University of Maryland. *Minorities at Risk Data Set*. www.cidcm.umd.edu/mar/data.asp

Conflict Sensitivity Consortium. www.conflictsensitivity.org

Global Partnership for the Prevention of Armed Conflict, Peace Portal. www.gppac.net

Governance and Social Development Resource Centre. www.gsdrc.org

Human Security Report Project. www.hsrgroup.org

International Crisis Group. *CrisisWatch*. www.crisisgroup.org/en/publication-type/crisiswatch.aspx

International Peace Institute. www.ipacademy.org/publication.html

International Peace Research Institute Oslo (PRIO). www.prio.no

Interpeace, *Peacebuilding and Policy Resources*. www.interpeace.org/index.php/publications/cat_view/8-publications/23-peacebuilding-and-policy-resources

OECD-DAC Network on Conflict and Fragility (INCAF). www.oecd.org/dac/conflictandfragility

Peace Direct, *Insight on Conflict*. www.insightonconflict.org

Swisspeace. *Resources on Statehood & Conflict*. www.swisspeace.ch/topics/statehood-conflict/resources.html

Stockholm International Peace Research Institute (SIPRI). www.sipri.org

U.S. Agency for International Development (USAID), *Development Experience Clearinghouse*. https://dec.usaid.gov/dec/home/Default.aspx

United States Institute of Peace (USIP). www.usip.org

Uppsala Conflict Data Program (UCDP) and Peace Research Institute Oslo (PRIO), *Data on Armed Conflict*. www.prio.no/CSCW/Datasets/Armed-Conflict

INDEX

ABOUT THE AUTHOR

Matthew Levinger is visiting professor of international affairs and director of the National Security Studies Program at The Elliott School of International Affairs, George Washington University. Among his previous positions, he was a senior program officer at USIP's Academy of International Conflict Management and Peacebuilding, director of the Academy for Genocide Prevention at the U.S. Holocaust Memorial Museum, a William C. Foster Fellow at the U.S. Department of State, and associate professor of History at Lewis & Clark College.

UNITED STATES INSTITUTE OF PEACE PRESS

Since its inception, the United States Institute of Peace Press has published over 175 books on the prevention, management, and peaceful resolution of international conflicts—among them such venerable titles as Raymond Cohen's *Negotiating Across Cultures*; John Paul Lederach's *Building Peace*; *Leashing the Dogs of War* by Chester A. Crocker, Fen Osler Hampson, and Pamela Aall; and *The Iran Primer*, edited by Robin Wright. All our books arise from research and fieldwork sponsored by the Institute's many programs, and the Press is committed to extending the reach of the Institute's work by continuing to publish significant and sustainable works for practitioners, scholars, diplomats, and students. In keeping with the best traditions of scholarly publishing, each volume undergoes thorough internal review and blind peer review by external subject experts to ensure that the research and conclusions are balanced, relevant, and sound.

—*Valerie Norville, Director*

BOARD OF DIRECTORS

Members ex officio

Also Available from the United States Institute of Peace Press

From the Academy Guide Series

Peace Economics

A Macroeconomic Primer for Violence-Afflicted States

Jurgen Brauer and J. Paul Dunne

Creating sound economic policy and a stable macroeconomic framework is essential to societies recovering from violent conflict. This volume provides practitioners with a concise yet broad overview of macroeconomic fundamentals as they touch on violence-afflicted states and extends into the wider realm of social reconstitution, social contract, and social capital.

174 pp. • 6 x 9

Paper: 978-1-60127-138-9 eBook: 978-1-60127-139-6

Books on Mediation from Crocker, Hampson, and Aall

Taming Intractable Conflicts

Mediation in the Hardest Cases

224 pp. • 6 x 9

Paper: 978-1-929223-55-8 eBook: 978-1-60127-089-4

Grasping the Nettle

Analyzing Cases of Intractable Conflict

432 pp. • 6 x 9

Paper: 978-1-929223-60-2

Herding Cats

Multiparty Mediation in a Complex World

768 pp. • 6 x 9

Paper: 978-1-878379-92-4 eBook: 978-1-60127-120-4

Chester A. Crocker is the James R. Schlesinger Professor of Strategic Studies at Georgetown University. **Fen Osler Hampson** is distinguished fellow and director of the global security program at the Centre for International Governance Innovation (CIGI). **Pamela Aall** is the provost of the Academy for International Conflict Management and Peacebuilding at the U.S. Institute of Peace

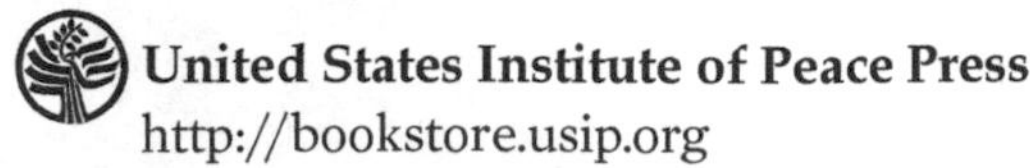